Reproductive Health Status of Women in Tamil Nadu

Reproductive Health Status of Women in Tamil Nadu

Dr K. Jothy

Dr S. Vasuki

KALPAZ

First Published, 2017

Published by

Kalpaz Publications
C-30, Satyawati Nagar,
Delhi – 110052
E-mail: kalpaz@hotmail.com
Ph.: 9212142040

Printed at: G. Print Process, Delhi

Cataloging in Publication Data—DK
Courtesy: D.K. Agencies (P) Ltd. <docinfo@dkagencies.com>

Jothy, K. (Kanagasabai), author.
Reproductives health status of women in Tamil Nadu / Dr K. Jothy.
pages cm
Includes bibliographical references.
ISBN 9789351282563

1. Women—Health and hygiene—India—Chidambaram (Taluk) 2. Generative organs, Female—Diseases—India—Chidambaram (Taluk) 3. Reproductive health—India—Chidambaram (Taluk) 4. Women's health services—India—Chidambaram (Taluk) I. Title.

RA564.85.J68 2017 DDC 613.0424095482 23

Contents

Acknowledgement

This book is based on research conducted to assess the Reproductive health status of rural women in Tamil Nadu. The authors are grateful to a number of friends and colleagues in encouraging us to start the work, preserve with it and finally to publish it. The authors are grateful to the authorities of Annamalai University for granting permission to publish this book. Words cannot fathom the depth of gratitude that my heart is filled with to be associated with this prestigious institution.

Foreword

It is my great pleasure to write a few lines about the book "**Reproductive Health Status of Women in Tamil Nadu**" by **Dr K. Jothy** and **S. Vasuki**. To write a book on reproductive health is tough in the sense that it encompasses many topics to cover diverse disciplines as well as it needs conceptual explanations for the beginners. Although there are some good textbooks available in India, these do not meet the requirements of all readers because of absence of some essential topics. Their book is a welcome improvement upon the existing texts in this respect.

The book is well written and presented in a lucid, easily understandable manner and it covers many topics to satisfy the needs of the students and researchers of many disciplines. Explanations and illustrations are primarily made with Indian data. This is also an additional advantage to understand the subject clearly. Moreover, the wide coverage of issues and multidisciplinary approaches, this book will be of interest to policy makers, researchers and students in the fields of health and development, demography and gender studies, and programme managers in women's and men's health projects both within and outside the government.

In fine, I must thank the authors for writing such a good book and hope that the book will attract the attention of all concerned.

Professor Dr Md. Nazrul Islam Mondal
Department of Population Science and
Human Resource Development
University of Rajshahi; BANGLADESH

Preface

Women's health in India can be examined in terms of multiple indicators, which vary by geography, socioeconomic standing and culture. To adequately improve the health of women in India multiple dimensions of well-being must be analysed in relation to global health averages and also in comparison to men in India. Health is an important factor that contributes to human wellbeing and economic growth.

The global concern on reproductive health emerged in the 1994 International Conference on Population and Development at Cairo. In this reproductive health defined as 'a state complete physical, mental and social well-being and not merely the absence of disease of infirmity, in all matters relating to the reproductive system and to its functions and processes' (United Nations, 1994).

Currently, women in India face a multitude of health problems, which ultimately affect the aggregate economy's output. Reproductive health status of women has been largely neglected over a long period of time. The population control programmes hardly focused on reproductive health needs. The recent focus on reproductive health marks the need to reorient existing programmes. These new programmes are women based, respond to women's health needs and are sensitive to the socio-cultural constraints that women and adolescent girls face in acquiring services and expressing health needs. India has made extensive efforts to reduce maternal mortality and to increase access to reproductive healthcare and in some regions much progress has been achieved. However, the progress made has been uneven and inequitable, and many women still lack access to maternal and reproductive healthcare. In India, as in many other settings, social structures prevent women from having access to maternal and reproductive healthcare. These structures, defined by the WHO as 'social and structural determinants of health', vary between different contexts and influence access to and availability of care differently in different societies. This well-researched volume provides an understanding of various dimensions of reproductive health status of rural women in India.

In these circumstances, an in-depth analysis has been made in this book about the Reproductive Health Problems of Women in various stages of their reproductive life before marriage, during pregnancy, during delivery, immediately after delivery and within seven days and General Gynecological Problems and the Health Care Seeking Behaviour of rural women and the linkages with their socio-economic statuses. The contraceptive Practices and Reproductive losses of the rural women have also been examined.

Unique in its wide coverage of issues and its multidisciplinary approach, this book will be of interest to policy-makers, researchers and students in the fields of health and development, demography and gender studies, and programme managers in women's and men's health projects both within and outside the government.

K. Jothy
S. Vasuki

List of Tables

Chapter – I

Introduction

1.1 Introduction

Reproductive health refers to mortality, morbidity and quality of life attributable to the reproductive system, process and events experienced by men and women at all ages. Conceptually, the term should include reproduction related mortality, morbidity and quality of life issues of both men and women. But discussion about women's health problems usually gets larger attention in the context of pregnancy and child birth related morbidity and mortality. For example, Zurayk (1993) defined reproductive health as "The ability of women to live through the reproductive years and beyond with reproductive choice, dignity, and successful childbearing, and to be free of gynecological disease and risk".[1] The International Conference on Population and Development (ICPD, 1994) defined reproductive health in generic terms but stressed the importance of women's reproductive health.[2] The consensus view, in ICPD (1994), of reproductive health was that; (a) people have the ability to reproduce, (b) women are able to go through pregnancy and child birth safely, (c) the outcome of pregnancy is successful in terms of maternal and infant survival and well being, and (d) couples are able to have sexual relations free of the fear of pregnancy and of contracting disease (Fathalla, 1988).[3] The World Health Organisation (WHO, 1998) defines reproductive health as "a state of physical, mental and social well-being in all matters relating to the reproductive system at all stages of life."[4] The term reproductive age group refers to the active reproductive years in women starting with menarche around

12-14 years and ending with menopause around 45-49 years. For demographic purposes, reproductive age group is usually defined as 15-49 years or 12-49 years.[4] Reproductive health may at times be, confusedly, restricted to problems of women in the reproductive age group. The "...at all ages of life" part in the WHO definition is to remind us about the reproductive tract related mortality and morbidity experienced beyond the reproductive age group. For example, carcinoma of cervix, prolapse uterus, etc.

- An estimated 1,600 women die every day from complications caused by pregnancy and child birth, 99 per cent in developing countries.
- Each year, approximately two million girls are at risk of female genital mutilation.
- About 70,000 women die every year from unsafe abortions, and many more suffer infections and other consequences.
- Women are more likely than men to contract HIV through sexual encounters and about 42 per cent of all persons infected with HIV are women.
- Fifty-one per cent of all pregnant women suffer from iron-deficiency anemia.
- In many countries of South Asia, Africa, Latin America, and the Middle East, one-third to one-half of women are mothers before the age of 20.
- Cancer of the cervix, the most common form of cancer in developing countries, is often linked to the sexually transmitted human papilloma virus.
- Domestic violence, rape and sexual abuse are a significant cause of disability among women.

Reproductive health status of third world women as indicated by various available this indicator of maternal mortality is very alarming. The figures concerned highlight not only the enormity of the poor health status of women, but also the sharp disparity between the developing and developed countries in the context. The limitation of the population control approach was recognised through experiences of women all over the world, including India. It was also recognised that women suffer silently from a large number of reproductive illness, which were termed as the silent emergency. This understanding lead to women's health researchers and activists focusing more on women's health, especially in the field of reproductive health.

Reproductive morbidity is a broad concept that encompasses health problems related to reproductive organs and functions, including and outside of childbearing. Reproductive morbidity can be broadly categorised into three subgroups: obstetric morbidity, gynecological morbidity and contraceptive morbidity. Obstetric morbidity refers to ill health in relation to pregnancy and childbirth. Gynecological morbidity includes health problems outside pregnancy such as RTIs, menstrual problems, cervical ectopic, infertility, cancers, prolepses and problems related to intercourse. Contraceptive morbidity includes conditions, which result from efforts to limit fertility, whether they are traditional or modern methods. Reproductive morbidity in general, is an outcome of not just biological factors but of women's poverty, powerlessness and lack of control over resources as well. Malnutrition, infection, early and repeated childbearing and high fertility also play an important role in poor maternal health conditions in India.

India's maternal mortality ratio (MMR) is highest in South Asia: 540 deaths per 100,000 live births or one woman dying roughly every five minutes. An estimated 1,36,000 women die in India every year due to pregnancy-related setbacks. The number of maternity-related deaths which occur in a week in India is equivalent to what occurs in a whole year in Europe. However, government has not taken any effective measures till date. Despite the fact that an high fatalities occur among women in a year due to poor reproductive health practices no one is exercised enough to create a movement for improving women's health.

One of the reasons why women succumb to reproduction related complications is lack of timely transportation to the nearest hospital. Experts estimate that 70 per cent of the maternal-related deaths are preventable. Tetanus and anemia claim a large number of women because mothers get very little or no care in the post-natal period. Anaemia can be overcome with proper nutrition and supplements.

In US, MMR has dropped by 99 per cent in recent years largely because of improvements in sanitation and post-natal care rather than new medication. Good sanitation and nutrition and avoiding overwork and stress will improve the health of the women here. The need is to shift focus from the medical to the social, beginning with healthy antenatal care. But cultural, social and economic barriers delay or prevent women from seeking reproductive healthcare at any stage-antenatal, delivery or post-natal. Safe maternity is a vital social indicator which requires immediate attention.

Women's health issues have attained higher visibility, public interest and adequate political commitment in recent times. Generally, most women suffer from one or other kind of health problem, in her life time as she passes through various stages of life and faces new and variety of life experiences. It may be in the early years of life childhood women faces societal neglect, in the period of adolescence during which she attains puberty; in the adulthood when she is definitely in the married life a women participates in the reproduction and in the old age (particularly, after the age of 45) when her reproductive capacity ceases. Also women, in general, at their old age are dependent on others for their livelihood.

It could be observed that every year it is estimated that worldwide more than 500,000 women die due to complications of pregnancy and childbirth. Further at least seven million women who survive childbirth suffer from serious health problems and a further 50 million women suffer from adverse health consequence after childbirth. The overwhelming majority of these deaths and complications occur in developing countries.

More specifically, in developing countries, women continue to face major challenges to meeting women's reproductive health needs including the poor quality of health services, widespread ignorance about reproductive health issues, financial gender inequality (Aoyema, 2001). In reality, women's reproductive health problems are rather preventable but they are compounded by social and economic conditions and gender bias. Yet, failure to address women's reproductive health needs increases both healthcare costs and social inequalities.[5]

Owing to this new development of targeted policies and programmes implemented in many countries of the world and that have enabled the women to lead relatively healthier lives of course, with limited access to education and employment in many nations. However, at the same time, as a result of high illiteracy rates and increasing poverty levels leads further to deteriorating the socio-economic conditions of women. Realising the importance of women health and great concern for woman folk, the International Conference on Population and Development held at Cairo in 1994, resolved to implement the reproductive and child health programme focusing on women and newborn and young children.

Reproductive health (RH) is explained as a state of complete physical, mental and social well-being and not merely the absence of diseases, in all matters relating to reproductive system. It is pestinent to point out the reproductive health implies that people are able to have responsible a satisfying and safe sex life and that they have the capability to reproduce and freedom to decide their reproductive choices. Further, reproductive health problems such as early and unwanted childbearing, HIV and other sexually transmitted infections, and pregnancy-related illness and death account for a significant part of the burden of disease among adolescents, adults and married of both sexes in developing countries. According to the World Development Report 2006, sexual and reproductive health problems account for 18 per cent of the total global burden of diseases and 32 per cent of the burden among women of reproductive age. In other words, at least 18 per cent of all disability adjusted life years were caused by reproductive health problems.

Reproductive health problems are particularly concentrated among the poor who often lack access to minimum reproductive healthcare. An estimated 120 million women wish to space and limit fertility but lack access to family planning (WDR, 2006). Prevention is the most cost-effective approach to addressing most reproductive health problems. Series problems are costly and very difficult to solve once manifest. The adverse consequences of poor reproductive health and the benefits of good reproductive health, extend well beyond health, and have an impact at the societal level. For example, early childbearing can have negative health and social consequences for young mothers and lasting health-related effects on their children. On the other hand, good reproductive health increases productivity and well-being of the people, family and ultimately the nation and world at large.[6]

Globally, 51 per cent of pregnant women and a third of women of reproductive age who are not pregnant are anemic. This causes fatigue reduces productivity and lowers their resistance to disease. In pregnancy and childbirth it means greater risk for the life and health of both mother and child.

The United Nations Decade for Women (1975-1985), Maxico Population in 1984, the Nairobi Conference on Women in 1985 and the Cairo Population Conference in 1994, all brought the world's attention to the issue of women's reproductive health problems.

While referring the about the overall aim of reproductive health programme is to protect the reproductive health of women folk, it prevent health hazards of reproductive system and thereby sustain healthy sexual and reproductive life. In other words, the reproductive health aims at facilitating safer sex, safe delivery, free from anxiety of excessive fertility or infertility, prevention of the risk of sexual morbidity and premature degenerative defects and thus, pave way for happy and joyful life. The concept of reproductive health as adopted at the International Conference on Population and Development held at Cairo in 1994 include various aspects of women health. These may include: Sexual and reproductive behaviours, Family planning services, maternal care and safe motherhood, Reproductive tract infection (RTI), Infertility, Genital tract malignancies and HIV infection/AIDS.

The different features of the reproductive health programmes specifically focuse on improving adolescent reproductive health, reduces unwanted pregnancies and the risk of contacting HIV and other sexually transmitted infections. It improves the chances of girls continuing in school and expands their life options. Providing life coping skills including reproductive health education for boys and girls has long-term positive impacts. Prevention and management of sexually transmitted infections (STI's) prevent sexual spread of HIV. Integrating HIV prevention activities in mother and child health (MCH) and family planning (FP) programmes address missed opportunities to curb the HIV epidemic in the general population. Reproductive and child health provides opportunities to choose when to get pregnancy, apart from being a health issue, greatly influences population growth, and environmental conditions. Increasing contraceptive choices and access leads to fewer unsafe abortions-arguably the most easily avoidable cause of maternal death. Life saving care for complications from abortion is an excellent opportunity to provide contraception, avoiding another unwanted pregnancy. Reducing pregnancy-related death and illness in mothers increases the survival probabilities of newborn and child survival and hence improves productivity. Reducing maternal deaths depends on a functioning health system. Strengthening the RCH system to improve maternal health brings benefits in many other areas of health.

The Global Commission on Women's Health considers reproductive health as referring to all aspects of well being related to the reproductive system throughout the life cycle. It encompasses fertility, infertility and the enjoyment of sexual health without fear of disease or unwanted pregnancy. Women's reproductive health was one of the central themes at the 1994 Cairo World Conference on Population and Development. Its programme of action clearly states that all countries should strive to make reproductive healthcare including Family Planning, counselling, information, education, services for prenatal care, safe delivery and postnatal care, accessible to all through the primary care system.

1.2 Reproductive Health Problems of Women in India

Reproductive health has till recently been a neglected area in the public health domain of several developing countries including India. Only after the International Conference on Population and Development (ICPD), Cairo in 1994, it was recommended that the participating countries should implement unified Reproductive and Child health (RCH) Programmes. After ICPD reproductive health received worldwide recognition. In fact, if should be mentioned that the ICPD only formalised the growing international consensus that improvement of reproductive health (including family planning) is an essential element of human welfare and development. It is well known that the new population policy adopted at Cairo Conference promoted gender equity and reproductive health lessening the importance of reducing the rates of population growth. Among a wide range of issues concerning population and development, which were discussed in the programme of Action adopted by the ICPD, reproductive rights and reproductive health were two important issues and in the final Cairo policy document, both gender equity and reproductive health are comprehensively defined (Luke and Watkins, 2002).[7] Reproductive health includes not only the earlier items of family planning and maternal and child health but also sexually transmitted Diseases (STDs) including HIV/AIDS and Reproductive Tract Infections (RTIs), infertility, post-abortion care, reproductive cancers, gender-based violence and reproductive and sexual rights (UNFPA, 1999).[8] One important vision of ICPD was every sex act should be free of coerce in (Tsui *et al.,* 1997)[9].

India adopted the RCH programmes in April 1996. The package of essential RCH services recommended for implementation in India includes prevention and treatment of RTI's and Sexually Transmitted Infections (STI's) (Pachauri, 1995).[10]

The International Conference on Population and Development (ICPD), held in Cairo in 1994, drew the attention of the international community and of national governments to the need for improved reproductive healthcare, particularly in low income countries. The ICPD Programme of Action recommends the "comprehensive and factual informal information and a full range of reproductive health-care services, including family planning, should be accessible, affordable and convenient to all uses." It also states: "All countries should take steps to meet the family planning needs of their populations as soon as possible and sound, in all cases by the years 2015, seek to provide universal access to a full range of safe and reliable family planning methods and to related reproductive health methods services which are not against the law.

As a part of Indian delegation to International Forum on Population Development India presented the report on "Population and Development: 10 years since ICPD" on 7th September 2004 in Wuhan, China. India, being a signatory to the Programme of Action (POA), which was endorsed by the 179 participating countries in the Conference held in Cairo, has responded positively and had taken several initiatives since 1994.

Further, ICPD (1994) had stressed the need for implementation of Reproductive and child health programme for various countries. According to the ICPD (1994), "People have the ability to reproduce and regulate their fertility, women are able to go through pregnancy and child birth safely, the outcome of pregnancies is successful in terms of maternal and child health survival and well-being, and couples are able to have sexual relation free of fear from poignancy and contracting diseases."

Many countries have subscribed to the Programme of Action drafted at the International Conference on Population and Development held in Cairo in 1994, and these countries must now move beyond policy statements to actually implement integrated to reproductive health programmes.

The POA centred on considerations like population but of reproductive health, reproductive rights and gender equity. The concerns over education of girls, gender equity and empowerment of women reduction in infant, child and maternal mortality reduction; and the provision of universal access to reproductive health services, including family planning and sexual health were conference. Apart from the ICPD, POA another noteworthy development report was of the National Committee on Population, headed by M.S. Swaminathan, which submitted its recommendations in June 1994. The National Committee on Population was critical of the earlier target oriented approach and mentioned that the target oriented approach had led to large scale statistical manipulations of official data, offered poor quality of couples and was also anti-women. The report clearly recommended that India's population policy should be pro-poor pro-women and pro-nature. Historical perspective of India's population policies since Independence by Professor Srinivasan had rightly categorised earlier target oriented approach until 1976 as HIT's model that is to say that health department operated, incentive-based, target-oriented, time-bound and sterilisation-focused programme; and thereafter coercion approach during the emergency period from June 1975 to March 1977, and thereafter recovery period and finally the RCH approach since 1994 (Srinivasan, 2001).[11] However, such critical reports and evaluation studies, and deliberations and recommendations of the ICPD conference provided background and were instrumental for the paradigm shifts in India's population policy since 1994. Several initiatives undertaken by the Government of India since ICPD had been highlighted in the country report presented at Wuhan, China.

The major paradigm shift from earlier target-oriented to target-free approach (TFA) in April 1996 and then to client centred and demand-driven-Community-Needs-Assessment (CAN) approach, which was later renamed as Reproductive and Child Health (RCH) approach into policy and programme of actions in India. The essential components of the RCH were prevention of unwanted pregnancies by promoting contraception for both spacing and limiting children, providing services for safe motherhood improvement in child survival by expanding immunisation coverage, treatment of diarrhoeal diseases and acute respiratory infections, etc. Most of these concerns that were raised in the ICPD conference and the evaluation reports were under active consideration of the population policy committee formulating the National Population Policy.

The National Population Policy (NPP), announced by the Government of India on 15th February 2000, had clearly enunciated short, medium and long-run objectives of the policy. The immediate objective enshrined in the NPP–2000 document was to address the unmet needs for contraception healthcare infrastructure, and health personnel, and to provide integrated service delivery for basic reproductive and child healthcare.[12]

1.3 Adolescent Reproductive Health

The reproductive health of adolescents is of growing concern today. At the global level, the Programme of Action of the International Conference on Population and Development, held in Cairo in 1994, placed great emphasis on the health problems and health needs of adolescents. Until recently, the reproductive health needs of adolescents as a group were largely ignored by the existing reproductive health services.

It is highly important to mention that the information and services on reproductive health be made available to adolescents to help them understand their sexuality and protect them from unwanted pregnancy, Sexuality Transmitted Diseases (STD's) and the subsequent risk of infertility. It is noticed that motherhood at a very young age entails high risk of maternal morbidity and mortality that far exceeds the average. The children of young mothers tend to have higher levels of childbearing continues to be an impediment to improvements in the educational, economic and social status of women worldwide. Furthermore, sexually active adolescents are increasingly at risk of contracting and transmitting STDs, including Human Immunodeficiency Virus/Acquired Immuno Deficiency Syndrome (HIV/AIDS). Typically, there are poorly informed on how to protect themselves from such diseases.

The Programme of Action adopted at the International Conference on Population and Development stressed that it was important to "address adolescent sexual and reproductive health issues, including unwanted pregnancy, unsafe abortion and sexually transmitted diseases, including HIV/AIDS, through the formation of responsible and healthy reproductive and sexual behaviours, including voluntary abstinence, and the provision of appropriate services and counselling specifically suitable for that age group" (United Nations, 1994).[13] In particular the programme of Action called for a substation reduction of adolescent pregnancy.

According to the United Nations (1997), adolescence is defined as the stage of life during which individuals reach sexual maturity; it is the period of transition from puberty to maturity. Since the age range implied by this description is imprecise, operational definitions also vary. The age group 10-19 identifies the period of adolescence. But for the purpose of this study "adolescents" refers to the age group 15-19, as data on reproductive health are most commonly available for this age group. Furthermore, the reproductive health problems and needs of adolescents tend to be more distinct than those of youth aged 20-24[14].

1.4 Components of Reproductive Health

Antenatal Care

Antenatal care is the care and help you receive from health professionals during the course of your pregnancy. It is important that you take good care of your own health and that of your unborn baby during pregnancy and making the most of the antenatal care available to you is a big part of that.

As soon as you find out that you are pregnant you should get in touch with your GP or midwife to get information on the services and support that are available and to organise antenatal care. This will include:

- antenatal appointments–regular health appointments with your midwife or doctor to check your health and the development of your baby,
- antenatal screening–tests that assess whether your unborn baby is at risk of certain conditions or abnormalities, and
- antenatal classes–classes and workshops that prepare you and your partner for the birth of your baby.

Antenatal appointments are check-ups to assess the health of you and your baby.

The antenatal period is an extremely important time during pregnancy. It is well recognised that good antenatal care improves maternal, perinatal and neonatal outcomes. Most women will progress through pregnancy in an uncomplicated fashion and deliver a healthy infant with little medical intervention. However, a significant number will develop medical or fetal complications.

The current challenge in antenatal care is to identify those women who will require specialist support while allowing uncomplicated pregnancy to proceed with minimal interference.

The Aims of Antenatal Care are to:

- provide high-quality information that can be easily understood in the current climate of ethnic and social diversity;

- provide an informed choice about the pathways of antenatal care;
- identify and screen for maternal complications;
- identify and screen for fetal complications;
- assess maternal and fetal wellbeing throughout pregnancy;
- provide advice and education on the normal symptoms of pregnancy.

The First Trimester

The first trimester of pregnancy is the time period after conception to the end of the 13th week of pregnancy. It is very important to initiate prenatal care as soon as pregnancy is confirmed and routine prenatal visits should begin occurring monthly. Women should be enrolled in prenatal care, WIC, home visiting, HANDS, and Resource Persons, if applicable. (It is necessary to document in the medical record the patient's verbalisation of understanding of the services covered under the prenatal programme, if the prenatal/postpartum services are to be provided by the health department.)

The estimated date of confinement (EDC) or estimated date of delivery (EDD) is calculated by taking the first day of the last menstrual period (LMP) adding nine months plus seven days. The LMP method is less reliable in predicting the EDC than first trimester or early second trimester ultrasound dating. The majority of women will deliver between 38-41 weeks gestation. Delivery prior to the beginning of the 38th week is considered preterm, and delivery occurring after 42 weeks is called post-dates or post-term.

The Second Trimester

The second trimester of pregnancy is the time period beginning with the 14th week through the 27th week of gestation. Routine prenatal visits should occur monthly. Women should be enrolled in prenatal care, WIC, home visiting, HANDS, and Resource Persons if applicable. Typically the mother-to-be feels best in this trimester. The nausea has usually subsided and her energy level increases. This is a most favourable time to provide anticipatory guidance and counselling as her focus has shifted from herself to her developing baby. Usually the mother and her significant other are ready for new learning opportunities as they prepare to become parents.

The Third Trimester

The third trimester of pregnancy is the time period beginning with the 28th week of pregnancy until delivery. Routine prenatal visits begin taking place every two weeks until the 36th week when they become weekly visits until delivery. Women should be enrolled in WIC, home visiting, HANDS, and Resource Persons if applicable. Mothers-to-be tend to become anxious as well as physically uncomfortable toward the end of the third trimester. Many mothers-to-be anticipate delivery by their EDC date but only approximately five per cent actually deliver on their due date.

The Fourth Trimester

The time period from delivery until the six weeks postpartum checkup is sometimes referred to as the fourth trimester. This transitional period for the new parent(s) may be very challenging. Attention has shifted from the mother (also father and other children) to the newborn with his/her numerous needs. Maternal expectations may be unrealistic increasing the likelihood of postpartum depression. Emotional support from the significant other, family members, friends and healthcare providers is essential for sustaining the mother during this trimester. Mother and/or infant should be enrolled in WIC, home visiting, HANDS, Resource Persons, Family Planning, and other LHD services if applicable.

Intranatal Care

Intranatal care refers to the process of childbirth. Intranatal care is of extreme importance for every pregnancy. Such level of care strongly emphasises on great deal of safe procedures on the following:

- Clean surrounding of the Labour Room and the other rooms connected to it.
- Clean hands and hygienic practices.
- Following safe and hygienic delivery practices.
- Maintaining highest standards of sterility of tools and instruments.

If you happen to go for labour or to assist someone whom you know, make sure the above mentioned points are followed or else places not keeping above standards would not be a good place for delivery.

Postnatal Care

The care of the mother and the newborn child after delivery is known as postnatal care. It is also called postpartal care.

Objectives of Care to Mother

- To prevent complications of postpartal period.
- To provide care for the rapid restoration of the mother to optimum health.
- To check adequacy of breast feeding.
- To provide family planning services.
- To provide basic health education to mother and family.

Essential Physical Care for Mother

It should be made sure the mother has three checkups a day for three days after delivery.

Frequency of Post Natal Checkups

Three times a day for three days after delivery

Once or twice a week for first few weeks

Once a month for first six months

Once in two-three months for end of one year.

1.5 Reproductive and Child Health and National Population Policy

The National Population Policy of 2000 articulated the sexual reproductive health needs of the adolescent in India. About 22 per cent of India's population falls into the adolescent age group of 10-19 years. Despite the rising age at marriage, and laws prohibiting early marriage (Child Marriage Restraint Act of 1929 and its amendment in 1978) the average age at marriage for girls continue to be 19.2 for girls still about 31 per cent of the girls marry below legal age at marriage with substantial rural-urban and inter-state differentials. Culturally for younger women in India, sexual relations occur overwhelmingly within marriage. But it is alarming to know almost 50 per cent of all new HIV infections occur amongst younger people between the ages of 10-25 years. In a culturally sensitive Indian situation the knowledge about sexual health, reproductive tract infections, sexually transmitted diseases, usage of contraception, etc. counselling for adolescents is imparted to female health workers in rural areas but data from district level Rapid Household surveys indicate that 15 per cent of the rural women, or households for that matter, were visited by the ANM/LHV at household during three months prior to the survey. Thus, programme and schemes need to be focus more on adolescents to impart knowledge about contraception, sexual health and HIV/AIDS. In the developing world, programmes of reproductive health aimed at teenagers are often small scale and not centrally coordinated, although some countries such as Indonesia and Sri Lanka have a systematic policy framework for teaching about sex within schools. Non-governmental agencies such as the International Planned Parenthood Federation provide contraceptive advice for young women worldwide.

Maternal and prenatal health is of particular concern among teens who are pregnant or parenting, since the worldwide incidence of premature birth and low birth weight is higher among adolescent mothers. Adolescents also face at least a 20 per cent greather likelihood of maternal of infant death than women in their twenties. The risks increase several fold for women under age 16. Despite their high risk, most unmarried adolescents lack the requisite knowledge and services to prevent pregnancy. Studies in Guatemala and Kenya found that fewer than one in ten unmarried youth could correctly identify the fertile period (CDC, 1991; Aiayi and others, 1991) Research indicates that pregnant teens are less likely to receive prenatal care, often seek it at very late stage of pregnancy may be in the third trimester, if at all for instance, the Guttmacher Institute reports that one-third of pregnant teens receive insufficient prenatal care and that their children are more likely to suffer from health issues in childhood or be hospitalised than those born to older women. However, studies have indicated that young mothers who are given high-quality maternity care bear significantly healthier babies than those that do not.[15] In most developing countries a majority of young women have heard of at least one modern contraceptive method, but they generally do not have adequate knowledge about correct usage. National surveys in several African countries found that although at least one in four women aged 15 to 19 was single and sexually experienced, few were using contraception. Among those who were using contraception, large proportions were relying on ineffective traditional methods such as rhythm and withdrawal (Population Reference Bureau, 1992; Yinger and others, 1992).[16]

It may be noticed that many of the health-issues associated with teenage mothers, many of whom do not have health insurance, appear to result from lack of access to high-quality medical care. Many pregnant teens are subject to nutritional deficiencies from poor eating habits which is quite common in adolescence, including attempts to lose weight invariably through dieting, skipping meals, food faddism, snacking, and consumption of fast food.

Very importantly, it may note that inadequate nutrition during pregnancy is an even more marked problem among teenagers in developing countries. Complications of pregnancy result in the deaths of an estimated 70,000 teen girls in developing countries each year. Young mothers and their babies are also at greater risk of contracting HIV. The World Health Organisation estimates that the risk of death following pregnancy is twice as great for women between 15 and 19 years than for those between the age of 20 and 24. The maternal mortality rate can be up to five times higher for girls aged between 10 to 14 than for women of about twenty years of age.[17]

Many unmarried adolescents seek abortions–whether legal or not–to avoid expulsion from school and social condemnation. Because they often seek clandestine abortions and delay in obtaining the procedure and seeking attention for associated problems, adolescents have a higher rate of abortion complications. Studies of hospital records in several African countries found that between 38 and 68 per cent of women seeking care for complications of abortion were under 20 years of age.

Unplanned pregnancy is common in every country. In most developing countries, about 20 to 30 per cent of married women– or about 120 million women–with to avoid becoming pregnant but are not using contraception (Westoff and Ochoa, 1991).[17] This number would increase substantially if unmarried women who need a better or more suitable contraceptive method, and women who use abortion services were included. One in five birth in these countries is unwanted.[18]

Worldwide, an estimated 40 million to 60 million women resort to abortion to end unwanted pregnancies. Because the majority of abortions are unsafe, the procedure carries a higher risk of injury and death, accounting for 125,000 to 200,000 female deaths annually (Dixon Mueller, 1990; Rosenfield, 1989; WHO, 1992C).[18] Abortion-related mortality is highest in countries where abortion is legally restricted, access to family planning and safe abortion services in limited, and overall maternal mortality is high. About 40 per cent of the world's population lives in countries with no restrictions abortion, 23 per cent where abortion is permitted for social and medical reasons, 12 per cent where abortion is permitted when the woman's life and health are at stake or there are injuries to the foetus, and 25 per cent where abortion is permitted only to save the life of the woman or is not permitted at all (Hensaw, 1990).[19] The cost of treating abortion-related complications is much greater than the cost of safe abortion.

Each year more than 150 million become pregnant, more than 50 million experience acute pregnancy-related complication, and 15 million develop long-term disabilities (WHO, 1992a). Half a million of these women die as a result. In developing countries, more than one-fourth of all deaths of women of reproductive age are pregnancy-related, caused mainly by hemorrhage, sepsis, unsafe abortion, hypertensive disorders and obstructed labour. While maternal mortality has fallen in parts of Latin America and in South-east and West Asia, it remains high in Africa and South Asia. Even though the risk of dying as a result of pregnancy or childbirth has declined globally, the number of pregnancy-related deaths has continued to rise as the number of women in their prime childbearing years also rises.[20]

Risks for medical complications are greater for girls at the early teens say 14 years of age or earlier as an underdeveloped pelvis can lead to difficulties in childbirth. Obstructed labour is normally dealt with by Caesarean section in industrialised nations; however, in developing regions where non-availability of appropriate medical services can lead to eclampsia, obstetric fistula, infant mortality, or maternal death. For mothers in their late teens, age in itself is not a risk factor, and poor outcomes are associated more with socio-economic factors rather than with biology.

Reproductive life is a very personal, private and secret matter in our society. Done to this culture people often don't discuss matters related to reproductive health problems. Due to the socio-cultural taboos attached to reproductive health and ignorant attitudes; women are often the silent suffers of many reproductive health problems than can be easily detected, caused and prevented.

Reproductive health is the healthy sexual and reproductive life of individual's lights through their life cycle and not just in the reproductive age group. It addresses the physical, social, emotional and psychological dimensions of sex and reproduction and not just the presence or absence of disease of reproductive organs, it attempts to address the problems originating for irresponsible sexual behaviour, myths and misconceptions.

Women in poor health are more likely to give birth to low weight infants. They also are less likely to be able to provide food and adequate care for their children.

1.6 Maternal Morbidity and Mortality

In India, nearly 10,00,000 women die every year due to abortion and child birth, two-thirds of pregnant women in India are anemic. The complications of pregnancy due to high fertility leads to placenta praevia in one per cent, abruptio placenta in two per cent prolonged pregnancies in ten per cent, ectoctopic gestation in 0.5 per cent, eclampsia in eight per cent not to mention of thousand of cases of malpresentations of the fetus, post partum hemorrhage and rupture of uterus. It is well known that pregnant women lose immunity to malaria are more susceptible to viral infections like infectious hepatitis.

Pregnancy also precipitates development of overt leprosy and child birth triggers off episodes of major psychiatric pathology, like schizophrenia, manic depression and acute psychosis.

India's maternal mortality rate estimated at 4-5 per 1000 live births (UNICEF, 1991) is about 50 times higher than that of developed countries. However, levels as high as 13 were also noted in certain rural areas. The actual risk of Indian women dying from maternity related causes is high due to their larger number of pregnancies (five or six compared to one or two in developed countries). Maternal age and parity have a strong effect on maternal mortality. A woman giving birth to children at the optimum age 20-35 years faces a much lower risk than women below 20 and over 35 years. The level of risk from this factor alone can be inferred from the fact that an estimated eight per cent of around 26-27 million annual births in India, are on account of mothers below 19 years. It is observed that maternal illness and deaths rise significantly with the fourth pregnancy and reach a high level after the fifth. In India, as in many developing countries, maternal mortality accounts for the largest or near largest proportion of deaths among women in their prime year.[21]

Shatrugna *et al.,*. (1993) recently reported that attention to the poor health status of women in India has been inadequate. Macro data analysis suggests that apart from literacy, women's income may be an important determinant women's health status. A study was therefore undertaken to explore the relationship between women's work, income and women's utilisation of health services. It is sad to note that women's work for income resulted in an increase in women's morbidities. There were gynecological problems, back pain, upper respiratory tract infection etc. However, except in case of fevers where private services were utilised in over 70 per cent of cases, and the government hospital which were popular for antenatal care over 60 per cent (80 per cent) women's illnesses did not receive any healthcare.[22]

In India, 50 per cent of all women and two-thirds of all pregnant women are anemic. It is well known that serve anaemia per se is associated with a high incidence of premature birth, puerperal sepsis and teromoembolic phenomenon in the mother.

According to records of the National Institute of Nutrition 10 to 20 per cent of all maternal deaths are due to nutritional anaemia.

Poor nutrition during pregnancy or during the child's first two years can slow a child's mental and physical development for life. From birth to age two, children should the weighted every month. If a young child does not gain weight over a two months period, something is wrong.

The right to health is the most basic of all human rights. This means that every human being has the light to live in an environment with minimum health seeks and to have access to services that can prevent or alleviate diseases, promote good health throughout the individual's life. Women or developing countries are being denied this basic human right.

In India, Majority of women in India are in the age group of 15 to 49 years put the percentage by 2001 census. Without proper healthcare service, this group is highly vulnerable of many health problems arising from reproductive causes. It is now universally accepted that health status of the women in reproductive age has an impact on health of their clouding, the family, the community and the nation.

Maternal and child health services in India are very poorly developed. Only 40-50 per cent of pregnant women at present received antenatal care, less than 15 per cent are delivered by trained birth attendants only about 20 per cent receive tetanus toxoid a mere 30 per cent are covered by the nutritional supplement (iron and folic acid) programme.

1.7 Summary

In this chapter, brief introduction about meaning of reproductive health, reproductive health problems of women in India. Adolescent reproductive health, components of reproductive health, (Antenatal care, Intranatal care and Postnatal care), Reproductive policy, maternal morbidity and mortality are clearly explained followed by objective of the study. In the proceeding chapter–II, the necessary review of literature for the present study were given in detail.

The reproductive health scenario of the world and India, the emerging pattern of the concept reproductive health have been described so as to enable to understand the importance of the regional level studies relating to reproductive health status of women.

Notes

1. Zurayk. *"Concepts and Measures of Reproductive Morbidity".* Health Transition Review, 1993, 3(1): 17-39.
2. United Nations (UN). Report of the International Conference on Population and Development, Cairo: UN, 1994.
3. M. Fathalla, Research Needs in Human Reproduction in E. Diczfalusy, P.D. Griffin and J. Kharina (eds). *Research in Human Reproduction.* Geneva: World Health Organisation, 1988.
4. WHO. Division of Reproductive Health, 1998. Who, Geneva.
5. Aoyama A.S. "Rproductive Health in the Middle East and North Africa: Well-being for all" Washington, DC: The World Bank, 2001.
6. World Development Report 2006.
7. Luke, Nancy and Watkins, Susan Cotts. *Reactions of Developing Country Elites to International Policy,* Population and Development Review, 28 (4); 2002.
8. UNFPA. *Reproductive Tract Infection in India: The HIV / AIDS connection,* New Delhi, 1999.
9. Tsui, A.O., Wasserheit, J.N. and Hagga, J.G (eds.). *Reproductive Health in Developing Countries,* Expanding Dimensions Building Solutions National Academy Press, Washington DC, 1997.
10. S. Pachauri. *Relationship Between AIDS and Family Planning Programmes: A ratio native for developing integrated reproductive health services,* Health Transition Review, Supplement to No. 4, 331-347, 1995.
11. Srinivasan, K. *et al.,* (2001). Population profile of the state of Uttaranchal Paper Presented at the State Level conference on *"Health Development and Population Stabilisation Issues in Uttaranchal,* Dehradun, 22-23 May, 2001.
12. Govt. of India. National Population Policy Department of Family Welfare, Ministry of Health and Family Welfare, GOI, New Delhi, 2000.
13. United Nations (1994). Population and Development Review, New York.
14. United Nations 1999. Demographic Year Book, 1997, New York.
15. CDC–*Trends in Fertility and Infant and Maternal Health-United States,* 1980–1988, MMWR, 1991; 40: 381-3, 389-90. Ajayi *et al.,* (1991) "*Adolescent sexuality and fertility in Kenya : A survey of knowledge perceptions and practices"* Studies in Family Planning 22(4) : 205-16.

16. PRB. 1992. *Adolescent Women in Sub-Saharan Africa.* Washington, D.C. Yinger and other PRB, Demographic and Health surveys project of Macro international and the division of RH of the centers for Disease control. 1992. *Adolescent sexual activity and childbearing in Latin America and the Caribbean: Risks and consequences.* Wessington D.C. international programs.
17. Westoff and Luis Hernando Ochoa 1991. *"Unmet Need and the Demand for Family Planning".* DHS, Comparative Studies No.5 Columbia, Md. Macro Systems / Institute for Resource Development.
18. WHO, 1992c. *Women's Health, across Age and Frontier:* Geneva.
19. WHO, 1992a. *Approaches to Adolescent Health and development:* A compendium of projects and programming Geneva.
20. Department of family welfare, Ministry of Health and Family Welfare, GOI, New Delhi, 2000.
21. Shatrugha (1993). Govt. of India, *National Nutrition Policy,* 1993, Department of Women and Child Development, Ministry of Human Resource Development, GOI, New Delhi.
22. UNICEF. The Progress of Nation, 1991, New York, p. 21.

Chapter – 2

Review of Literature

2.1 Introduction about Review of Literature

Reproductive health problems have been recognised with the development and change in social, economic and demographic characteristics at global level. References elaborate different approaches relating to reproductive health problems; discussed within socioeconomic and demographic context. The international community regards reproductive health as a basic human right. To exercise this right within the social and cultural limits, the people must have access to complete reproductive health information and services.

2.2 Adolescent Health Care

Studies by Bongaarts and Cohen (1998) suggest that sub-Saharan Africa, the incidence of premarital sex among women aged 20-24 ranged from 5 per cent in Nigar to 81 per cent in Botswana. In Latin America, this percentage ranged from 10 per cent in the Dominican Republic to 40 per cent in Brazil.[1] Premarital sexual activity is found to be relatively rare in the Asian region. Nonetheless the prevalence of premarital sexual activity is on the rise in Asian societies (Blanc and Way, 1998).[2]

In India, very few studies tried to explore the nutritional status and anemia with its related factors among women in general and among adolescent girls in particular. Based on both anthropological and empirical evidences Khan *et al.*,. (1988) in Uttar Pradesh observed that the majority of the rural women suffer from sever malnutrition.

They were unable to take and nourishing food because of poverty.[3] Thangaleela and Vijayalakshmi (1994) in their study in Coimbatore city noticed that the prevalence of anemia was found to be high in those mothers who had ante-partum and post-partum hemorrhage in their previous pregnancies, and also definite correlation. Could be established between anemia in pregnancy, poor economic status, illiteracy, advancing age, teenage pregnancy, and multi-gravida closed spacing and poor ante-natal care.[4]

In some parts of the developing countries where fertility rates are high, teenage pregnancy and early marriage are common and adolescents have more than 14 million births each year, and more than 90 per cent of these occurs in developing countries (AGI, 1998).[5]

Demographic health survey, (1998-1999), found that nearly 15 per cent of ever-married adolescent women were stunted, and about one-fifth had moderate to severe anemia with poor nutrition. The adverse health consequences of poor nutrition due to low income, poverty and early childbearing can include damage to the reproductive tract infection, maternal mortality, pregnancy complications, prenatal and neonatal mortality and low birth weight.[6]

In this context, the present shift of the national family welfare programme from one that had been aimed at meeting the health and family planning needs of the population to one that currently seeks to address the reproductive health needs of women is indeed a welcome move. In a nutshell, the Reproductive and Child Health (RCH) programme seeks to cover women's health needs across their life cycle from puberty to menopause. It also seeks to implement two new programme services viz. management of reproductive tract infections and adolescent reproductive health (Government of India, 1998). To facilitate the implementation of this new programme, the government has adopted a "Community Needs Assessment Approach", formerly known as "target free approach", the basic philosophy of which is to address individual needs of the clients for health and family welfare, ensure quality of these services and ultimately client satisfaction with the same (Government of India, 1998).[7]

In India, although traditional norms oppose premarital sex, some studies, indicate a growing trend towards premarital sexual activities among adolescents (Sharma, 2000) Limited information from Bangladesh revealed a very high incidence of premarital sex: 61 per cent of males as compared with 24 per cent of females had premarital sexual activity among adolescents, and this percentage was much higher in urban than in rural area (Uddlin, 1999).[8]

Senderowitz (2000) discussed the problems youth concerning reproductive health problems and family planning organisations in Latin America have attracted adolescent clients by creating special spaces for young people and hiring staff specially trained to work with teens and adolescents. In Pakistan, discussion on reproductive health issue among the unmarried young males and females regarded as vulgarity and cultural belief system.[9]

A recent study of young married women aged 16-22 years in a rural community in Tamil Nadu reports a very high level of morbidity. The study shows that more than half of the women were suffering from at least one or more RTI/STDs. Clinical examination also confirmed STDs among majority of them (Joseph *et al.,* 2000). Kulkarni and Adhikari in a study of adolescent women in India and Nepal report relatively high rates of gynecological morbidities, especially in the settings where girls have limited excess to adequate healthcare (Jejeebhoy, 2000).[10]

Adolescent pregnancies (15-19) Contribute to 19 per cent of total fertility in India and record the highest maternal mortality rates. Low birth weight is the major adverse outcome for the infant and an important determinant of increased child mortality. The adolescent population constitutes more than one-fifth (23 per cent) of the total population in India. (NFHS-2, IIPS, ORC Macro, 2000).[11] Among the SAARC countries also, adolescents comparise a sizeable proportion (one-fifth) of the total population as a whole the total population will increase by 18 per cent by 2020 (UNFPA, 1990) early than pointed out. The risks of early pregnancy are exacerbated by poverty and inadequate access to maternal and child health services.[12]

Studies by the Population Reference Bureau found that adolescent women are especially vulnerable to reproductive health problems, and they are more likely than older women to die from problems related to pregnancy and childbirth. Mostly adolescent women face increased risks during pregnancy and childbirth because they have less information and access to prenatal, delivery post partum care as compared with older women (Ashford, 2001).[13] A survey carried out in Matlab, Bangladesh relieved that the maternal mortality rate of girls aged 10-14 was five times higher than for women aged 20-24, and for women aged 15-19 the rate was twice as high as for women aged 20-24. (Chen and Others, 1974).[14] Studies by UNESCO also suggest that in Bangladesh the high incidence of teenage pregnancies has contribute to high maternal mortality among adolescent girls under 18, the maternal mortality rate is three to four times higher than among older women (Uddlin, 1999).[15]

And adolescent mother who is already malnourished and if she is an urban slum dweller, the competing nutritional needs of pregnancy and growth will affect the growth of the fetus and hence the birth weight of the child (UNICEF, 2001).[16]

UNICEF (2001), report revealed age at marriage is an important factor in child bearing. Global estimates suggested that girls aged 15-19 are twice as likely to die from childbirth compared with women in their twenties, while girls younger than age 15 face a risk that is five times great. Indeed, more adolescent's girls at early age die from pregnancy-related causes than from any other cause (PRB, 2000).[17]

Akhtar (2002) disclosed that fear; shame and lack of resources inhibit adolescents from seeking safe and early abortions on one hand and from seeking care when complications occur on the other. Research in selected areas of Bangladesh found that while adolescents constitutes nine per cent of those who received menstrual regulation services, they constituted 15 per cent of those turned away because they sought services too late in their pregnancy.[18]

In many parts of India, adolescents are likely to marry considerably older men and more sexually experienced for example, women who married at the age of 15 or below have an average spousal age gap of 7.3 compared to a gap of 4.7 for women who married at the age between 21 and 25 (Jensan and Thornton, 2003).[19] Women who marry *considerably* older men may be *more vulnerable* than other young women for two reasons. First, older husband may be more likely infected themselves than *younger men,* for example, Studies in Zambia have noted that *having an* older partner was associated with increased risk of HIV infection among the (Gregson *et al.,* 2002; Sturdevant *et al.,* 2001)[20] and Second, where spousal age difference is considerable, the young women may be less capable of asserting themselves or denying sex. (Jensen and Thornton, 2003; Nurse, 2003; Martin *et al.,* 1999; Maman *et al.,* 2002, Van Derstraten *et.al.,* 1998).[21]

The proportion of teenage women who are mothers or currently pregnant is greatest in sub-Saharan Africa (20-40 per cent) (Wesoff *et al.,* ORC Macro, 2003). The proportions are low on other regions; 6-21 per cent in Asia with Bangladesh on outlier at 35 per cent and 13-25 per cent in Latin America.[22]

Wang *et al.,* (2003) explores the factors using Multiple logistic regression analysis identified six factors associated with adolescents reproductive health of different teenagers include: poor contraceptive knowledge' poor contraceptive self-efficacy, low effective contraceptive use, low socio-economic status, more frequent mating and older age. The result provide health professional to develop more effective prevention to mitigate this problem. The results also could be used for effective policy formulation.[23]

Baridalyne and Redderiah (2004) found that almost half of the women (48 per cent) attained menarche at 13 years of age, and 35 per cent at 14 years. All the women refrained from worshipping and participating in religious activities during their menstrual period. However, none of them were at rest during menstruation and majority of them (60 per cent) reported to have used home-made pads made of cloths, while 11 per cent of women used both clothes and sanitary napkins. Only 28 per cent women found to have exclusively used napkins. Only eight per cent of women preferred washed and cleaning clothes among those using clothes as absorbent. The rest used any kind of cotton cloth available and 18 per cent used dirty clothes since they regard menstruation as unclean. There is a statistically significant association between the educational status of the mother and the use of absorbent materials. It was also observed that women of young age group (20-29) years were more likely to use sanitary napkins compared to the older woman (30+years).[24]

As a result of high levels of early childbearing in developing countries, pregnancy and child birth are the leading causes of death among women aged 15-19. Compared with older women, teenages are at increased risk for poor maternal and infant outcomes (Senderowit *et. al., 1995).*[25] The rise of maternal death during child birth is 2-4 times as high among adolescents younger than 18 as among women aged 20 or older (MC Cauley and salter *et .al.,* 1995).[26] Compared with babies born to women aged 20-29, babies born to women younger than 20 have a 34 per cent higher risk of death in the neonatal period, largely because of their increased risk of being low-birth weight (UN, 1989) and a 26 per cent higher risk of death by age five (Bicego, Ahmed and Calvetlom).[27]

In the study of adolescent girls in Rajasthan it is found that large proportions of girls were not aware of menstruations when they first experienced it (Khanna and Goyal, 2005).[28] A study conducted in Ahmednagar in Maharashtra (Barua and Kurzk, 2001) shows that the married adolescent girls often went untreated in case of menstrual problem and RTI.[29]

2.3 Ante-natal Care

Ford (1945) also pointed out the importance of cultural factors for having children. He stated that although human reproduction is a biological phenomenon, it is supported by a belief system. Childbearing is not a charming experience. Bitter experience of gestation and labour pain, risk of stillbirth, chance of death of mother and baby, rearing and looking after children and problems associated with childbearing. The author states that desire for children is not the natural drive, but it is reinforced by the social system through rewards and punishment.[30.]

Easterlin (1986) central thesis was related to economic models that support advancement in economic realities to understand reproductive health behaviour. These models have been a source of inspiration to many population scientists. The discussion revealed that many decision-making styles are habitual and characterised by a culture economy of family. The economic level varies within and between societies. Hence, decision-making processes and patterns vary within and between societies, and from those that prevailed in the past. Variations in decision styles from the past depend upon the degree and speed of assimilation of a new code of behaviour. The overall decision sequence can act to counterbalance change resulting from the introduction of new alternatives under the light of income and explained how the decision styles change due to the assimilation of a new code of behaviour. The author argued, that social pressures against a particular set of decisions grows, tension develops in the decision-making pattern. Women may continue to behave in accordance with the common pattern in spite of this tension, because of the strength of the overall logic of the sequence, the whole structure of decision-making changed. This led to the point that the decision-making process was changing and shifting from collectivism to individualism.[31]

Freedman (1987) viewed that the relation of education to reproductive health becomes attenuated when other socio-economic variables are controlled. He argued that education might be considered as a broad socioeconomic indicator. They also found high birth intervals among the children of mothers who were educated than the mothers who were illiterate. It also reflected from the study that high birth intervals has also important factor of children nutritional level.[32]

Studies in Indian women of the upper income group have shown that their dietary intakes range between 2000-2500 kcal per day in pregnancy. In this group women generally do not perform hard physical work and there is a reduction in the activity during pregnancy. The average weight of this population group ranges between 45-55 kg and the mean weight gain during pregnancy is about 11 kg (Ramachandran, 1989).[33] Studies in urban women of low income group showed that their dietary intakes range from (1200-1600 Kcal) per day. The average per-pregnancy weight of these women is around 43 Kg and they gain 6 Kg during pregnancy. In rural India, dietary intakes of women are slightly higher (1600-1900 Kcal) than those of urban women. However; rural women have spend more energy in daily household chores.

He reported that anaemia is common among pregnant women, the prevalence rates ranging from 40-50 per cent in urban areas and 50-70 per cent in rural areas. A significant fall in birth weight has been observed with decrease in haemoglobin levels.[42] In a study reported by Sarma and Rao (1992), incidence of low birth weight was 40 per cent in anaemic women with haemoglobin less than 8 gm/dl as against 23 per cent in women with normal haemoglobin level.[34]

Shatrugna *et.al.,* (1993) recently reported that attention to the poor health status of women in India has teen inadequate. Macro data analysis suggests that apart from literacy, women's income may be an important determinant women's health status. A study was therefore undertaken to explore the relationship between women's work, income and women's utilisation of health services. It is said to note that women's work for income resulted in an increase in women's morbidities. There were gynecological problems, back pain, upper respiratory tract infection etc. However, except etc., fevers where private services were utilised in over of per cent of cases, and the government hospitals which were popular for antenatal (18 per cent). over 60 per cent of women illnesses did not receive any healthcare.

Accurate assessments of maternal morbidity are not available but evidence from available studies points to an appallingly high incidence of pregnant women not in contact with health services. Around 71.1 per cent of deliveries in rural areas and 29.2 per cent of deliveries in urban areas are conducted by untrained personnel outside the health system. In Rajasthan, one-third of pregnant women reported illnesses lasting on an average for over two weeks. The maternal mortality rate was 592 per 100,000 live births; for every maternal death some 60 episodes of illness occurred. Of these, on an average, 16.5 episodes were related directly to pregnancy and childbirth and together represented both the leading cause and over a quarter of overall morbidity.[35]

In a study "Determinants of maternal healthcare utilisation in India: Evidence from a recent household survey" Abusaleh Sheriff and Geeta Singh (1994) have made an attempt to discuss the issues associated with the demand and supply of the five measures of maternity care, antenatal care, blood pressure check up, place of delivery, use of trained help at the time of delivery and postnatal care. Econometric analysis is undertaken to find out the determinants of the use of reproductive healthcare services among rural Indian households. Rural data from 32,000 households belonging to 1765 villages across all parts of India was collected by National Council of Applied Economic Research in 1994. The multi-model survey was conducted both at the national and state level. The analysis pertains to 7635 women in the reproductive age group who delivered a child in the year before the survey. The focus on the role of education, information and economic factors as determinants of healthcare accessibility and their utilisation is the specialty of this analysis. Analysis shows that education and information variables significantly increase the utilisation rates for prenatal, child delivery and postnatal healthcare. Women with primary education are more likely to use maternal health services as compared to illiterate women, even after controlling for income and healthcare supply factors. From this we find that access to locally available health services significantly increases maternity care use.[36]

In a study by Jodie M Dodd, Jeffrey S Robinson and Caroline A Crowther entitled "Guiding antenatal care", they state that antenatal care includes screening asymptomatic pregnant women, with the aim of detecting, and thereby preventing, both maternal and neonatal adverse events. Ballantyne at the University of Edinburgh suggested that the high maternal and prenatal mortality rates observed at the beginning of the twentieth century reflected inadequate maternity care during pregnancy and lack of supervision of the progress of labour.

The falling mortality rates corresponded with a gradual increase in the number of antenatal visits recommended. Breech presentation and pre-eclampsia were the only complications reliably detected in the antenatal period, and the benefit in the detection of pre-eclampsia was confined to prime gravid women beyond 34 weeks gestation. Most antenatal admissions, apart from admissions for labour and birth, were for conditions that had arisen despite routine antenatal care-conditions that had not been prevented or detected by it. These studies repeatedly emphasise antenatal care and thus preventing high maternal and prenatal mortality.

Some 'hot' food items are meat, egg, fish, onion, garlic, papaya, pineapple, mango, black berry, suran and so on. The general concept of avoiding these food items was that they caused premature delivery, miscarriage, or abortion. Some of the 'cold' food items are custard apple, coriander, coconut water, peas, radish, yogurt and so on. Some people believe that cold diets could cause cold and cough to the mother and child. Pulses in general should be avoided during pregnancy or eaten in small quantity, after adding herbs and spices that would reduce the heating and gaseous effect. Adding methi seeds (fenugreek) or seasoning it with garlic or hinge (asafetida) would help reduce the gaseous effect. Sour buttermilk is recommended during pregnancy to help digestion. Women also believe that eating cold foods particularly during the last three months would lead to cold labour pains and cause delay in childbirth. The health education programmes in India are trying to take cognizance of the popular beliefs regarding food during pregnancy and trying to use innovative means to minimise their negative and maximise their positive nutritional effects.

A survey was conducted by students on Beliefs and Practices of Antenatal mothers in a rural setting. This survey was conducted among mothers who had children from birth to three years or were currently pregnant. The study aiming at to know the utilisation or healthcare facilities during antenatal period, specially health check-up, immunisation and diet, to find out the prevalence of performance of religious ceremonies during pregnancy, beliefs, practices and superstition related to pregnancy. This survey revealed that in this rural community most of the mother had a low educational standard and belonged to low socioeconomic groups. The maximum number of mothers got married in early age and many mothers had got more than three pregnancies. Fifty per cent of mothers recognised that addition of food stuff was required in this period. All mothers practiced some kind of rituals and in many cases one mother practiced more than one ritual. Mothers utilised sub-centre services like check-up and immunisation. Gradually, their attention has to be diverted towards scientific practices.[37]

An overview of women's health status presents a sobering picture. Death and illnesses from reproductive causes are highest among poor women the world over. In developing countries the burden of reproductive problems is particularly severe for women since they are almost always illiterate, disproportionately poor and politically powerless. According to the World Bank, about one-third of the total disease burden among women aged 15 to 44 years in the developing countries is linked to health problems associated with pregnancy, childbirth, abortion, HIV, and reproductive tract infections and among the diseases for which cost-effective interventions exist, reproductive health problems account for the majority of the disease burden in women of this age group (World Bank, 1993).[38]

Munjanja, S.P. *et al.,* (1996) conducted a Randomised controlled trial of a reduced-visits programme of antenatal care in Harare, Zimbabwe, the goal of this randomised controlled study was to determine whether a new programme of antenatal care with fewer goal-oriented visits would result in equivalent *or* better pregnancy and delivery outcomes compared to the standard programme. The new programme consisted of fewer but more objective oriented visits and fewer procedures per visit. Women were recruited from seven primary healthcare clinics, which were randomly assigned to the two programmes. A total of 15,532 women participated in the study: 9,394 from the four clinics that followed the new programme and 6,138 from the three clinics with the standard programme. Results showed that, as planned, women in the new programme made fewer visits than those in the standard one (median four versus six, respectively). In addition, there were significantly fewer referrals for pregnancy-induced hypertension and for severe hypertension or eclampsia during labour. The risk of preterm delivery (less than 37 weeks) was also significantly lower for women in the new programme (10.1 per cent versus 11.5 per cent).[39]

Mc Donagh M, 1996. "Is antenatal care effective in reducing maternal morbidity and mortality?" Health policy and planning 11(1): 1-15 who appear to use antenatal care frequently are less likely to use services for a mistimed pregnancy. Long distance to the nearest antenatal care facility is an obstacle to antenatal care. The data show that women are highly consistent in their use or non-use of antenatal care services, even when services are within easy access. The reasons remain unexplained by this study, but may include personal beliefs. In-depth qualitative studies may help identify the barriers to use of antenatal care services.[40]

Addressing the aspect of obstetric morbidity, an exhaustive review to understand maternal health status, including maternal mortality, in India by Jejeebhoy (1997) reveals some grim facts associated with pregnancy and childbearing. Maternal mortality levels in India were found to be among the highest in the world with maternal mortality ratio ranging from 437 to 568 per 100,000 live births. Neonatal mortality was also disturbingly high at 52.7 per 1000 live births and is a cause of concern since it is a direct consequence of poor maternal health and reflects maternal conditions like malnourishment, anemia, inadequate care and lack of rest during pregnancy often accompanied by heavy work loads. A striking finding was the lack of information on women's experiences during pregnancy, delivery and the postpartum stage. Such information assumes great significance as an overwhelming majority of Indian women continue to give birth at home, often attended by untrained persons.

While the picture with regard to women's reproductive health, gynaecological as well as obstetric, is indeed grim, what is equally frightening is that poor health gets perpetuated from mother to daughter over several generations as part of a continuous process. It therefore becomes crucial to break this vicious cycle and formulate policies and programmes that are sensitive to women's health needs.[41]

Ahmad *et al.,*. (1998) used the demographic surveillance which has been maintained by an agency since 1966, provided the information for the treatment and comparison areas on pregnancy outcome, live birth, miscarriage, induced abortions, still birth, deaths, migrations and marriages. They applied logistic regression model and compared odds ratios for induced abortion, miscarriage and stillbirth by explanatory variables. They found that the incidence of abortion is higher among women who had six or more births and became pregnant before 12 months after the previous pregnancy with low degree relation. They found large family size as an important indicator of women's reproductive health.[42]

Maternal death and injury rates throw into sharp relief the impact of poverty and gender inequity on reproductive health. Every minute one woman dies needlessly of pregnancy-related causes. This adds up to more than a half million mothers lost each year- a figure that has hardly improved over the past few decades. (Koblinsky *et. al.*, 2000).[43] Another eight million or more suffer *life-long* health consequences from the complications of pregnancy. (Bacci *et. al.*, 1993).[44] Every woman, rich or poor, faces at 15 per cent risk of complications around the time of delivery, but maternal death is practically nonexistent in developed regions (Zabin and Kiragu, 1998). The lack of progress in reducing maternal mortality in many countries highlights the low value placed on the lives of women and testifies to their limited voice in setting public priorities. The lives of many women in developing countries could be saved with reproductive health interventions that people in rich countries take for granted.[45]

"The quality of risk factor screening during antenatal consultations in Niger" a study conducted by Prual, A. *et.al.*, (2000). Has assessed the frequency of risk factors among a sample of pregnant women receiving antenatal care in Niger and to assess the quality of the screening of those risk factors.

A total of 330 pregnant women were enrolled in the study. Each woman was examined twice: the first time by a midwife, the second time by one of the authors but without knowledge of the results of the first consultation. Study results showed that 55 per cent of pregnant women had at least unrisk factor, and 31 per cent had more than one. Ninety-one per cent of the risk factors were detected at interview. The following risk factors were not systematically searched for by midwives: height (48.5 per cent), blood pressure (43.6 per cent), glycosuria (40.6 per cent), vaginal bleeding (38.2 per cent), odema (37.3 per cent), parity (17 per cent), age (16 per cent), previous cesarean section (15.2 per cent), previous stillbirth (15.2 per cent) and previous miscarriages (14.8 per cent). Based on the study findings, the authors conclude that the quality of screening for risk factors during antenatal consultation is poor. Antenatal care can only play a limited role. The most efficient action for decreasing maternal and neonatal mortality is the implementation of essential obstetric care at the primary or secondary level of the health system.[46]

A study was carried by Acharya, L.B. and Cleland, J. (2000), on "Maternal and child health services in rural Nepal: Does access or quality matter more?" This study evaluated the relative importance of access and quality on the utilisation of preventive health services in the western and middle-western hill region of Nepal. Access was measured by travel time to the nearest health posts and coverage by outreach workers. Quality was defined by physical infrastructure, number of staff, availability of drugs, and the holding of special maternal and child health clinics. The adjusted odds ratios of using some form of antenatal care were 6.6 times higher in the catchment areas of high-quality posts than in areas served by low-quality posts. Travel times to the nearest post had less effect. Regular monthly visits by outreach workers also had a significant effect on service utilisation. These results suggest that investing in the quality of health posts is more important than further increases in the number, and expansion of outreach services should be a priority.[47]

Beard, J. (2000) in his study on "Effectiveness and strategies of iron supplementation during pregnancy" he reported that the iron deficiency anemia is the leading single-nutrient deficiency in the world, and the majority of the more than two billion people affected live in developing countries. Pregnancy depletes iron stores, and can lead to increased anemia. At least half of anemia cases occurring during pregnancy are due to nutritional iron deficiency. Scientific opinions differ as to the effects of iron deficiency on the mother and the fetus.

Similarly, there is no clear evidence of the benefit of iron supplementation during pregnancy. There are known health risks associated with excess iron intake. Because of side effects and cost, compliance with daily iron supplementation is low, even in more developed countries. Successful iron supplementation requires substantial investments in infrastructure, personnel training, targeting of at-risk groups, quality control of supplements and the delivery systems, and monitoring of compliance. Given the high global prevalence of iron deficiency anemia during pregnancy, there is need to better understand how iron supplementation can be used to address this deficiency.[48]

A study "Prenatal screening in rural Bangladesh: From prediction to care" carried out by Vanneste, A.M. *et. al.,* (2000), assessed whether prenatal screening can identify women at risk of severe labour or delivery complications in a rural area in Bangladesh. Antenatal risk markers, signs, and symptoms were assessed for their association with severe maternal complications including dystocia, malpresentation, hemorrhage, hypertensive disease, twin delivery, and death. The results showed that antenatal screening by trained midwives fails to adequately distinguish women who will need special care during labour and delivery from those who will not need such care. The majority of the women with dystocia or hemorrhage no warning signs during pregnancy. Women who had an antenatal visit were four times more likely to deliver with a midwife than women who had no antenatal visit. The authors conclude that antenatal care may not be an efficient strategy for identifying those most in need for obstetric service delivery, but if promoted in concurrence with effective emergency obstetric care, and delivered in skilled hands, it may become an effective instrument to facilitate better use of emergency obstetric care services.[49]

Gender discrimination related to education, healthcare and lack of control over economic resources and reproductive decisions further increase pregnancy related risks. High levels of maternal mortality are associated with gender inequality. (AYARH, 2001).[50]

Abrahams, N. *et. al.,* (2001) conducted a study entitled "Health care-seeking practices of pregnant women and the role of the midwife in Cape Town, South Africa" during 2001.This study is based on 103 interviews with 32 pregnant women in a peril-urban area of Cape Town, South Africa. The findings indicate that women's perceptions of the quality of care greatly influence their healthcare-seeking practices. Women generally thought antenatal care to be beneficial, particularly to avoid being scolded by staff should they arrive in labour without prior antenatal care. The women's interactions with staff were generally poor, and women expected to be treated badly by the midwives. The women's own needs for information were not met during antenatal care they were given little information about the status of the baby or when they might expect to deliver, and given no test results. While obstetric outcomes are good in Cape Town, this study shows the need to improve the quality of services, improve staff-patient communication, and make services more patient-oriented.[51]

"Understanding users' perspectives of barriers to maternal healthcare use in Maharashtra India" a survey conducted by Griffiths, P. and Stephenson, R. during 2001. Using in-depth, semi-structured interviews of women in two rural and urban areas of Maharashtra, India, this study examined utilisation of maternal healthcare services and aimed to identify social, economic, and cultural factors influencing.[52]

In 2001, WHO published the conclusions of a randomised controlled trail of a new model of antenatal care and also carried out a systematic review of other randomised trails that looked at the effectiveness of different models of antenatal care, this work had led to a growing consensus around key elements of antenatal care that are likely to improve maternal and perinatal health outcomes, though it is important to note that these outcomes tend to be either maternal and perinatal health or perinatal survival, not maternal survival.

The new WHO model of antenantal care separates pregnant women into two groups: those likely to need only routine antenatal care (some 75 per cent of the total population of pregnant women), and those with specific health conditions or risk factors that necessitate special care (25 per cent of pregnant women). For the first group, a standard programme of four antenatal visits in recommended (with additional visits should conditions emerge which require special care). The WHO guidelines are also specific as regards the timing and content of antenatal care visits according to gestational age. The guidelines stipulate that "only examinations and tests that serve an immediate purpose and that have been proven to be beneficial should be performed" these examinations include measurement of blood pressure, testing of urine for bacterial and proteinuria and blood test to detect syphilis and severe anemia. Routine weight and height measurement at each visit is considered.[53]

Navaneetham K and A Dharmalingam (2002) presented a paper on "Utilisation of maternal healthcare services in southern India" which examines the patterns and determinants of maternal healthcare utilisation across different social settings in South India: in the states of Andhra Pradesh, Karnataka, Kerala and Tamil Nadu. Data from the National Family Health Survey carried out during 1992-93 across most states in India are used. Results show that the utilisation of maternal healthcare services is highest in Kerala followed by Tamil Nadu, Andhra Pradesh, and Karnataka. Utilisation of maternal healthcare services is not only associated with a range of reproductive, socio-economic, cultural and programme factors but also with state and type of health service. The interstate differences in utilisation could be rarely due to variations in the implementation of maternal healthcare programme as well as differences in availability and accessibility between the states, in the case of antenatal care, there was no significant rural-urban gap, thanks to the role played by the multipurpose health workers posted in the rural areas to provide maternal healthcare services. The findings of this study provide insights for planning and implementing appropriate maternal health service delivery programmes in order to improve the health and well being of both mother and child.

Nearly two-third of the sample perceived the services to be excellent or good regarding their awareness, convenience, utilisation and satisfaction, 22.5 per cent felt that it was satisfactory and 16.0 per cent thought it was poor or very poor. Categorising them according to age revealed no definite pattern, but younger mothers seemed to be less satisfied. Excellent or good scoring was obtained more for multiparas than null primiparas and significantly more for Muslims than Hindus, housewives than working women and illiterates than literates, least being with those most highly educated. Maximum utilisation was found in case of immunisation, followed by investigations. Utilisation was minimum in case of antenatal care. Of the total sample 62.75 per cent had availed all the services at this centre only. The MCH services rendered by the centre had succeeded in generating awareness regarding this service, achieving satisfaction and ensuring utilisation among majority of the studied sample.[54]

Magadi. *et al.,* (2003) discussed the negative effects of early pregnancy and unplanned birth, that has for reaching effects on mother and child. The all over aim of the study was to generate data on the maternity care and social support provided by health professionals. The doctors; the contraceptive counselling in order to prevent pregnancy at young age and also to improve their sexual and reproductive health statuses paid special attention to adolescent sexual and reproductive health needs.[55]

Pathamanathan *et al.,* (2003) discussed and reveals the study regarding Sri Lanka and Malaysia concerning maternal mortality death, that has improved in both peer developing countries. The maternal mortality has decreased due to building of health infrastructure improved in per capita income and getting rid of uneven distribution of wealth, along with improvements in service delivery system.[56]

A study was carried out by Pallikadavath S, Foss M, and Stones RW (2004) on Antenatal care: "Provision and inequality in rural north India". The objectives of his study are to examine factors associated with use of antenatal care in rural areas of north India, to investigate access to specific critical components of care and to study differences in the pattern of services received via health facilities versus home visits. They used the 1998-1999 Indian National Family Health Survey of ever-married women in the reproductive age group and analysed data from the states of Bihar, Madhya Pradesh, Rajasthan, and Uttar Pradesh (n = 11,369). Overall, about three-fifths of rural women did not receive any antenatal check-up during their last pregnancy. Services actually received were predominantly provision of tetanus toxoid vaccination and supply of iron and folic acid tablets. Only about 13 per cent of pregnant women had their blood pressure checked and a blood test done at least once. Women visited by health workers received fewer services compared to women who visited a health facility. Home visits were biased towards households with a better standard of living. There was significant under-utilisation of nurse/ midwives in the provision of antenatal services and doctors were often the lead providers. The average number of antenatal visits reported in this study was 2.4 and most visits were in the second trimester.

Higher social and economic status was associated with increased chances of receiving an antenatal check-up, and of receiving specific components including blood pressure measurement, a blood test and urine testing but not the obstetric physical examination, which was however linked to ever-use of family planning and the education of women and their husbands. Thus, pregnant women from poor and uneducated backgrounds with at least one child were the least likely to receive antenatal check-ups and services in the four large north Indian states. Basic antenatal care components are effective means to prevent a range of pregnancy complications and reduce maternal mortality. The findings indicate substantial limitations of the health services in overcoming socio-economic and cultural barriers to access.[57]

The analysis by Anuratha Mathu (2005) women's health- a major area of concern on bring out the idea in Indian women's health status is very poor due to various reasons. Among all the reasons poverty place one leading role. Alone with poverty, illiteracy among women cannot be put aside which means due to lack of education there is lack of awareness among women regarding health though they are literate or illiterate. It is reported that at "least 75 million pregnancies each year are unwanted" they result in 45 million abortions, 20 million of which are Unsafe -resulting in 70,000 women dying and an unknown number of women suffering from infection. Invariably women's health programme are translated into maternal and child health, the idea bring that a women's health is important only when she is carrying out the all important task of producing a new generation. As a matter of fact, it is clearly shown how poverty and illiteracy paves the way to the destruction of women and their health.[58]

2.4 Intra-Natal Care

Where pregnancy is defined as a "women's issue", the participation of men in the decisions and responsibilities are limited. Yet helping men and communities appreciate the risks of pregnancy which can improve women chance of obtaining life-saving care (CEDPA, 2001).[59] In Uganda, educating fathers about safer childbirth and unsafe home deliveries yielded some results. In India, training physicians to involve men in maternity care resulted in more husbands accompanying their wives to antenatal clinics. In rural China, a survey found that husbands shared domestic chores and parenting responsibilities, women were more likely to receive prenatal care, to reduce their workloads before giving birth and to deliver under more sanitary conditions. The Mother Friendly Movement in Indonesia-along with the Alert Husband programme-has helped communities recognise the need for maternal support and establish emergency transport for women in labour (Mmari and Magnani, 2003).[60]

Joshi and Pai have observed that there has been a close correlation between maternal age and low birth weight. Their study revealed the fact that marriage at young age leads to low birth weight. This has been found in their study made at the slums of Mumbai.[61]

A report by Sivaraman has examined the reasons for postponing the marital age of girls. It showed that the women who got married below the age found at risk at the time of delivery. But at the same time the women who got married after the age 20 have very low risk at the time of delivery. (Programmes and Policies adopted in Tamil Nadu T.V. Antony; p. 190).[62]

Poverty increases the risks inherent in childbearing, and maternal mortality and morbidity deepen poverty. In sub-Saharan Africa, where high fertility multiplies the dangers mothers face over a lifetime 1 in 16 women is likely to die as a consequence of pregnancy; in some of the poorest parts, as many as one in six face this risk. By comparison, in industrialised countries the lifetime risk is only 1 in 2,800. Ninetynine per cent of maternal deaths occur in developing countries, almost all-95 per cent-in Africa and Asia. (Carroli *et al.,* 2001) Wealth matters: Two-thirds of maternal deaths in 2000 occurred in 13 of the world's poorest countries, and one quarter of these were in India alone.[63] (Stoltzfus, 2001) Within countries, the wealthiest women have much better access to skilled obstetric care than the poor.[64]

"Safer maternal health in rural Uttar Pradesh: Do primary health services contribute?" A study conducted by Ramarao, S. *et. al.,* (2001) emphasised that the Government of India failed to achieve its goal of a reduction in maternal mortality from 407 to 2000 per 100,000 live births by the year 2000 and examined utilisation of maternal and child health services and the readiness of primary healthcare facilities to provide maternity services to determine why the state of Uttar Pradesh continues to have one of the highest levels of maternal mortality in the country. Less than half of pregnant women in rural Uttar Pradesh sought any antenatal care. Almost 90 per cent of deliveries took place at home, and nearly half were attended by family or relatives. While the primary healthcare system has rudimentary equipment and some staff competency in detecting and managing maternal complications, there is need for improvement.[65]

"Access to care and maternal mortality in Jamaican hospitals" 1993-1995 a study carried out by Mc Caw-Binns, A (2001). The Ministry of Health in Jamaica all maternal deaths in public hospitals for 1993-1995 as part of its reproductive health quality-assurance programme. In Jamaica, 89 per cent of births are attended by a skilled practitioner, and 82 per cent of all births take place in public hospitals. The review of hospital records found a maternal mortality ratio of 106.2 deaths per 100,000 live births. This level is virtually unchanged from the levels observed in 1986-87 (119.7) and 1981-83 (118.6). Regional differences in mortality levels suggest that re-allocating personnel and improving quality of care can reduce mortality by at least 50 per cent.[66]

Analysis of factors associated with maternal mortality in Kenyan hospitals by Magadi, M. *et.al.,* (2001), in this analysis of hospital records for 58,151 obstetric admissions in sixteen public hospitals in Kenya showed 182 maternal deaths. This is one of the few studies that attempts to understand maternal mortality in hospitals on the national.[67]

A longitudinal population-based study was conducted by Hoj, L. *et al.,* (2002). In this longitudinal, prospective study, more than 15,000 women living in 100 clusters were visited at six-month intervals over a period of more than six years to determine risk factors for maternal death. Of the 10,931 pregnancies, 85 resulted in a maternal death. Maternal mortality increased as distance from the regional hospital increased. The risk of death was greater for a multiple pregnancy, and the risk of subsequent maternal death was greater if the fetus was stillborn. This study did not find any increase in maternal mortality associated with a class of age or parity. Screening and referral based on these factors would not reduce maternal risk. The distance to an Emergency obstetric care facility is an important factor in determining the outcome of complicated deliveries.[68]

"Are socially and economically weaker sections deprived of maternal healthcare in Tamil Nadu, India?" a study conducted by Sivakami M and P.M. Kulkarni in 2003 investigates whether women from economically, socially, and educationally weaker sections of the society receive adequate maternal healthcare. Though most women in Tamil Nadu receive antenatal care, many do not get institutional and professional care at delivery. Logistic regression analysis shows that in both rural and urban areas only the economic factor, and not the social and educational factors, has a significant net effect on the ability to secure institutional delivery care.[69]

"Maternal care in India reveals gaps between urban and rural, rich and poor" a study conducted in West Bengal by Biswas, R during 2003 rate that in Calcutta it is common to see women in labour travelling on the backs of open, three-wheel "cycle vans" over pot-holed roads to distant rural health centres. Many other women opt for home delivery, often under dangerously unhygienic conditions. By contrast, upper- and middle-class women in metropolitan areas spend thousands of rupees for delivery at private nursing homes. These women would not venture to the government hospitals in the city, where, at times, two mothers with newborns must share a single bed. These and other scenarios illustrate the lopsided nature of maternal care in India, where maternity-related complications are leading causes of death and disability among women of reproductive age. In this country of roughly one billion people, where women have, on an average, about three children, some 440 women die of maternity-related complications for every 100,000 live births. The United Nations estimates that at current levels of fertility and mortality, one out of every 55 women in India faces the risk of maternal death, compared with one in 80 in Pakistan and one in 610 in Sri Lanka.[70]

Socioeconomic inequalities in use of delivery care services in India by Abdul Salam, S.A. Siddiqui notes that three is a positive association between socioeconomic status of women and the use of maternal health ocean services. Those men who were better educated, economically well off and resided in urban areas availed the delivery care services to the maximum. Poor women cannot afford the cost of healthcare services.[71]

A leading initiative is the Averting Maternal Death and Disability programme to improve emergency obstetric care in developing countries. UNFPA, WHO, UNICEF and many non-governmental organisations have partnered with. Governments across the developing countries to restructure health systems and capacity building exercise. UNFPA support programmes to expand access to skilled attendance at birth and emergency obstetric care for women in poor and rural areas, including health-provider training now being undertaken in 76 countries. Uganda is tackling several of the challenges commonly faced in reducing maternal deaths, including equipping and staffing health centres with doctors and nurses, and establishing referrals and transportation to handle emergencies. A radio communication system ('RESCUER') and ambulance services have been introduced in some areas. In three regions of Nicaragua, the proportion of women who received emergency obstetric care raised from 37 in 2000 to 50 per cent in 2003. In Senegal, 100 rural women were saved within a year of UNFPA support to a local health centre. In Yemen, the number of female providers has been increased, with 12,000 community midwives trained (WHO, 2003).[72]

In spite of the government's effort to reach out to women in reproductive age in all parts of the country to provide all components of healthcare free or with nominal charges, utilisation of reproductive healthcare remains low in the country. For example, institutional delivery according to NFHS-2 was as low as 34 per cent (UPS, 2000).[73] However, one of the important policy goal of the government is to achieve 80 per cent institutional deliveries by the year 2010 (National Population Policy, 2000). Though the government is committed to provide extensive free maternal healthcare under its top priority national health programme is low.[74]

2.5 Post-Natal Care

Everyone has the right to enjoy reproductive health, which is a basis for having healthy children, intimate relationships and happy families. Reproductive health encompasses key areas of the UNFPA vision that every child is wanted, every birth is safe, every young person is free of HIV and every girl and woman is treated with dignity and respect. But reproductive health problems remain the leading cause of ill-health and death for women of childbearing age worldwide. Impoverished women, especially those living in developing countries, suffer disproportionately from unintended pregnancies, maternal death and disability, sexually transmitted infections including HIV, Gender-based violence and other problems related to their reproductive system and sexual behaviour. Because young people often face barriers in trying to get the information or care they need, adolescent reproductive health is another important focus of UNFPA programming.

Mauldin and Segal, (1988, p. 341) give comparison between men and women about the use of contraception and disclose, that the vast majority of the women who use contraceptives are 155 million rely on sterilisation but it is the woman who has been sterilised in; two-thirds of these, i.e. 80 million use the IUD, and 61 million use hormonal methods. Only about 38 million men use condoms, despite their acknowledged safety, efficacy and potential for preventing sexually transmitted diseases because they are motivated to act upon husband advice, indicating the importance of communication of spouse in addressing the reproductive health issues.[75]

A reproductive health approach means that people have the ability to reproduce and regulate their fertility; women are able to go through pregnancy and childbirth safely; the outcome of pregnancy is successful in terms of s maternal and infant survival and well being; and couples are able to have sexual relations free of the fear of pregnancy and of contracting disease (Fathallah, 1988). The proponents of the reproductive health framework believe that reproductive rights and freedom, and to women's status and empowerment. Thus, the reproductive health approach extends beyond the narrow confines of family planning and to encompass all aspects of human sexuality and reproductive health needs during the various stages of the life cycle. Programmes must, therefore, be redesigned to address diverse needs at different stages of the life cycle.[76]

A pioneering study by Bang *et al.,* (1989) in a region in Maharashtra, India, has provided compelling evidence regarding the burden of gynaecological diseases among poor women. Subsequently, several community based studies within the country have also reiterated the grim scenario of reproductive morbidity among Indian women.[77] (Bang and Bang, 1991; Bhatia and Cleland, 1995; Ravindran, 1995). Some of the common morbidities that women were found to experience included white discharge, excessive and painful menstruation and weakness.[78]

Research suggests that one in ten pregnancies will end in an unsafe abortion, in Asia, Africa and Latin America accounting, for the highest numbers (Rutstein *et al.,* 1990). Pregnancies, skilled attendance at all births, appropriate and timely emergency obstetric care for all women who develop complications. Weak health systems, limited transportation in remote and rural areas, shortage of skilled health providers, and limited availability of contraceptives are among the major challenges. Gender discrimination can make it difficult to muster the political will and resources needed to implement the change.[79]

Unsafe abortions are a leading cause of maternal mortality and can result in permanent injuries. Lack of access to family planning results in some 76 million unintended pregnancies every year in the developing world alone. (Reynolds *et al.,* 2003).[80] Each year, 19 million abortions are carried out under unsanitary or medically unsound conditions. These result in some 68,000 deaths. Many women who seek abortions are married. They are usually poor and struggling to provide for children they already have. (Govindasamy *et al.,* 1993).[81]

There is ample data worldwide that underscores the high burden of reproductive morbidity among women. According to the World Bank, about one-third of the total disease burden in developing country women age 15-44 is linked to health problems related to pregnancy, childbirth, abortion, human immuno-deficiency virus (HIV), and reproductive tract infections (World Bank, 1993). Among diseases for which cost effective interventions exist, reproductive health problems account for the majority of the disease burden in women of this age group.[82]

Sundari Ravindran (1993) disclosed the values formulation regarding use of contraception in a family was the agenda with clear methods especially in India, where collaboration with the government produced national, push, against pregnancy. For millions of women, these population controllers, did open up access to contraception. However, the services were usually applied with little sensitivity to different culture context and frequently abused the rights of both women and men. Success was evaluated only it terms of numbers accepting contraception, with little concern for unsure, satisfaction or for the long-term effects on their health.[83]

Although using contraceptives can prevent 20 to 35 per cent of maternal deaths, (Scholl *et. al.,* 1994) limited family planning supplies and services, as well as social norms, often for women from-using them. Inadequate education often leaves women with little or no understanding of childbearing risks and other health matters, including how to navigate the health system or negotiate timely lifesaving care within the family. Informing women about their right to free care (where it exists) can be critical. High service costs can push families into poverty and deepen impoverishment. Fees may thus better families from seeking services, especially when the quality of care provided is considered to be better than that of trusted traditional birth attendants.

In India, women more so in the society do not enjoy an independent social status. Her social status is linked with that of her father or her husband. This has deep-rooted and traditional origins. In almost all religious faiths, women are regarded as inferior to men. They are here primarily to reproduction much as and as quickly in Indian families. But ironically, this unique reproductive potential of a female has never been considered as a case for receiving in her role of mother and housewife she has in fact been detrogated to the role of a self of mother and house citizen family first before herself and to suffer in silence on all matters.

Abortion has been legalised in India as a health measure since 1972 by the Medical Termination of Pregnancy Act. 1971. Even so, because of non-availability of MTP services within easy reach for most of the rural population and ignorance of the law; 'illegal' abortions continue to be performed by incompetent persons under unhygienic conditions. As a result, abortion-related mortality and morbidity remain major problems. Only 507,719 terminations were performed through the health services in 1986-87, which is around nine per cert of the induced abortions that were likely to have been performed during the same period. Since the inception of the programme, 5.1 million abortions have been performed under the MTP programme, which is less than the total number of induced abortions likely to be performed in one year. Induced abortions indicate an unmet need of women for family planning, highlight a gap between the availability of services and their accessibility to those in need, and demonstrate women's inability to make use of the services they need accurately.[84]

Substantial data to show that the Indian women bear a high burden of reproductive ill health (Bang *et. al.,* 1989; Bang and Bang, 1991; Pachauri and Gittlesohn, 1994; Jejeebhoy and Rama Rao, 1002). Studies show that the heavy load of reproductive morbidity among Indian women is an outcome of their poverty, their powerlessness, low social status, malnutrition, infection, high fertility and lack of access to healthcare. Thus, socio-economic and biological determinants operate synergistically throughout the lives of poor women to undermine their health, resulting in right levels of morbidity and mortality.[85] There is, therefore, an urgent need to design and implement services to address women's reproductive health needs. Women centered, gender-sensitive services must be organised and implemented (Pachauri, 1995).

Unsafe abortion is one of the main reasons women and girls seek emergency care: In sub-Saharan Africa, post-abortion care takes up one-fifth to half of all gynecological beds. (Thaddeus and Maine, 1994) Fearing exposure and judgmental attitudes from providers, many women delay seeking life-saving treatment until, it is too late. The many costs of unsafe abortions far outweight the price of the contraceptives that could prevent such suffering.[86]

It is indeed heartening that India has taken a lead to begin the process of translating these concepts into its national programme. The first major step that the government took was to remove contraceptive targets and Implement a reproductive health approach. However, to translate reproductive rhetoric into reality, two important issues must be addressed. First, a paradigm shift is essential. And second, packages of good quality services must be designed and implemented to address reproductive health needs of people. A shift in paradigm implies a change in the focus: from a population control approach of reducing numbers to developing programmes designed to address the reproductive health needs of people. A change in the culture of the programme from one that focused on achieving targets to one that now aims at providing a range of quality services is essential (Pachauri, 1995).[87]

Zafar *et al.,*. (1995) argued the significance of cultural factors in influencing fertility and contraceptive behaviour. The study indicated the importance of social forces such as education of both spouses, age at marriage, family size, sex preference, beliefs and values regarding family life in predicting fertility and contraceptive behaviour in Pakistan.[88]

Poverty and gender discrimination exacerbate reproductive health problems throughout the life cycle. The foundation for good reproductive health begins early in life. For instance, stunted growth in underfed girls increases the risks of obstructed labour later in life. Malnourished mothers and their babies are vulnerable to premature death and chronic disability. Anaemia, which can lead to post partum hemorrhage, afflicts 50 to 70 per cent of pregnant women in developing countries (Steketee *et.al.,* 1996).[89]

Utilisation of Reproductive healthcare depends not only on the availability of services but also on different other factors such as distance of healthcare facility; perception of women and their families regarding the need for care; social restrictions on freedom to movement; the opportunity cost of accessing healthcare; and the interaction between the client and the provider of formal healthcare system (World Population Monitoring, 1998; UPS, 2000).[90] Also as a woman's social status and her health are intrinsically related:

These studies have revealed the almost apathetic attitude that women have in seeking treatment for their health problems (Gittlesohn, *et al.,* 1994; Kapadia *et al.,* 1997). Women resorted to treatment seeking only when it caused great physical discomfort or when it affected their work performance. Moreover, the treatment seeking was better when women received advice and support from significant others especially husband, mother or neighbor.[91]

World Bank (1999) reports about youth in Uganda that nearly half of young people ages 15 to 19 never having had sex and need awareness about reproductive health problems may lead them to psychological harm. It was stated in the above stated report that the proportion for the use of contraception was higher in the developed regions, where 70 per cent of the 170 million married or in-union women were using contraception, compared to 60 per cent of the 880 million in the less developed regions. Worldwide, 62 per cent are using contraception.[92]

Adamchak, *et al.,* (2000) revealed that; community-based studies in Cameroon, India, and Nepal disclosed that how and why, young people often use home remedies, traditional methods of contraception, contraceptives provided by friends or relatives, and contraception and medication purchased without a doctor's prescription reflects the traditional society with conservative behaviour.[93]

The Government of India had established a wide network of Reproductive healthcare facilities all over the country. In rural areas, where a large majority of 72 per cent live (Government of India, 2001), government sponsored healthcare facilities function as a three tier system-Sub-centre, Primary Health Centre (PHC) and Community Health Centre (CMC)-and cover almost all the rural population. As on 1998, there were 137,006 Sub-centres, 23179 PHCs, 2913 CHCs in India (MOHFW, 1999). In the urban areas, state government or municipalities, and private and non-governmental organisations (NGO) provide Reproductive healthcare. Recently, Mother and Child Health Programme been broadened into reproductive and child health (RCH) programme.[94]

"Utilisation of reproductive and child healthcare services: some observations from Kerala" a study carried out by Dilip TR (2002), at Kerala, based on the data from the National Family Health Survey to show how the same cohort of women utilises facilities in the private sector for delivery care services, sterilisation care and treatment of their children. The preference of public/private sector depends on nature of service in demand. The role of private providers in healthcare was found to be limited in the case of family planning services, but almost 50 per cent availed delivery care services from the private sector. A majority of women were found to prefer treatment from the private medical providers if their children were suffering from fever or cough. Class differentials were severe; with the public sector bring the major.[95]

A qualitative analysis of maternal and child health services of an urban health centre, by Banerjee, B (2003) in his article has assessed the client perception in terms of awareness, satisfaction and service utilisation, regarding the MCH services rendered by the centre and to analyse the demographic and socio-cultural barriers to higher levels of perception. Study design; Cross-sectional, community-based study.[96]

Recognising the impact of unsafe abortion as "a major public health concern", the ICPD Programme of Action urges governments to spare no effort in preventing unwanted pregnancies and reducing "the recourse to abortion through expanded and improved family planning services" (Chowdhury, 2003).[97] The efficacy of this strategy is proven: Access to safe and effective contraception decreases the incidence of induced abortion (CEDPA, 2001).[98] In several countries of Central and Eastern Europe, abortion rates declined rapidly with the establishment of family planning information and services, increased supplies of contraceptives and the active involvement of civil society and religious groups.

India is one of the few countries where males significantly out-number females, and this imbalance have increased over time. India's maternal mortality rates in rural areas are among the world's highest. From global perspective, Indian accounts for 19 per cent of all live births and 27 per cent of all maternal deaths.

According to Sen (2004), the direct impact of the paradigm shift was the repudiations of targets in the family planning programme and the attempt to introduce an approach to service delivery based on community needs assessment. A new programme on Reproductive and Child Health (known as RCHI) was introduced with major donor funding and with significant new programme elements included.

The right to reproductive health is a key component of women and men's reproductive and sexual rights. Moreover, the achievement of reproductive health is inextricably linked to women's men's ability to exercise reproductive and sexual rights, which includes, besides the right to reproductive health, the right to

- Reproductive decision-making including voluntary choice in marriage, family formation and determination of the number, timing and spacing of one's children; and the right to have access to the information and means needed to exercise voluntary choice;
- Equality and equity for men and women to enable individuals to make free and informed choices in all spheres of their life, free from discrimination based on gender;
- Sexual and reproductive security including freedom from sexual violence and coercion, and the right to privacy.

The ICPD Programme of Action also identifies the empowerment of women as central to the achievement of reproductive health. "Advancing gender equality and equity and the empowerment of women, and the elimination of all kinds of violence against women, and ensuring women's ability to control their own fertility, are corner-stones of population and development programmes."[99]

Amita Pitra and Bhogyashree Khaire (2004) in the article need for a gender-sensitive healthcare system share their experience from their research, "As part of the homework we received information from 36 primary health centres from 20 districts of Maharashtra through this process. The most striking finding was that out of 36 PHCs, only 2 reported availability of MTP services on a regular basis. Upto 18 per cent of all *maternal mortality* is caused due to unsafe abortions, which means more than twenty five thousand women die every year in India due to this. More than one-third of activists reported that women in their areas were not satisfied with services available to them. They gave the following reasons for their dissatisfaction the behaviour of hospital/PHC staff is not responsible/good, they feel that good care is not taken especially after conducting MTPs and sterilisation, absence of female doctor, health personnel expect to get paid for services, all required facilities are not available, absence of health education which results in women not coming out with their illnesses, all medicines not available free of cost at the health centre, women are referred to the general hospital for delivery, doctor is often not available from time to time in the hospital intentionally reduced dietary intake during pregnancy has been reported in Tamil Nadu and it is also observed that less food intake was due to the fear of a big foetus, causing obstruction and pain during pregnancy. In Indian communities food items perceived as 'hot' are often believed to be harmful for pregnant women and those perceived as 'cold' believed to be beneficial.[100]

Recent trends in public and policy awareness about women's health needs and concerns and their actual access to the means and services to address such concerns show complex and contradictory tendencies (Sen, 2004). Sen argues that the country's poor record in improving women's health is due to a critical absence of focused attention. However, the period of the post-1990's saw a number of policy shifts and changes with direct and indirect implications for women's health. These include (i) the overarching economic reforms agenda, with its emphasis on liberalising controls different industries, and controlling the fiscal deficit through real expenditure cuts; (ii) a contested paradigm shift in the national population policy in line with the new ICPD those of meeting the reproductive and sexual health needs of individuals and couples; (iii) growing concern over HIV/AIDS and its increasing "feminisation" as it spreads from high risk groups into the general population; and (iv) growing recognition of violence against women as a major health and human rights problem.[101]

The critical importance of reproductive health to development has been acknowledged at the highest level. At the 2005 World Summit, world leaders agreed to integrate access to reproductive health into national strategies to attain the Millennium Development Goals. UNFPA is fully committed to mobilising support and scaling up efforts to make reproductive health for all a reality by 2015. Babies an increased maternal morbidity/mortality. Malnourished mothers give birth to underweight babies. Early marriage leads to early onset of childbearing occurring before the female is physically fully developed. Complications of pregnancy, prenatal and neonatal mortality and low birth weight are much higher among adolescent women than among older women. From this we observe that the age of marriage is the main reason behind the above-mentioned issues. The condition is prevalent among the women of most of the villages of India. Though the government had taken several efforts in creating awareness and even framing laws to emphasise the Oabi Dr Parakh Manish, *et. al.*, entitled "A study of maternal vitamin "A" status and its relationship with intrauterine growth restriction" quotes the following. It aims to determine the prevalence of vitamin "A" deficiency in mothers of intrauterine growth restriction (IUGR) neonates and to evaluate the relationship of vitamin "A" levels with birth weight. The findings of the study shows vitamin A deficiency during pregnancy may be a very important factor for growth hindered of the fetus. In malnourished mothers, besides interim. Many other factors also have an influence on intrauterine growth restriction but vitamin A deficiency appears to be a key factor in mothers who are otherwise not severely aroused.

Though safe motherhood has been high on the international agenda for nearly two decades, progress has been uneven, and in some countries maternal mortality rates are considered to be rising. More is known about which strategies are most effective in averting maternal death and injury. They are family planning to reduce unintended communities play a key role in reducing maternal mortality. Trusted local health workers can refer women to the formal health system and encourage them to deliver in safe settings. In poor countries, communities can pool resources to arrange emergency transport for women with complications, for example, by working with taxi, bus or truck drivers and their unions. In Honduras, community-based efforts helped cut maternal mortality by 37 per cent between 1990 and 1997 and increased skilled attendance at delivery by 33 per cent in rural areas. In Senegal, Imams have been enlisted to promote safe motherhood.[102]

2.6 Summary

Various studies relating to the components of reproductive health of women such as health status during antenatal period, intra-natal and post-natal period have been review in this chapter on the basis of the previous studies reviewed; majority of the studies emphasised more on the reproductive health status of women on a whole. Studies relating to the reproductive health of women with varying socio-economic and demographic background rural very limited. Studies relating to the reproductive health status of the rural women have also very limited. Hence this study in a free of research work in the direction to explore the reproductive health status of rural women in the control part of Tami Nadu.

In this chapter the necessary review of literature for the present study are clearly given. In the next chapter the research methodology are given briefly.

Notes

1. Bongaarts, John and Barney Cohen. "*Introduction and overviews*" Studies in Family Planning, 1998, 29(2), pp. 99-105.
2. Blanc, Annk. And Anna. *"Way Sexual Behaviour and Contraceptive Knowledge and use Developing countries"* Studies in Family Planning, 1998, 29(2), pp. 99-105.
3. Khan, M.E., Ghosh Dastitar S.K., and Ratanjeet Singh. *"Nutrition and Health practices Among Rural Women: A case study of Uttar Padesh, India"*. The Journal of Family Welfare, 1998, 33(1): pp. 3-18.
4. Thengaleela, T. and P. Vijayalakshmi. *"Prevalence of Anemia Pregnancy"*. The India Journal of Nutrition and Dietetics, 1994, 31(2), pp. 26-29.
5. Alan Guttmacher Institute (AGI). Into a New World: *Yoting Woolens Sexual and Reproductive Lives.* New York, NY: AGI, 1998.
6. Demographic Development in Europe Belgium 1998-1999.
7. Government of India. National Population Policy. *Department of Family Welfare. Ministry of Health and Family Welfare,* GOI, New Delhi, 1998.
8. Bang, R. and Bang, A. *"A Community Study of Gynecological Diseases in Indian Villages in Zeidenstein and Moore (eds.) Learning about Sexuality: A Practical Beginning"*. New York: Population Council, 1989.
9. Senderwiz, J. A Review of Programme Approaches to *Adolescent Reproductive Health* Poptech Assignment Number 200–176, June 1, 2000, review on 13 May 2005.

10. Jejeebhoy, Sthireen. *"Adolescent Sexual and Reproductive Behaviour: A Review of the Evidence from India in Ramasubban and Jejeebhoy"*, (eds.). Women's Reproductive Health in India, New Delhi: Rawat Publications, 2000.
11. NFHS–2, India. National Family Health Survey (NFHS-2) 1998-99, India, *International Institute for Population Sciences,* Mumbai and ORC Macro, USA, 2000.
12. UNFPA, The South Asia Conference.
13. Ashford, Lori S. *"New Population Policies: Advancing Women's Health and Rights",* Population Bulletin, 2001, 56(1): 1-44.
14. Chen, Lincoth C., Melitia C., Gesche, Shamsa Ahmed, A.I. Chowdhury and W.H. Mosley. *"Maternal Mortality in Rural Bangladesh",* Studies in Family Planning, 1974, 5(11), pp. 334-341.
15. Uddlin, Nassir. Case study, Bangladesh, *Communication and Advocacy Strategies,* Adolescent Reproductive and Sexual Health Bangkok, UNESCO PROAP, 1999.
16. UNICEF. *The Progress of Nations 2001,* New York, United Nations Children's Fund.
17. PRB. *The World's Youth, Washington DC,* Population Reference Bureau, Measure Communications, 2000.
18. Akhter, H.H. *"Menstrual Regulate Among Adolescents in Bangladesh; Risks and Experiences",* in S. Bott and other (eds), Adolescent Sexual and Reproductive Health, Evidence and Programme Implications for South Asia, (Geneva, WHO), 2002.
19. Jensen, R and A Thornton. *Early Female Marriage in the Developing World,* Gender and Development, 2003, 11(2) : 9-19.
20. Gregson, S.C.A. Nyamukapa, G.P Gaehtt. *et al., Sexual Mixing Patterns and Sex Differentials in Teenage Exposure to HIV Infection Rural Zimbabwe,* The Lencet, 2002, 359 (9321) : 1896-1903.
21. Van Der Straten, A.R., King O. Grinsteal *et al., Sexual Coerction, Physical in Steady Relationship in Kingali,* Rwanda, AIDS and Bahaviours, 1998, 2(1) : 61-73.
22. Westoff, C.F., *Trends in Marriage and Early Childbearing in Developing Countries,* Calverton, M.D., U.S.A.: ORC Macro, 2003.
23. Wang *et al., Access to Adolescent Reproductive Health Services Financial and Structural Barriers to Care Prospect Sex Report Health,* 2003, May: 35(3): 144-7.
24. Baridalyne, N., and V.P. Reddaian. *"Menstruation: Knowledge,* Beliefs and Practices of Women in the Reproductive Age Group Residing in an Urban Resettlement Colony of Perspectives and Issues, 2004, 27(1): 9-16.
25. Senderowit, Z J. *Adoleseent Health Reassessing the Passage to Adulthood,* Washington, D C World Bank, 1995.

26. Mc Cauley, A P and Salter, C. Meeting the Needs of Young Adults, Population Reports, 1995, Series J, No. 41.
27. United Nations. *Adolescent Reproductive Behaviour*. Vol. II Eviolence from Developing Countries, New York: UN,1989.
28. Khanna, Anoop and Goyal R.S. *"A study of Adolescent Girls in Rajasthan"*, Journal of Health Management, 2005, Vol. 7 (1), pp : 91-107.
29. Barua, A and Kurtz, Cathleen. *"Reproductive Health Seeking by Married Adolescent girls in Maharashtra, India"*, Reproductive Health Matters, 2001, Vol. 9(17).
30. Ford, Clellans. S. A comparative study of human reproduction. *Yale university publications in anthropology*. No. 32 New Haven Yale University Press, 1945.
31. Easterly, R.A and Crimmins, EM: The Fertility Revaluation the University of Chicago Press. *Pilanesberg National Park.* South Africa, 1985.
32. Freedman, R. Fertility Determinants. In the World Fertility Survey: *An Assessment (Ed. J. Cleland and C. Scott),* pp. 773-795. Oxford University Press, Oxford, 1987.
33. Prema Ramachandran. Nutrition in Pregnancy. In Gopalan. C, Kaur. S., editors. *Women and Nutrition in India.* Special Publication No. 5, New Delhi. Nutrition Foundation of India, 989, pp. 153-93.
34. Rameshwar Sarma K.V. and Prahlad Rao. N. Strengthening Nutrition Programme for *Women IASSI quarterly,* Oct–Dec 1992.
35. Shatrugha. Government of India, National Nutrition Policy, Department of Women Child Development, Ministry of Human Resource Development, *GOI,* New Delhi, 1993.
36. Abusaleh Sharriff and Geetha Singh. *"Determinants of Maternal Health Care Utilisation of India; Evidence from a Recent Household,"* "www.ncaer.org/wp.pdd. Recent publication, 1994.
37. Jodie Dodd, M, S. Jeffery Robinson and A. Carolis Gowther, *"'Guiding Antenatal Care"* www.i-nja.comau/public/issues/I 76-06-180302/dod 10052.html
38. World Bank, *World Development Report: Investing in Health Oxford University* Press, New York, 1993, pp. 117, 216
39. Munjanja, S.P. *et al., "Randomized Controlled Trial of a Reduced Visits Programme of Antenatal care in Harare Zimbabwe"*. Lancet, 1996, 348:364-9.
40. McDonagh, M., *et al., Reproductive health and health sector reform: opportunities and challenges.* John Snow International UK forthcoming, 2000
41. Jejeebhoy, S.J., *Maternal Mortality and Morbidity in India, Priorities for Social Science Research.* The Journal of Family Welfare, 1996, 43(2): 31-51.

42. Ahmad, *et al., "Induced abortions in Mat lab, Bangladesh: Tends and determinates"* International Family Planning Perspectives, Vol. 24, No. 3 (Sep. 1998) pp. 128-138, Published by: Guttamacher Institute.

43. Koblinsky, M, Conroy, C, Kureshy, N, *et al.,. Issues in Programming for Safe Motherhood.* Arlington, VA: MotherCare/john Snow, Inc., 2000.

44. Bacci, A, Manhica GM, Machungo F, *et al., Outcome of Teenage Pregnancy in Maputo,* Mozambique. International Journal of Gynaecol Obstetrics, 1993, 40(1):19-23.

45. Zabin, LS. Expiration, K., *The health consequences of Adolescent sexual and fertility behaviour in sub-Saharan Africa* in the Studies Family Journal Planning 1998, 29(2) : 2010-232.

46. Prual, A. *et al., The Quality of Risk Factor Screening during Antenatal Consultations in Niger. Health Policy and Planning,* 2000, 15(1): 11-16.

47. Acharya, L.B. and Cleland, J. Maternal and Child Health Services in Rural Nepal: Does Access or Quality Matter More? *Health Policy and Planning,* 2000, 15(2):223-229.

48. Beard, J. *"Effectiveness and Strategies of Iron Supplementation During pregnancy".* American Journal of Clinical Nutrition, 2000, 71 (Suppl): 12885-12945.

49. Vanneste, A.M. *et al., Prenatal Screening in Rural Bangladesh; from Predication to Care.* Health Policy and Planning, 2000, 15(1): 1-10.

50. AYARH. Population Reference Bureau, the World's Youth 2000. Washington, P.C Population Reference Bureau, 2001.

51. Abrahams, N, *Jewkes R and Laubser R. "I do not Believe in Democracy in the Home".* Men's Relationships with and Abuse of Women (Technical Report). South Africa: Medical Research Council, 1999.

52. Griffiths, P. and Stephenson, R. *Understanding users Perspectives of Barriers to Maternal Health Care use in Maharashtra,* India. Journal of Biosocial Science, 2001, 33; 339-359.

53. WHO. *"Antenatal care Randomised trial Manual for the Implementation of the new Model,"* World Health Organisation, Department of Reproductive Health and Research 2001.

54. Naveneetham, K and A Dharmalingam. *"Utilisation of Maternal Health Care Services in Southern India".* Social Science and Medicine, 2002, 43: 459-471.

55. Magadi, M. *et al. "Analysis of Factors Associated with Maternal Mortality in Kenyan Hospital".* Journal of Biosocial Science, 2001, Vol. 33(3): July 2001. pp. 375-389.

56. Indra Pathamanathan, Jerker Kiljestrand. *"Investing in Maternal Health: Learning from Malaysia and Srilanka".* World Bank Publications 01, March, 2003, p. 182.

57. Pallikadavath, S. Foss. M., and Stones. R.W. Antenatal Care: *"Provision and Inequality in Rural North India"*. Social Science and Medicine (1982), 2004, 59(6): 1147-1158.

58. Anuratha Mathu. *"Women's Health a major area of concern"*. Social welfare, 52(1), April 2005, pp. 5-9

59. Centre for Development and Population Activates (CEDPA). *Adolescent Girls in India Choose a Better Future : An Impact Assessment,* Washington DC : CEDPA, 2001.

60. Mmari, KN, Magnani, RJ. *Does Making Clinic-Based Reproductive Health Services More Youth-Friendly Increase Service use by Adolescents? Evidence from Lusaka, Zambia.* Journal of Adolescent Health, 2003, 33 (4):259-70.

61. Sumedha, M. Joshi, (Mrs.) N.P. Pai. *"Effect of the Maternal Biosocial Determinates on the Birth Weight in a Slum Area of Greater Mumbai",* Indian Journal of Community Medicine, 2000, Vol. XXV, No. 3, July–Sept.

62. T.V. Antony. *"Population Policy and Reproductive Health Proceedings of the Seminar on Policy Direction and Strategy of Action in Population and Reproductive."* Health in India, New Delhi, December 1995, Edited by K. Srinivasan, Hindustan, Pub. Cor. (India) New Delhi (marry Martin Book sellers), 2001, XVI, 361, p. 123.

63. Carroli, G, Rooney, C, Villar, J. *How Effective is antenatal care in preventing maternal mortality and serious morbidity? An overview of the evidence.* Pediatrics Perinatal Epidemiology, 2001, 15(1 Suppl): 1-42.

64. Stoltzfus, Rj. *Iron-Deficiency Anemia: Reexamining the Nature and Magnitude of the Public Health Problem.* Summary: Implications for Research and Programmes. NWr, 2001;131 (2S-2):697S-701S.

65. Ramarao, S. *et al. "Safer Maternal Health in Rural Uttar Pradesh: Do primary Health Services Contribute?"* International Programmes Division, Population Council, New York. 10017, USA. Health Policy and Planning (Impact Factor: 2.65), 2001, 10/2001: 16(3) : 256-63.

66. Mc. Caw–Binns, A. "Access to care and Maternal Mortality in Jamaican hospitals": 1993–1995. International Journal of Epidemiology, 2001. Aug. 30(4) : 796-801.

67. Magadi, M. *et al., "Analysis of Factors Associated with Maternal Mortality in Kenyan Hospital"*. Journal of Biosocial Science, 2005, Vol. 52(1): April 2005, pp. 5-9.

68. Hoj, L. *et al., Factors Associated with Maternal Mortality in Rural Guinea–Bissau. A Longitudinal Population–Based Study.* British Journal of Obstetrics and Gynecology, 2002, 109: 792-299.

69. Sivakami, M., and Kulkarni, P.M., *Are Socially and Economics Weaker Sections Deprived of Maternal Health Care in Tamil Nadu,* Indian, Journal of Health and Population in Developing Countries, 2003, Aug. 7:15.

70. Biswas, R. Maternal Care in India Reveals Gaps between Urban and Rural Rich and Poor, *West Bengal World Health Organisation (WHO) United Nations Children's Fund (UNICEF) and United Nations Population Fund (UNFPA),* Maternal Mortality Database (1995) Accessed Online at www.child info.org/eddb/mat_mortal/database.htm, 2003, on May 7, 2003
71. Abdul Salam, S.A Siddiqui. *Socio-economic Inequalities in use of Delivery care Services in India.* The Journal of Obstetrics and Gynecology of India Vol. 56, No.2 : March/April, 2006, pp. 123-127.
72. WHO, World Population Report, 2003.
73. UPS, International Institute for Population Sciences (UPS) and ORS Macro. NFHS–2, 1998–99 Mumbai UPS 2000.
74. Government of India. National Population Policy. Department of Family Welfare, Ministry of Health and Family Welfare, GOI, New York, 2000.
75. W. Parker Maudlin and Sheldon J. Segal. *"Prevalence of Contraceptive use: Trends and Issues".* Studies in Family Planning, Vol. 19, No. 6 (Nov–Dec, 1988), pp. 335-353.
76. M. Fathalla, *Research Needs in Human Reproduction,* in E. Direfully, PD. Griffin, and J. Kharlne (eds), *Research in Human Reproduction.* Biennial Report (1986-87), World Health Geneva, 1988 IIPS (2000), National Family Health Survey India 1998-99 MOHFW Population Polity Government of India, 2000.
77. Bang, R. and Bang, A. *"A Community Study of Gynecological Diseases in Indian Villages"* in Zeidenstein and Moore (eds.) *Learning about Sexuality:* A Practical Beginning, New York: Population Council, 1989.
78. Bhatia, J.C and Cleland, J. *"Self Reported Symptoms of Gynecological Morbidity and their Treatment in South India",* Studies in Family Planning, 1995, Vol. 26(4), pp. 203-216.
79. Rutstein *et al., "Unsafe Abortion Higher no of Pregnancies".* National Institute of Population Studies 1992, Pakistan Demographic and Health Survey 1990-91. Islamabad, 1990.
80. Reynolds *et al., World Health Organisation Unsafe Abortion. Global and Regional Estimates of the Incidence of Unsafe Abortion and Associated mortality in 2003,* 5th ed. Generva: World Health Organisation: 2007.
81. Govindasamy, P. Stewart, MK, Rutstein, SO, *et al., High–Risk Births and Maternity Care.* Columbia, MD: Macro International, Inc., 1993.
82. World Bank, Investing in Health. Oxford University Press, 1993.
83. T.K. Sundari Ravindran 1993. *"Women and the Polities Population and Development in India".* Reproductive Health Matters. Vol. 1, No. 1. Population and Family Planning Policies: Women–Centred Perspectives May (1993), pp. 26-38. Published by: Reproductive Health Matters (RHM).

84. Thersa, O. Scholl *et al.,* "Prenatal Care and Maternal Health During Adolescent Pregnancy: A Review and Meta–Analysis. Journal of Adolescent Health, Vol. 15, Issue 6, pp. 444-456, Sept. 1994.

85. S. Pachauri and J. Gittlesohn, Summary of Research Studies and Implications for Health Policy and Programmes New Delhi, 1994.

86. Thaddeus Dudes, S. Marine D. *Too Far to Walk : Maternal Mortality in Context,* Social Science and Medicine. 1994: 38(8): 109-110.

87. S. Pachauri, *Relationship between AIDS and Family Planning Programmes: a Ratio Native for Developing,* Integrated Reproductive Health Services, Health Transition Review, Supplement to No.4 331-347,1995.

88. Zafar, M.I. *et al., Significance of Beliefs and Values in Predicting Fertility and Contraceptive Behaviours.* Bio-social Science, Cambridge, 1995, 27(3): 145-170.

89. Steketee, RW,Wirima, JJ, Slutsker. L, *et al., The problem of Malaria and Malaria Control* in Pregnancy in Sub-Saharan Africa. Ain J Trop Med Hyg 1996, 55(1 Suppl): 2-7.

90. World Population Monitoring. Population and development review 24(4) : 697-737, December, 1998.

91. Gittelsohn, J., Bentley, M.E., Pelto P. J., Nag, *M., Paachauri S., Harrision,* A.D. and Landman, L.T. (eds.) Listening to Women Talk about their Health: Issues and Evidence from India, New Delhi : Har Anand Publication, 1994.

92. World Bank. *"Safe Motherhood and the World Bank: Lessons from Ten Years of Experience".* Draft Washington, D.C, 1999.

93. Adamchak, S. *et al.,* "A guide to Monitoring and Evaluating Adolescent Reproductive Health Programmes", Washington, DC FOCUS on Young Adults, 2000.

94. Government of India. National Population Policy Department of Family Welfare, Ministry of Health and Family Welfare GOI, New Delhi, 2001.

95. Dilip, T.R. *"Utilisation of RCH Care Servicers: Some Observations from Kerala".* Journal of Health Management April–2002, 4:19-30.

96. Banerjee, B. "*A Qualitative Analysis of Maternal and Child Health Services of an Urban Health Centre, Indian Journal of Community Medicine".* 2003; 28: 153-156.

97. Chowdhury, S. *Pregnancy and Postpartum Experience Among First-Time Young Parents in Bangladesh:* Preliminary Observations. In Boa So Jejeebhoy S, Shah I, *et al.,* eds. *Towards Adidthood: Exploring the Sexual and Reproductive Health of Adolescents in South Asia* (Geneva: World Health Organisation, 2003) 59-61.

98. Centre for Development and Population Activates (CEDPA), Adolescent Girls in India Choose a Better Future : An Impact Assessment Washington DC : CEDPA, 2001.

99. Sen, G. (2004). Whether Women Health, www. India–seminar. Com/ 2004, 25 August.

100. Amita Pitra and Bhogyashrec Khaire (2004). Gender Sensitive Health Care System. Need for a Gender Sensitive Health Care System, Health Action, Vol. 17, No. 9, Sept. 2004. pp. 17-19.

101. Sen, G. *Whether Women Health,* www. India–seminar. Com/2006, 25 August.

102. Dabi, DR, Parak Manish *et al.,* "A Study of Maternal Vitamin 'A' Status and its Relationship with Intrauterine Growth Restriction". The Journal of Obstetrics and Gynecology of India, Vol. 56, No. 6, November/December 2006, pp. 489-497.

Chapter – 3

Methodology and Design of the Study

3.1 Introduction

Researching Reproductive Health Status of Women is one of the potentially difficult areas as it is open to all sorts of misunderstandings and objections. While the picture with regard to women's reproductive health, gynecological as well as obstetric, is indeed grim, what is equally frightening is that poor health gets perpetuated from mother to daughter over several generations as part of a continuous process. It therefore becomes crucial to break this vicious cycle and formulate policies and programmes that are sensitive to women's health needs. The term reproductive health is often equated with one aspect of women's lives, viz, motherhood; Complications associated with various maternal issues are indeed major contributors to poor reproductive health among millions of women worldwide. Women's poor reproductive health in India is affected by a variety of socio-economic, demographic, cultural and biological factors. Underlying poor Reproductive health among Indian women is their poor status on the one hand and an inadequate delivery system to cater the needs of scheduled, devalued and rural women on the other. The previous Chapter discusses the various studies undertaken in assessing the Reproductive Health Status of Adolescents and adult women. Analysis of review of previous literature enables the researcher to identify the research gap in the previous studies. Under the economic conditions prevailing in rural areas and the poor utilisation of health services the problem of motherhood being linked with child survival and maternal mortality. Untrained persons attend more than 60 per cent of the deliveries in rural areas. This affects both infant mortality and maternal mortality. The maternal mortality rate in 15-19 age groups is one of the highest in India. This is due to frequent pregnancy, which affects the health of the mother who becomes anemic with the consequence of delivering underweight children (Santhya and Jejeebhoy, 2003). With this background the present study aimed at assessing the Reproductive health status of the rural women by thorough examination of the Reproductive health problems of the rural women with the following objectives.

3.2 Statement of the Problem

In order to address women's reproductive health as envisaged under the national programme, it becomes necessary to assess the magnitude of reproductive morbidity among the women across the country. While the studies reviewed earlier have provided valuable insights into women's health and treatment seeking patterns, most of them are in depth studies and the magnitude of morbidity among various groups of women cannot be ascertained. Thus, data are needed on the varied health problems of women in all regions of the country as well as the magnitude of these problems. The feedback to the programme can be further made better if such assessments are made available periodically.

It is in this context an attempt has been made to study the Reproductive Health Status of the Rural Women in Tamil Nadu with the following objectives.

3.3 Objectives

The prime objectives of this study are to

- Analyse the Socio-economic and Demographic Profile of the women in the study area.
- Analyse the Reproductive Health Problems of the women before marriage.
- Examine the Reproductive Health Problems of women during pregnancy.
- Examine the Reproductive Health Problems of women at the time of delivery.

- Examine the Reproductive Health Problems of women immediately after delivery.
- Assess the General Gynecological Problems of the women.
- Discuss the Contraceptive behaviour of women.
- Elucidate the linkages between the Socio-economic and Demographic Characteristics of the women and their Reproductive Health behaviour.

The methods and procedures used in conducting this research study are presented under the following headings.

3.4 Locale of the Study

Chidambaram Taluk of Cuddalore district was selected as the locale of the study.

3.5 Study Population

All women in the Reproductive Age Group (15-45 years), irrespective of their marital status were interviewed for this study.

3.6 Selection of the Sample

Sampling is the procedure of selecting a portion of the population to represent the entire population in the study. It is proposed to select Cuddalore district among other districts of Tamil Nadu, as Cuddalore is one among the most backward districts of Tamil Nadu, and it lags behind in all the socio-economic and demographic and health indicators when compared with other districts of Tamil Nadu. In the second stage, Chidambaram taluk was selected as the locale of the study. Chidambaram taluk is one among the biggest taluks of Cuddalore district. It has the highest number of revenue villages (193) compared to Virudhachalam (167), Kattumannarkoil(161), Titakudi (130), Panruti (102), Cuddalore (84) and Kurinjipadi (64). In the third stage, five villages in Chidambaram taluk of Cuddalore district, viz., Usuppur, Meethikudi, Sivapuri, Nandhimangalam and Kattukudalur were selected. Finally, from each village 60 respondents were selected randomly as sample for this study. Totally, 300 respondents within the age group of 15 to 45 were selected as sample.

3.7 Data Collection Tools

As it was planned to obtain information from the women through interview method, a detailed schedule was prepared, pretested and finalised. The schedule which was finalised for this purpose contains the following aspects.

Section-1: Identification Particulars,

Section-2: Socio-economic and demographic details,

Section-3: Reproductive health problems before marriage,

Section-4: Reproductive health problems during pregnancy,

Section-5: Reproductive health problems during delivery,

Section-6: Reproductive health problems during post-partum period,

Section-7: General Gynecological morbidity,

Section-8: Contraceptive practices.

3.8 Data Collection

The detailed schedule for adoption of interview method to elicit information on various aspects of women in the study area to assess the reproductive health status was administered to all the selected women for this study.

3.9 Methods

Though the schedules were administered to all the women (300) selected in the sample villages for this study, 40 women were identified as unmarried and 260 women were married. Hence, the information regarding all the aspects including reproductive health problems before marriage were elicited from 260 women and the remaining 40 women were probed to obtain information regarding the reproductive health problems before marriage as they were unmarried. Editing, coding and feeding the data in to the computer have been done after obtaining the data from the women in the study area. The tabulated data were analysed with the use of SPSS. The association between the reproductive health problems at various levels reported by the mothers in the study area and their socio-economic and demographic background were established with the use of Chi square test.

Chapter – 4

Socio-economic and Demographic Profile

4.1 Introduction

The Socio-economic and Demographic Profile of the respondents provides a logical basis to understand their health. Socio-economic and Demographic Characteristics of Women have a strong influence on their Reproductive Health Behaviour. Many studies reviewed earlier have established the powerful influence of the socio-economic and demographic factors such as religion, place of residence, income, employment status and education exercise on fertility behaviour and reproductive health and healthcare seeking behaviour. Before analysing the factors determining the reproductive health status, it is essential to understand the socio-economic and demographic background of the sample respondents in the rural areas of Chidambaram.

Hence, this Chapter gives an analysis of percentage distribution of Socio-economic and Demographic Characteristics of Women of Chidambaram Area of Cuddalore District, Tamil Nadu. Since the socio-economic and demographic background of the respondents are having strong bearing towards Reproductive Health Status and Health Care Seeking behaviour, it is necessary to study the socio-economic and demographic background of the respondents in the study area. This chapter is divided into Seven Sections. Section-I deals with socio-economic and demographic characteristics of respondents in the sample area. Section-II deals with the Health Problems of Women Before Marriage, Section-III deals with Problems During Pregnancy and Health Care Seeking Behaviour, Section-IV deals with the Health Problems During Delivery and Postpartum Care Services, Section-V deals with the General Gynecological Problems of the Women and Section-VI deals with the Contraceptive Practices and Reproductive Losses of the Women in the sample area.

Section - I

4.2 Socio-economic and Demographic Profile

Religion is an important factor influencing the fertility and health seeking behaviour of women. The examination of Table-4.1, revealed that 96.0 per cent of the respondents were Hindus and a meager of 4.0 per cent was belonging to Christians and Muslims. The caste of the respondents has been classified broadly SC/ST and Others as it is a study of analysing the Reproductive Health Status of Women in General. Nearly one-fourth of the respondents were belonging to Scheduled Castes and Tribes. Broadly speaking, there is two types of families in India, namely nuclear and joint families. The type of family, its size and composition are usually considered important in the analysis of demographic behaviour because the fertility level of a society is expected to be influenced by its dominant family structure. In the study area more than two-third of the women belong to nuclear families. Distribution of women on the basis of their household size reveals that 28.0 per cent of the women belongs to households with size 4 followed by 27.7 per cent of households with size 6+. Considerable proportions of women (23.7 and 20.8 per cent) were belonging to the households with size 5 and ≤ 3 respectively. The mean household size of the sample area has been calculated as 4.6. From the table it was found that, majority (71.0 per cent) of the respondents was found to be engaged in agriculture and as agricultural coolies labourers followed by employed (18.7per cent) in other than agriculture. About annual income of the family, 37.3 per cent of the families had annual income below ₹ 10,000. Another 36.0 per cent of the families had income between ₹ 10,000-20,000. 8.3 per cent of the families fall in the category of ₹ 20,000-30,000.The remaining 18.4 per cent of the families had income more than ₹ 30,000. The average annual household income of the families in the study area has been calculated as ₹ 19,133.33.

The information on the expenditure pattern of the respondents on various items have also been obtained and tabulated. On the basis of the table it can be revealed that the annual household expenditure of 38 per cent of the respondents were ₹ $\leq$10,000. Forty-one per cent of the families expenditure was between ₹ 10,000-20,000. Remaining 21 per cent were lies between ₹ 20,001-60,000. The distribution of respondents by their present age shows that 55.3 per cent of the respondents belong to the age group of 20-29 years. The average age of the respondents has been calculated as 26.7 years. Place of birth is an important factor which will determine the reproductive health status of women. The women in the sample area have been distributed according to their place of birth and the distribution shows that 97.0 per cent were rural born respondents. Age at marriage is an important variable because early age at consummation of marriage leads to early child bearing, which is considered as a risk factor for reproductive health of women. The table revealed regarding age at marriage that 13.0 per cent of the married women have got married before the legal age at marriage of 18 years. The mean age at marriage has been calculated as 20.9 years. The distribution of respondents by their educational status revealed that 9.3 per cent of the women in the sample area were illiterate. Nearly 24.0 per cent of the respondents were educated up to primary level of education.

Table-4.1: Distribution of Respondents by Socio–economic and Demographic Variables

SED Variables	*Sub-variables*	*No. of Respondents*	*Percentage*
Religion	Hindu	288	96.00
	Christian	8	2.67
	Muslim	4	1.33
	Total	**300**	**100.00**
Caste	SC/ST	74	24.67
	Others	226	75.33
	Total	**300**	**100.00**
Family Type	Nuclear Family	205	68.33
	Joint Family	95	31.67
	Total	**300**	**100.00**

(Contd...)

Household Size	≤ 3	62	20.67
	4	84	28.00
	5	71	23.67
	Above 6	83	27.66
	Total	**300**	**100.00**
	Average Household size- 4.6		
Occupation	Agriculture	109	36.33
	Coolies/wages	104	34.67
	Business/ Trade	31	10.33
	Employed	56	18.67
	Total	**300**	**100.00**
Household income (Annual)	≤ 10,000	112	37.33
	10,001-20,000	108	36.00
	20,001-30,000	25	8.33
	30,001-40,000	12	4.00
	40,001-50,000	9	3.00
	50,001-60,000	10	3.33
	Above 60,001	24	8.00
	Total	**300**	**100.00**
	Average annual Household Income ₹ 19,133.33		
Household expenditure (Annual)	≤ 10,000	114	38.00
	10,001-20,000	123	41.00
	20,001-30,000	25	8.33
	30,001-40,000	12	4.00
	40,001-50,000	7	2.33
	50,001-60,000	19	6.33
	Total	**300**	**100.0**
	Average household expenditure ₹ 16,066.67		
Age Group	≤ 19	35	11.7
	20-24	96	32.0
	25-29	70	23.3
	30-34	48	16.0
	Above 35	51	17.0
	Total	**300**	**100.0**
	Average age- 26.73 years		
Birth Place	Rural	291	97.00
	Urban	9	3.00
	Total	**300**	**100.00**

(Contd...)

Age at Marriage	Below 18	39	13.00
	18-20	110	36.70
	21-23	88	29.30
	Above 24	23	7.70
	Unmarried	40	13.30
	Total	**300**	**100.00**
	Average age at marriage-20.90 years		
Educational level	Illiterate	28	9.33
	Primary	71	23.67
	Middle	55	18.33
	High school	78	26.00
	Hr. Secondary	25	8.30
	Graduate	37	12.30
	Professional	6	2.00
	Total	**300**	**100.00**
Spouse's Age at Marriage	≤24	69	26.54
	25-29	133	51.15
	30-34	41	15.77
	Above 35	17	6.54
	Total	**260**	**100.00**
	Average age at marriage for spouses-27.11 years		
Age at Menarche	≤12	20	6.67
	13	34	11.33
	14	39	13.00
	15	92	30.67
	Above 16	115	38.33
	Total	**300**	**100.00**
	Average age at menarche-14.83 years		
Age at First Birth	≤ 20	32	12.30
	21-22	30	11.54
	23-24	90	34.62
	25-26	43	16.54
	Above 27	65	25.00
	Total	**260**	**100.00**
	Average age at first birth-24.11 years		
Age at Last Birth	≤21	7	2.71
	22-24	80	30.76

(Contd...)

	25-27	95	36.53
	Above 28	78	30.00
	Total	**260**	**100.00**
	Average age at last birth-25.82 years.		
Children Surviving	1	106	40.77
	2	106	40.77
	Above 3	48	18.46
	Total	**260**	**100.00**
	Average Children – 1.5		
Children Ever born	1	64	24.62
	2	78	30.00
	3	67	25.77
	4	33	12.69
	Above 5	18	6.92
	Total	**260**	**100.00**
	Average-1.6		

Only 22.6 per cent of the respondents have got higher education such as Higher Secondary, Graduation and Professional courses. Distribution of Spouses with their age at marriage shows that, a majority (51.2 per cent) of the spouses married at the ages between 25-29 years. The average age at marriage of the spouses has been calculated as 27.1 years. In rural areas of India, most of the parents think that their daughters are ready to start reproductive life as soon as the daughters attain menarche which hinders all the opportunities like education and employment in their life. Hence they will be deprived from these opportunities and face many problems in their future life as they were sent to their husband's house by the parents as soon as they reach menarche. Thus, age at reaching menarche decides her future reproductive life. An examination of the table revealed regarding age at menarche that, higher percentage (55.0 per cent) of respondents reached menarche when they were in the age group of 13-15 years and the mean age at menarche was found to be 14.8 years. Sooner the adolescent become pregnant, higher the complication she has to face during pregnancy and delivery. Most of the studies revealed that most of the married adolescent mothers experienced their first pregnancy and child birth before they reached the age of 18 years. In the sample area, regarding age at first birth, it was found that majority of the respondents (58.46 per cent) had their

first birth before 25 years of age. The mean age at first birth was found to be 24.1 years in the sample area. The results of the distribution of respondents by their age at last birth were that a higher percentage (36.5 per cent) of women had their last birth between 25-27 years. But a considerable (30 per cent) proportion of women had their last birth only after the age of 30 years. The number of living children is an important demographic variable influencing the reproductive health and acceptance of contraceptive methods of women. The average number of living children of women in the sample area was found to be 1.5. Majority (40.77 per cent) of the respondents in the sample area had only one living children. The analysis of children ever born also shows that 24.62 per cent of the respondents had only one ever born child. A small percentage (6.92 per cent) of women had more than five ever born children. The average number of children ever born in the sample area has been found to be 1.6.

Section – II

4.3 Reproductive Health Problems of Women before Marriage

In this section, Reproductive health problems of women before marriage, Duration of illness, Proportion of Women taken treatment, Type of treatment, Health personnel consulted, Type of medicine taken, and Duration of treatment taken were analysed. Out of 300 women assessed, 195 (65 per cent) reported reproductive health problems during their premarital stage. It can be found from the Table 4.2 that, abdominal pain, profuse bleeding, irregular periods, breast tenderness, painful menstruation, leg pain and back pain, vomiting sensation and headache and white discharge were the common reproductive health problems experienced by the women in the sample area. Among the 195 respondents who have experienced problems, more than two-third of women had abdominal pain and leg pain and back pain. Profuse bleeding was also a common problem experienced by 60 per cent of the women. White discharge, irregular periods and vomiting sensation were also the problems reported by 50 per cent of the women. As far as the duration of the problems is concerned that most of the problems mentioned above last long for three days of their menstruation. Very few problems last long for more than five days.

Table-4.2: Distribution of Respondents by Nature of Reproductive Health Problems before Marriage

Nature of Reproductive Health Problems before Marriage	*Sub-variables*	*Number of Respondents*	*Percentage*
Any health problems before marriage	No	105	35.00
	Yes	195	65.00
	Total	**300**	**100.0**
Health problems before marriage (*The percentage of women reproductive health problems adds to more than 100 due to multiple responses*)	Abdominal Pain Profuse Bleeding Irregular Periods Breast Tenderness Painful Menstruation	132 117 94 42 51	(67.69) (60.00) (48.21) (21.54) (26.21)
	Pain in legs/ backache	130	(66.67)
	Feeling of Headache/Vomiting	75	(38.46)
	White Discharge	97	(49.74)
Duration of Illness (Days)	1	63	32.31
	2	37	18.97
	3	44	22.57
	Above 4	51	26.15
	Total	**195**	**100**
		Average - 2.43	
Treatment Taken	No	133	68.20
	Yes	62	31.79
	Total	**195**	**100**
Type of Treatment	Government Hospital	12	19.35
	Private Hospital	40	64.52
	Traditional Practice	10	16.13
	Total	**62**	**100**
Persons Consulted	Govt. Doctor	12	19.35
	Private Doctor	40	64.51
	Traditional Method	10	16.14
	Total	**62**	**100**
Medicine taken	Allopathy	46	74.19
	Homeopathy	6	9.68
	Local Medicine	10	16.13
	Total	**62**	**100**

(Contd...)

Duration of Treatment (days)	1	23	37.10
	2	14	22.58
	Above 3	25	40.32
	Total	**62**	**100**
	Average - 2.03		

Inappropriate healthcare seeking behaviour of women coupled with perceived low services quality and cultural barriers are contributing factors to inadequate service utilisation and high maternal deaths. Of the 195 women reported reproductive health problems during premarital period, only 62 (32 per cent) women sought care for their problems with a majority (64.5 per cent) using private providers followed by (19.35 per cent) government providers. 16.13 per cent of women in the sample area still sought locally available traditional medicines for their illness. The average duration of treatment taken for their problems has been calculated as 2.03 days. Hence, women's reproductive health seeking behaviour appears far from optimum. Future intention for home delivery and unskilled child birth was highly indicated. Inadequate awareness and decision-making were obvious. Effective measures need to be considered at the community and health sector level.

Health Problems of Women Before Marriage

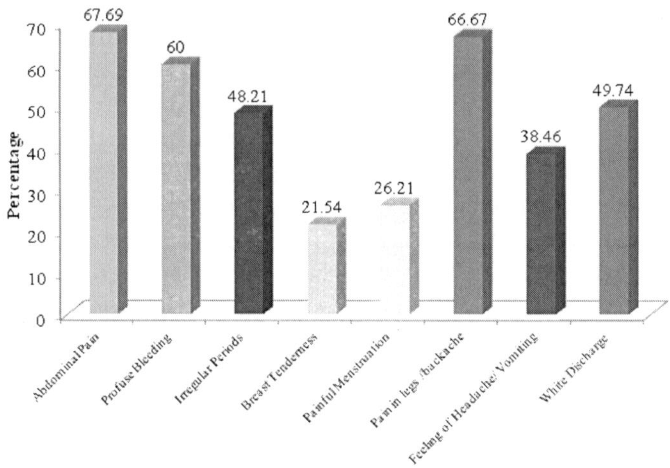

Note: The percentage of women reproductive health problems adds to more than 100 due to multiple responses.

Section - III

4.4 Problems During Pregnancy and Health Care Seeking Behaviour

Reproductive health problems of the women and their healthcare seeking behaviour in the sample area have been analysed in this section. Antenatal and postnatal care services are amongst the major interventions aimed at reducing maternal and newborn deaths worldwide. Antenatal care services help pregnant women to identify complications associated with the pregnancy or diseases that might adversely affect pregnancy. Antenatal visits benefit women as she is counselled about healthy lifestyle, provided iron/folic acid supplements and tetanus toxoid vaccine which are known to protect newborns against neonatal death.

From the Table 4.3, it was noted that majority 253 (97.3 per cent) of the women were reported to have at least one health problem related directly or indirectly to their pregnancy in the preceding three months of their antenatal period. This indicates high prevalence of reproductive morbidity. The important morbidities reported were swelling of feet and face 185 (73 per cent), White discharge 128 (50.6 per cent), Paleness/Aneamia 14 (5.5 per cent), Nausea/Vomiting 108 (42.6 per cent) and pregnancy-induced hypertension 60 (23.7 per cent). Other morbidities included morning sickness 68 (26.1 per cent), fever 36 (13.9 per cent), diarrhoea 7 (2.5 per cent), vaginal bleeding 4 (1.5 per cent) and urinary tract infections 29 (11.1 per cent). Hence the mothers require immediate treatment to overcome these problems. The duration of illness has last long for one to more than eight days. The average duration of illness has been calculated as 3.6 days. The above discussion show high prevalence of problems during prenatal period. These results are in line with the studies conducted by various researchers in India as well as in many countries.

Table 4.3: Distribution of Respondents by Nature of Reproductive Health Problems of Women During Pregnancy

Nature of Reproductive Health Problems of Women During Pregnancy	*Sub-variables*	*Number of Respondents*	*Percentage*
Any Problems of pregnancy	No	7	2.69
	Yes	253	97.30
	Total	**260**	**100**
Problems during Pregnancy (The percentages of women reported problems during pregnancy adds to more than 100 due to multiple responses)	Pregnancy Induced Hypertension	60	(23.72)
	Swelling of Feet/Face	185	(73.01)
	Paleness/Anemia	14	(5.5)
	Foetal Movement	67	(26.50)
	White Discharge	128	(50.60)
	Nausea/Vomiting	108	(42.60)
	Others	63	(24.90)
Duration of illness (Days)	≤1	61	24.11
	2-3	95	37.55
	4-5	43	16.10
	6-7	25	9.88
	Above 8	29	11.46
	Total	**253**	**100**
	Average –3.6		
Treatment taken	No	10	3.95
	Yes	243	96.05
	Total	**253**	**100**
Treatment of medical institution	Government Hospital	43	16.5
	Private Hospital	167	64.2
	PHC/Sub Centre	33	12.7
	Traditional practices	17	6.5
	Total	**243**	**100**
Persons consulted	GovernmentDoctor	80	32.92
	Private Doctor	115	47.32
	Private Nurse	4	1.65
	Government Nurse	3	1.23

(Contd...)

	Traditional method	41	16.87
	Total	**243**	**100**
Conformation of pregnancy for first ANC (months)	≤2	42	16.15
	3	99	38.08
	4	19	7.30
	Above 5	100	38.47
	Total	**260**	**100**
		Average - 3.68	
Times of ANC	≤3	28	10.77
	4	25	9.62
	5	68	26.15
	6	23	8.85
	7	54	20.77
	8	14	5.38
	9	37	14.23
	Above 10	11	4.23
	Total	**260**	**100**
		Average - 6.13	
Received ANC	Govt. Hospital/ Primary Health Centre	63	24.23
	Private Hospital	197	75.77
	Total	**260**	**100**
T.T Injection	No	14	5.77
	Yes	246	94.23
	Total	**260**	**100**
Taken IFA	No	25	9.62
	Yes	235	90.38
	Total	**260**	**100**
Health care advices	Nutrition advices	203	(60.96)
	Received health care advices	214	(82.30)
	Family Planning advices	181	(69.61)
Special food	Milk	192	(73.85)
	Green leafy vegetables	219	(84.23)
	Fruits	190	(73.08)

During pregnancy, timely medical advice for illness can minimise the ill effects to the mother and the foetus. The present study estimated that 253 (97.3 per cent) of the women experienced one or more episodes of the health problems during three months period preceding the study and 96 per cent of the affected women visited the health facility. About 64.2 per cent of the mothers visited private health facilities during illness, while 29.2 per cent visited government general hospital. But a considerable proportion of women (16.8 per cent) still sought traditional practices of healthcare.

Antenatal Health Care Check-Up

The first time of seeking antenatal healthcare consultation was the less than Two, Three, Four and 5+ months for 16.15, 38.08, 7.30 and 38.47 percentages of women respectively. Professional consultations sought by the respondents for antenatal healthcare visits have been classified by the number of visits. 89.3 per cent of the mothers sought consultations for more than four times. The most mentioned places of latest consultation were the private hospital (75.8 per cent) followed by government clinics. In the present study, only 54 per cent of the mothers sought antenatal healthcare checkup in first trimester which is lower than the NFHS-3 data of 75 per cent for the state of Tamil Nadu. The tetanus toxoid immunisation coverage of 94.23 per cent and regular intake of iron-foliate tablets of 90.38 per cent, were more or less similar to NFHS-3 data for Tamil Nadu. With regard to healthcare advices received by the mothers in the sample area, 61.0 per cent of the women reported that they have received advices relating to nutrition and nearly 70.0 per cent of them reported that they have received some sort of advices relating to family planning. More than 70.0 per cent of the mothers in the sample area reported that they have taken green leafy vegetables, milk and fruits as special food items during pregnancy.

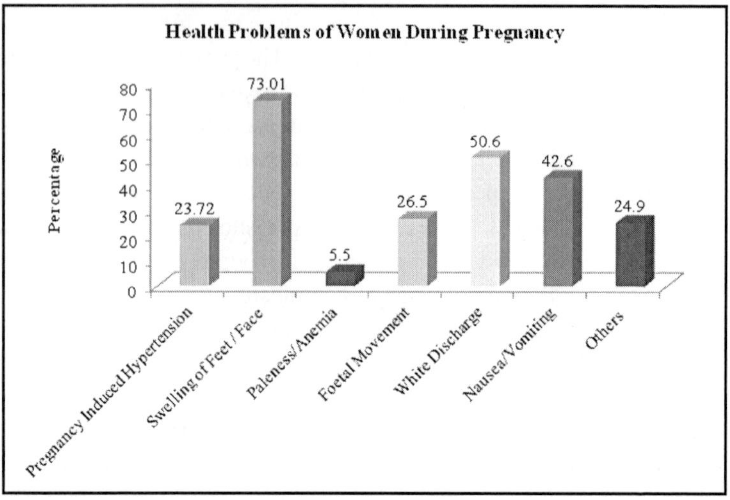

Note: The percentage of women reproductive health problems adds to more than 100 due to multiple responses.

Section – IV

4.5 Reproductive Health Problems During Delivery

The period from delivery and the first week of delivery lies in the perinatal period (from 28th week of pregnancy to 7th day of birth). During this period proper care is absolutely necessary. Poor nutritional status among mothers show high incidence of complications, which put them under risks. It was found in the present study that, more than half (51.2 per cent) of the respondents faced problems in this period. Among them majority (53.4 per cent) faced problems of Malpresentation. Rupture of Membrane was also a problem faced by 46.6 per cent of the respondents. Excessive bleeding and prolonged labour after delivery were the other problems reported by a considerable proportion of respondents. Episiotomy/Perineal tear and Retained Placenta were also the problems reported by some of the respondents.

Table-4.4: Distribution of Respondents by Nature of Reproductive Health Problems of Women During Delivery

Nature of Reproductive Health Problems of Women During Delivery	*Sub-variables*	*No.of Respondents*	*Percentage*
Problems at the Time of Delivery	No	127	48.84
	Yes	133	51.16
	Total	260	100
Problems Experienced during delivery (The percentage of women experienced problems adds to more than 100 due to multiple responses)	Rupture of Membrane	62	(46.62)
	Prolonged Labour	39	(29.32)
	Excessive Bleeding	61	(45.86)
	Malpresentation	71	(53.38)
	Episiotomy/ Perinea tear	18	(13.53)
	Retained Placenta	7	(5.26)
Place of Delivery	Govt.Hospital	103	39.6
	Private Hospital	141	54.2
	Maternity Home	2	0.78
	Home	14	5.38
	Total	**260**	**100**
Delivery Attended	Doctor	225	86.5
	Nurse	23	8.85
	ANM/LHV	4	1.54
	Family Members	8	3.08
	Total	**260**	**100**
Type of Delivery	Normal	205	78.8
	C-section	31	11.9
	Forceps	24	9.23
	Total	**260**	**100**
Complications of Last Delivery	No	194	74.6
	Yes	66	25.4
	Total	**260**	**100**
Type of Complications	Excessive	8	12.1

(Contd...)

	Bleeding		
	Prolonged Labour	55	83.3
	Delayed Delivery of Placenta	3	4.54
	Total	**66**	**100**
Weight of Last Baby (kgms)	≤2	17	6.53
	2-2.5	50	19.23
	2.5-3	96	36.9
	3-3.5	59	22.7
	3.5+	38	14.6
	Total	**260**	**100**
	Average – 2.85		

Regarding place of delivery in the present study majority (54.2 per cent) of respondents were found to have delivered at private hospitals. Nearly 40.0 per cent of the respondents delivered children at government hospitals. Interestingly, 5.4 per cent of the women in the sample area were still found to have delivered at home. Among these respondents, majority were assisted by their family members during their deliveries. As such, it was natural for some of the respondents in the sample area, to have suffered complications during child birth. In this context, women in the sample area were likely to be exposed to unhygienic delivery, which lead to the risk of morbidity and mortality of mother and child during and after the childbirth. The mothers were classified according to their type of last delivery. This classification shows that nearly 79 per cent of the mothers delivered normally their children. Around 12 per cent of them had Caesarean section type of births. Among 260 women assessed, more than one fourth (25.4 per cent) of them reported that they had some complications during the time of delivery. Out of 66 women with delivery complications, prolonged labour was the major complication experienced by 55 women (83.3 per cent). Excessive bleeding and delayed delivery of placenta were also the problems reported by a considerable proportion of women in the sample area. The classification of women with the weight of their last child at the time of delivery shows that, the weight of the children at the time of delivery was below 2.5 kilograms for more than one-fourth of the mothers in the study area. But the average weight of the children during delivery in the study area has been calculated as 2.85 kilograms.

Health Problems of Women During Delivery

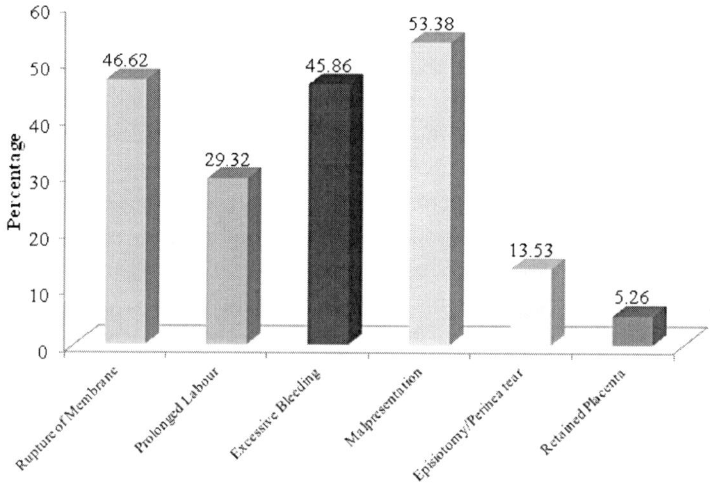

Note: The percentage of women reproductive health problems adds to more than 100 due to multiple responses.

Section – V

4.6 Problems Immediately After Delivery and Within Seven Days

The period from delivery and the first week of delivery lies in the perinatal period. During this period proper care is absolutely necessary. Poor nutritional status among mothers show high incidence of complications, which put them under risks. From the Table 4.5, results found that 71.2 per cent of the respondents faced problems during perinatal period. Nearly 50 per cent one-fourth of the respondents faced problems of excessive bleeding during this period, 61.08 per cent of the respondents reported that their lower abdomen pain and foul smelling discharge problem during this period were the other problems reported by a considerable proportion of respondents. All these problems were due to the improper or lack of treatment and care during pre and perinatal periods. The duration of illness ranges one day to more than 10 days. The average duration of these problems has been calculated as 6.4 days. Regarding treatment taken for these problems, among 185 women had problems during this period only 143 (77.3 per cent) women sought treatment. The remaining 42 (22.7 per cent) women did not seek any treatment for their problems. While probing about the general medical check up after delivery, 81 per cent of the women had general medical checks up after delivery. The remaining 35 women (19.0 per cent) did not go for any post natal checks up. Poor quality of medicines, non-cordial behaviour of the health personnel and unsuitable timings were the reasons reported by the respondents for their non-utilisation of health-care services. Poor quality of medicines resulted in poor recovery and dissatisfaction among the respondents, which lead to subsequent non utilisation of the facility. Regarding place of postnatal care services, in the present study majority of respondents (68.5 per cent) were found to have sought healthcare at private hospitals.

Table-4.5: Distribution of Respondents by Nature of Reproductive Health Problems of Women after Delivery

Nature of Reproductive Health Problems of Women after Delivery	*Sub-variables*	*Number of Respondents*	*Percentage*
Problems After Delivery	No	75	28.8
	Yes	185	71.2
	Total	**260**	**100**
Problems Experienced After Delivery (*The percentage of women experienced problems add to more than 100 due to multiple responses*)	Excessive Bleeding	88	(47.57)
	Lower Abdomen Pain	113	(61.08)
	Fainted	30	(16.22)
	Adherent Placenta	3	(1.62)
	Foul Smelling Discharge	7	(3.78)
	Pus Formation	5	(2.70)
	Fever More Than 3 Days	34	(18.38)
Duration of Illness (Days)	1-3	38	20.54
	4-6	53	28.65

(Contd...)

	7-9	65	35.13
	Above 10	29	15.68
	Total	**185**	**100**
	Average - 6.38		
Treatment Taken	No	42	22.70
	Yes	143	77.30
	Total	**185**	**100**
Medical Check up After Delivery	No	26	10.0
	Yes	234	90.0
	Total	**260**	**100**
Place of Post Partum Care service	Government hospital	74	28.47
	Private hospital	178	68.46
	Home Visit	8	3.07
	Total	**260**	**100**
How Long After Delivery did you First Put Your Baby to the Breast (Hours)	≤3 191	73.46	Hours
	3-6 Hours	45	17.30
	After 12 Hours	24	9.24
	Total	**260**	**100**
	Average 15.3 months		
Pre- Lactation Feeding Given to the Baby	Not Given	133	51.15
	Plain Water	112	43.07
	Sugar/Honey Water	13	5.01
	Liquid Items	2	0.77
	Total	**260**	**100**
Duration of Breastfeeding (months)	≤6	9	3.46
	7-9	19	7.30
	10-12	36	13.85
	13-15	71	27.30
	16-18	56	21.55
	19-21	47	18.08
	Above 22	22	8.46
	Total	**260**	**100**
Stoppage of Breast Feeding	Insufficient Milk	38	14.63
	Own Door Work	56	21.53
	Child Refused	42	16.15
	Wearing Age	54	20.77
	Became Pregnant	70	26.92
	Total	**260**	**100**

Only 28.5 per cent of the respondents sought postnatal healthcare services from government facilities. With regard to breast feeding, 191 women (73.5 per cent) were breast feed their children within three hours of delivery. The other 26.5 per cent of the women in the sample area breast feed their children only after 3 hours and some respondents breast feed their children even after 12 hours of delivery. During this period, the children were given plain water or water mixed with sugar/honey. The analysis of distribution of mothers with their duration of breast feeding shows that, nearly 24.6 per cent of the mothers in the sample area breast feed their children only up to 12 months. Nearly half of the women (48.9 per cent) in the study area breast feed their children up to 18 months. Only 26.5 per cent of women breast feed more than 19 months. The average duration of breast feeding of the mothers in the sample area has been calculated as 15.3 months. Women in the sample area reported reasons for the stoppage of breast feeding as became pregnant (26.9 per cent), own door work (21.5 per cent), wearing age (20.8 per cent), Child refused (16.2 per cent) and insufficient milk (14.6 per cent). Breast problem, Mother's sickness, Use of contraception were also the reasons reported by a considerable size of women in the sample area.

Health Problems of Women after Delivery

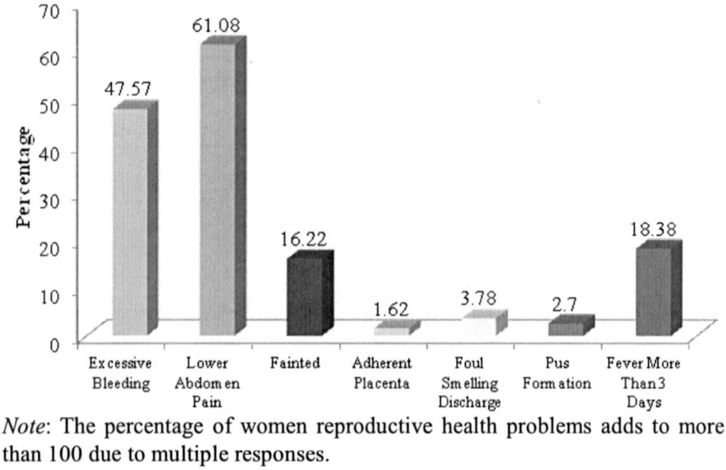

Note: The percentage of women reproductive health problems adds to more than 100 due to multiple responses.

Section – VI

4.7 General Gynecological Problems (other than those related to maternity)

In this section, the information collected relating to general gynecological problems of the women in the sample area were tabulated and analysed. Out of 260 respondents, 45 per cent (117) of the women reported that they had one or the other gynecological problems. Menstrual problem constitute one class of gynecological problems. One-third of the women reported that they had irregular periods of menstruation. Painful menstruation was also a problem reported by 8.6 per cent of the women. White discharge (60.9 per cent), Lower abdominal pain/Backache (34.2 per cent), Anemia (13.7 per cent), Excessive bleeding (38.5 per cent), Itching during menstruation (10.7 per cent), Foul smelling discharge (6 per cent), Burning and frequent urination (19.7 per cent), were the other problems reported by the respondents.

Table-4.6: Distribution of Respondents by Nature of Gynecological Problems of Women

Nature of Gynecological Problems of Women	*Sub-variables*	*Number of Respondents*	*Percentage*
Gynecological Problems	No	143	55
	Yes	117	45
	Total	**260**	**100**
General Gynecological Problems Experienced (The percentage of women experienced problems add to more than 100 due to multiple responses)	Irregular Periods	39	(33.33)
	Excessive Bleeding	45	(38.46)
	Painful Menstruation	10	(8.55)
	Foul Smelling Discharge	7	(5.98)
	Itching During Menstruation	12	(10.26)
	Scanty Bleeding	9	(7.69)
	Passes Clots	3	(2.56)
	Abdomen Pain\ Backache	40	(34.19)
	Prolapse Problems	8	(6.84)

(Contd...)

	Burning and Frequent Urination	23	(19.66)
	Anemia	16	(13.66)
	White Discharge	71	(60.88)
Duration of Illness (days)	≤ 3	10	8.62
	4-6	22	18.96
	7-9	36	31.06
	10-12	14	12.06
	13-15	18	15.51
	Above 16	16	13.79
	Total	**117**	**100**
		Average -9.40	
Treatment Taken	No	73	62.93
	Yes	43	37.07
	Total	**116**	**100**
Duration of Treatment (days)	1	25	58.13
	2	8	18.60
	3	3	6.97
	Above 4	7	16.27
	Total	**43**	**100**
		Average -1.81	

Prolapses problems, Passes clots and scanty bleeding were also some of the problems reported by a considerable proportion of the respondents. Regarding duration of the gynecological problems of the women in the study area, nearly 30.0 per cent of the women reported that the duration of their problems last long for more than 13 days. 43.1 per cent of the women reported that their illness duration last long for 7-12 days. The average duration of illness has been calculated as 9.4 days. Among 116 women with gynecological problems, 63.0 per cent of women did not seek any healthcare for their problems. Negligence, Laziness, Not serious problem, not get time were the reasons reported by the respondents for not taking any healthcare for the gynecological problems.

Gynecological problems of Women

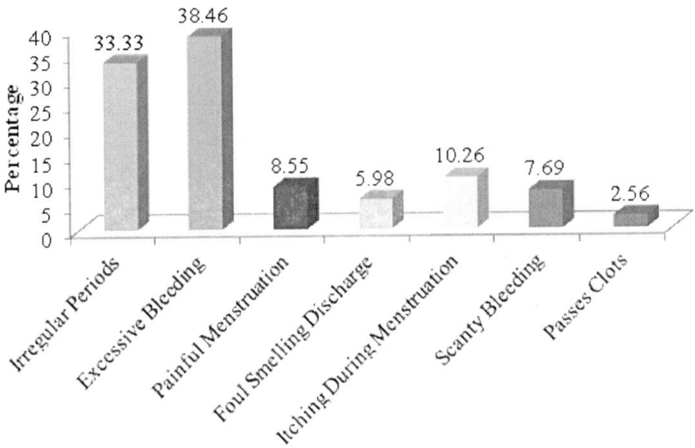

Note: The percentage of women reproductive health problems adds to more than 100 due to multiple responses.

Section - VI

4.8 Contraceptive Practices and Reproductive Losses

Utilisation of family planning measures both temporary and permanent methods influence the health status of women by delaying the future child bearing or stop the child bearing. In this section, the information obtained from the respondents on contraceptive practices and problems related to contraceptive use and reproductive loss was analysed. Among 260 respondents assessed, more than one-third (34.6 per cent) of the respondents used contraceptive methods. Female sterilisation was the most familiar method among the respondents which was used by 90.0 per cent of the users of contraceptives.

The analysis of duration of contraceptive use with the users of contraceptives shows that, 38.4 per cent of the users were under the protection of contraception for more than 24 months. 42.65 per cent of the users were under the protection of contraceptive for 12-24 months. Only 19.0 per cent were for less than one year. Government

Table 4.7: Distribution of Respondents by Nature of Contraceptive Practice Problems of Women

Nature of Contraceptive Practice Problems of Women	*Sub-variables*	*Number of Respondents*	*Percentage*
Contraceptive Method	No	170	65.38
	Yes	90	34.62
	Total	**260**	**100**
Method of Using	Pills	1	1.12
	IUD/Loop	4	4.44
	Sterillisation	81	90.00
	Rhythm /Safe period	4	4.44
	Total	**90**	**100**
Duration of Using Contraception (months)	≤ 5	8	8.98
	6-11	9	10.00
	12-17	16	17.97
	18-23	22	24.68
	Above 24	35	38.37
	Total	**90**	**100**
	Average - 3.70		
Source of Supply of Contraception	Govt. Hospital	64	71.11
	Private Hospital	19	21.12
	Shop	7	7.77
	Total	**90**	**100**
Period of Continuous use of IUD/Loop (months)	<6	1	25.00
	Above 12	3	75.00
	Total	**4**	**100**
Persons Inserted the IUD/Loop	Govt. Doctor	1	25.00
	Private Doctor	3	75.00
	Total	**4**	**100**
Institution Supply IUD/Loop	Govt. Hospital	1	25.00
	Private Hospital	3	75.00
	Total	**4**	**100**
Place of sterilisation	Govt. Hospital	63	77.77
	Private Hospital	18	22.23
	Total	**81**	**100**
Having any Problems due to any Contraception	No	40	44.45
	Yes	50	55.55
	Total	**90**	**100**

(Contd...)

Problems Faced After Using IUD/ Loop	No	1	25.00
	Excessive Bleeding	2	50.00
	Abdomin Pain	1	25.00
	Total	**4**	**100**
Problems of Sterilisation	Abdominal Pain	22	(27.16)
	Vaginal Discharge	21	(33.33)
	Pain/Backache/ Headache /Bodyache	29	(35.80)
	Pus Formation	15	(18.51)
	Irregular Periods	26	(32.10)
	Allergy	24	(29.62)
Sharing problems with experienced persons	Govt. Doctor	35	(38.88)
	Private Doctor	40	(44.44)
	PHN	25	(27.77)
	ANM/LHV	15	(16.66)
	H/F/R	20	(22.22)

health facilities played a vital role in providing contraceptive services to the respondents. Only four respondents used Intra Uterine Device as contraceptive. Out of which three were used it for more than 12 months. The IUDs were inserted by Private Doctors only. Most of the female sterilisations (77.8 per cent) were performed in government hospital and the remaining (22.2 per cent) performed by private doctors in private hospitals. Excessive bleeding and abdominal pain were the problems reported by the respondents using IUDs. Pain (Backache, Headache and Body pain), vaginal discharge, Irregular periods, Allergy, Abdominal pain, and Pus formation were the problems reported by the respondents because of sterilisation. Among 55 respondents had problems with the use of contraceptives, 44.4 per cent were consulted private doctors for their problems. 38.9 per cent of the respondents had consultations with government doctors for their problems relating to the use of contraceptives.

Contraceptive Practice Problems of Women

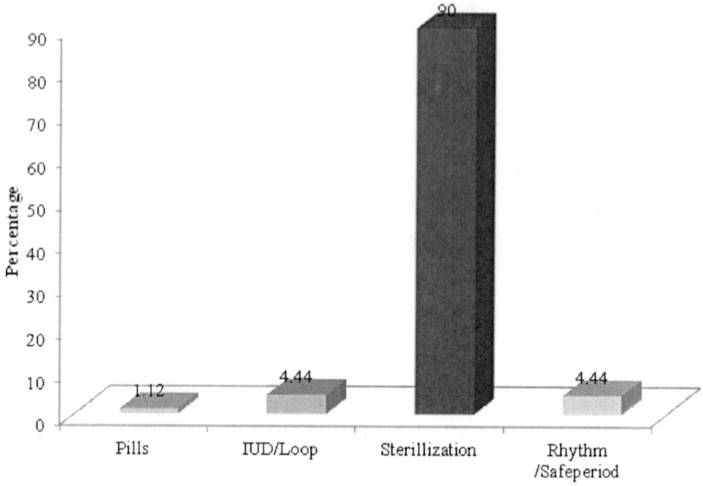

Note: The Percentage of Women Contraceptive problems adds to more than 100 due to multiple responses.

Table-4.8: Distribution of Respondents by Nature of Reproductive Losses

Nature of Reproductive Losses	*Sub-variables*	*Number of Respondents*	*Percentage*
Any Still Birth Spontaneous (or) Induced Abortion	Yes	57	21.92
	No	203	78.08
	Total	**260**	**100.00**
Reproductive Loss	Still Births	8	14.03
	SpontaneousAbortion	16	28.07
	Induced Abortion	33	57.89
	Total	**57**	**100.0**
No. of Still Births	1	5	8.77
	Above 2	3	5.26
	Total	**8**	**100**
No. of Spontaneous	1	9	15.79
	Above 2	7	12.28
	Total	**16**	**100**

(Contd...)

No. of Induced Abortion	1	21	36.84
	Above 2	12	21.05
	Total	**33**	**100**
Reasons for Induced Abortion	Immediately Pregnant After birth	23	40.35
	Doctor Advice Due to Health Problems	5	8.77
	Do not want another baby	29	50.87
	Total	**57**	**100**

Out of 260 women assessed, 21.9 per cent of them have experienced reproductive loss either in the form of still birth or abortion, out of the them 33 women (57.9 per cent) were experienced induced abortion, 16 women (28.07 per cent) were experienced spontaneous abortion. Only 8 women (14.0 per cent) were delivered dead children while probing women about the reasons for aborting children the reported that unwanted children, doctor due to health problem conceived immediately after birth were the reasons for induced abortion. In summing up, the socio-economic and demographic characteristics of the respondents reveal that they have profound influence over their reproductive health status and behaviour of the respondents.

Chapter – 5

Results and Discussions

In this chapter, the problems associated with premarital period, prenatal period, during delivery and postnatal period of the rural women in the sample areas were cross-classified with their socio-economic and demographic background. In the first part the reproductive health problems of women in the sample area before their marriage were analysed with their background characteristics. Duration of illness, Proportion of women taken treatment, Type of treatment, Health personnel consulted, Type of medicine taken, and Duration of treatment taken were analysed with the background variables. The association between the problems faced by the women during their antenatal, intranatal and postnatal periods and their socio-economic and demographic characteristics were analysed.

5.1 Health Problems before Marriage and Background Characteristics

The following table shows the distribution of respondents by their health problems before marriage and their socio-economic background. From the above table it can be inferred that among the 300 hundred women assessed, Majority of the respondents (65 per cent) suffered one or more health problems relating to reproduction before their marriage.

Women suffered by these problems were cross classified with their socio-economic and demographic characteristics and the inferences are as follows.

Table-5.1: Distribution of Respondents by Health Problems before marriage and their background Characteristics

SED/Sub-variables	*No*	*Yes*	*Total*	*Chi-square*	*df*	*P value*
Religion						
Hindu	104(35.6)	188(64.4)	292(100.0)	1.82	1	0.17
Christian	1(12.5)	7(87.5)	8(100.0)			
Total	**105(35.0)**	**195(65.0)**	**300(100.0)**			
Caste						
SC/ST	15(20.3)	59(79.7)	74(100.0)	9.36	1	0.002 (S)
Others	90(39.8)	136(60.2)	226(100.0)			
Total	**105(35.0)**	**195(65.0)**	**300(100.0)**			
Family type						
Nuclear family	57(33.5)	113(66.5)	170(100.0)	0.37	1	0.54
Joint family	48(36.9)	82(63.1)	130(100.0)			
Total	**105(35.0)**	**195(65.0)**	**300(100.0)**			
Education						
Illiterate	16(57.1)	12(42.9)	28(100.0)	19.85	6	0.003 (S)
Primary	30(42.3)	41(57.7)	71(100.0)			
Middle	22(40.0)	33(60.0)	55(100.0)			
High school	25(32.1)	53(67.9)	78(100.0)			
Hr. Secondary	7(28.0)	18(72.0)	25(100.0)			
Graduate	5(13.5)	32(86.5)	37(100.0)			
Professional	0(00.0)	06(100.0)	6(100.0)			
Total	**105(35.0)**	**195(65.0)**	**300(100.0)**			
Present Age						
≤19	7(20.0)	28(80.0)	35(100.0)	7.08	4	0.13
20-24	36(37.5)	60(62.5)	96(100.0)			
25-29	21(30.0)	49(70.0)	70(100.0)			
30-34	22(45.8)	26(54.2)	48(100.0)			
Above 35	19(37.3)	32(62.7)	51(100.0)			
Total	**105(35.0)**	**195(65.0)**	**300(100.0)**			
Age at Menarche						
≤12	5(25.0)	15(75.0)	20(100.0)	5.26	4	0.26
13	7(20.6)	27(79.4)	34(100.0)			
14	13(33.3)	26(66.7)	39(100.0)			
15	35(38.0)	57(62.0)	92(100.0)			

(Contd...)

Above 16	45(39.1)	70(60.9)	115(100.0)			
Total	**105(35.0)**	**195(65.0)**	**300(100.0)**			
Occupation						
Agriculture	42(38.5)	67(61.5)	109(100.0)	2.46	3	0.48
Coolies/wages	38(36.5)	66(63.5)	104(100.0)			
Business/Trade	10(32.3)	21(67.7)	31(100.0)			
Employed	15(26.8)	41(73.2)	56(100.0)			
Total	**105(35.0)**	**195(65.0)**	**300(100.0)**			
Annual Household Income						
≤10,000	42(37.5)	70(62.5)	112(100.0)	13.92	6	0.03 (S)
10,001-20,000	39(36.1)	69(63.9)	108(100.0)			
20,001-30,000	11(44.0)	14(56.0)	25(100.0)			
30,001-40,000	3(25.0)	9(75.0)	12(100.0)			
40,001-50,000	3(33.3)	6(66.7)	9(100.0)			
50,001-60,000	1(10.0)	9(90.0)	10(100.0)			
Above 60,000	6(25.0)	18(75.0)	24(100.0)			
Total	**105(35.0)**	**195(65.0)**	**300(100.0)**			
Medical Expenditure						
≤500	46(35.4)	84(64.6)	130(100.0)	14.66	5	0.02 (S)
501-1000	34(42.0)	47(58.0)	81(100.0)			
1001-1500	10(34.5)	19(65.5)	29(100.0)			
1501-2000	4(23.5)	13(76.5)	17(100.0)			
2001-2500	4(33.3)	8(66.7)	12(100.0)			
Above 2500	7(22.6)	24(77.4)	31(100.0)			
Total	**105(35.0)**	**195(65.0)**	**300(100.0)**			

Note: Figures in parentheses denote percentages (Row-wise).

As far as the Religion is concerned, nearly 65 per cent of the respondents belong to Hindu Religion were suffered by many of the reproductive health problems before their marriage. The percentage of women suffered by these problems among scheduled castes women (79.7 per cent) is higher than that of the women belong to other castes (60.2 per cent). It is also inferred that there is no significant variation among the percentages of women belong to Nuclear and Joint family suffered by reproductive health problems before their marriage. Surprisingly, the prevalence of problems was higher among the women with higher education than the women with relatively lower education and illiterates. While examining the women reported reproductive health problems with their present age, it was found that, more than 45 per cent of the women who suffered reproductive health problems were in the age group of less than 24 years. The age group wise analysis of the women who suffered one or more reproductive health problems revealed that higher percentage (70 per cent) of the women in the age group of 25-29 years reported reproductive health problems than the women in the other age groups. The analysis shows that there is no significant association between the occupational status of the respondents and the prevalence of reproductive health problems. As most of the respondents belong to the income category of less than ₹ 20,000 per annum, the women suffered reproductive health problems were also high among the women belong to low income category of less than ₹ 20,000. The medical expenses per annum of the family has been cross-classified with the prevalence of reproductive health problems among women. It was also found to be that more than 63.3 per cent of the women spending lesser amount of money as their medical expenses reported reproductive health problems. The percentages of women in the higher income and higher medical expenses categories were less in number it is not meaningful to corroborate these variables with the women reported reproductive health problems before their marriage.

The association between the prevalence of reproductive health problems and there socio-economic and demographic background were tested with the use of chi-square statistical test. The analysis shows that, caste educational level, annual household income and medical expenses of the household are significantly associated with the prevalence of reproductive health problems before marriage since the value of $p < 0.05$.

5.1.1 Types of Reproductive Health Problems and Socio-economic and Demographic Background

In this section, the problems reported by the respondents before their marriage, during pregnancy, during postnatal period, and general gynecological problems were analysed with their Socio-economic and Demographic Characteristics. Abdominal pain, Profuse bleeding, Irregular menstrual periods, Breast tenderness, Painful menstruation, Leg pain/Backache, Headache/Vomiting sensation and White discharge were the common problems reported by the respondents in the sample area. Among 300 women assessed, 195(65 per cent) were reported that they had one or more problems of this type before marriage.

5.1.2 Abdominal Pain and Background Characteristics

The following table analyses the women reported the health problem of Abdominal pain before marriage with their background characteristics. Among 195 respondents reported reproductive health problems, 132(67.7 per cent) responded that they had Abdominal pain before their marriage. The number of women reported abdominal pain was higher among non-SC/ST women. Women belong to Nuclear family, Younger age respondents, Women of higher menarcheal age, women engaged in Agricultural occupation and daily wages, women belong to families of low income groups and women belong to the families spending lesser money for medical expenses.

5.1.3 Profuse Bleeding and Background Characteristics

Profuse bleeding was also a reproductive health problem reported by 117(60 per cent) women among the women (300) assessed. While analysing the women reported profuse bleeding before their marriage with their socio-economic and demographic background, it was found to be that the prevalence of this problem was higher among non-SC/ST women, the women belonging to nuclear families, less educated women, women with younger ages, women with high menarcheal age, women engaged in agricultural occupation, women belonging to the families of lower income groups and women belong to the families spending lesser money for medical expenses.

5.1.4 Irregular Menstrual Periods and Background Characteristics

Among the 195 respondents reported reproductive health problems, 48.2 per cent (94) of the women responded that they had irregular menstrual periods before their marriage. Among the 94 women reported the reproductive health problems relating to irregular menstrual periods, majority (56.5 per cent) of them were belong to joint families. Similarly, illiterate women and women with lower educational status were reported more of the problem of irregular periods than the women with higher educational status. Higher the educational status lowers the problem of irregular menstrual periods. Hence, a negative association between educational status and the prevalence of the problem of irregular menstrual periods has been established. The analysis of women reported such problem with their age at menarche shows that there is an opposite relation between age at menarche of the women and the prevalence of the problem of irregular menstrual periods. The prevalence of the problem was higher among the women engaged in agriculture and Business/ Trade. Similarly the problem of irregular menstrual periods was higher among the respondents of low income categories and the families spending low money for their medical expenses.

5.1.5 Breast Tenderness and Background Characteristics

The problem of breast tenderness is a problem relating to reproduction of women faced by a considerable proportion of women in the rural areas of India as well as Tamil Nadu. In the study area, among 195 respondents reported reproductive health problems before their marriage, only 42 women (21.5 per cent) responded that they have suffered by breast tenderness problem before their marriage. More than 73 per cent of women reported breast tenderness were belong to nuclear families. The analysis shows that the problem of breast tenderness was higher among the women with higher menarcheal age. Women engaged in agricultural activities and daily wages were more among the women reported breast tenderness. Like the other problems, women from the families of low income groups and spending lesser money for their medical expenses were higher among the respondents reported the problems of breast tenderness.

5.1.6 Painful Menstruation and Background Characteristics

Painful menstruation is also a reproductive health problem reported by more than one fourth of the respondents who reported reproductive health problems in the study area. Among the women reported painful menstruation before marriage, majority were belong to the women of non-SC/ST category. Women of nuclear families were higher among those reported painful menstruation than the women belong to joint families. Unlike other problems, the problem of painful menstruation has no significant association with the educational status of the respondents. Since the number of respondents reported painful menstruation has been spread through all the educational categories. More than 68 per cent of the respondents reported painful menstruation was in the age group of less than 30 years.

Respondents with higher menarcheal age were likely to have the problem of painful menstruation. This inference has been established from the above analysis. The prevalence of the problem was also higher among the respondents engaged in agriculture occupation and daily wages/coolie. Higher percentage of women belongs to the families of low income groups and spending lesser money for their medical expenses reported the problem of painful menstruation.

5.1.7 Pain in Legs/Backache and Background Characteristics

Leg pain/back pain was also a health problem reported by the two-third of the respondents among 195 respondents who reported health problems before marriage. Among 130 respondents reported leg pain/back pain before marriage, 72.3 per cent of the women were belong to Nuclear families. It was found from the analysis that there is no significant association between educational status of the respondents and the prevalence of leg pain/back pain. The prevalence of this problem was higher among the young age respondents. Fifty per cent of the women reported leg pain/back pain were in the age group of below 24 years. Nearly 65.0 per cent of the women belong to higher menarcheal age (more than 15 years) group.72.3 per cent were engaged in agricultural occupation and as daily wagers/ coolies. Further the analysis shows that more than 74.0 per cent of the respondents belong to the families of low income groups (less than ₹ 20,000 per annum) and spending lesser amount for medical expenses.

5.1.8 Headache/Vomiting Sensation and Background Characteristics

Among the women reported headache/vomiting sensation in the study area, the percentage of women belong to nuclear families

(57.5 per cent) were higher than the women belong to joint families (42.5 per cent). The percentage of women reported headache/vomiting sensation was high among illiterates than other women of higher educational statuses. The Age-wise classification of women reported headache/vomiting sensation shows that the percentage of women was spreading through all the age groups and was high among the women with higher age at menarche. More than 50.0 per cent of the women reported headache/vomiting sensation were engaged in agricultural occupation and as daily wagers. Higher proportion of women in the families with lower income and spending more money for medical expenses were reported headache/vomiting sensation.

5.1.9 White Discharge and Background Characteristics

Out of 195 women reported reproductive health problems before their marriage, just above 50.0 per cent of the women reported that they have suffered by white discharge. Among these women, more than 59.0 per cent of the women belong to nuclear type of families. The analysis of the table shows that there is no significant association between educational status and the prevalence of white discharge. Younger age respondents and women with higher age at menarche reported more of the problem of white discharge in the study area. Similarly, women engaged in agricultural occupation and daily wagers were higher than other occupational category women among the women reported white discharge. Unlike other problems, the prevalence of the problem of white discharge was widespread irrespective of their household income and the amount of expenses spent on their household medical expenses.

It is also inferred from the table while correlating the reproductive health problems experienced by the women before marriage in the study area with the socio-economic and demographic characteristics, the variable like family type, annual household income are significantly related with the prevalence of various problems as the value of $p < 0.05$. the other variables do not significant associations with the prevalence of various problems.

Table-5.2: Distribution of Respondents Reported any Health Problems Before Marriage by their Socio-economic and Demographic Background

SED/Sub variables	Abdomen pain	Profuse bleeding	Irregular period	Breast Tender-ness	Painful menst-ruation	Pain in legs Backache	Feeling of Headache /Vomiting	White Dis-charge	Total	Chi-square	df	P value
Religion												
Hindu	125(66.49)	113(60.11)	92(48.94)	40(21.28)	48(25.53)	125(66.49)	74(39.36)	94(50.00)	188(64.4)	3.76	7	0.8
Christian	07 (100.0)	4(57.14)	2(28.57)	2(28.57)	3(42.86)	5(71.43)	1(14.29)	3(42.86)	7(87.5)			
Total	**132(67.69)**	**117(60)**	**94(48.21)**	**42(21.54)**	**51(26.15)**	**130(66.67)**	**75(38.46)**	**97(49.74)**	**195(65.0)**			
Caste												
SC/ST	44(74.58)	31(52.54)	24(40.68)	20(33.90)	15(26.42)	36(61.07)	20(33.90)	37(62.71)	59(79.7)	11.91	7	0.1
Others	88(64.71)	86(63.24)	70(51.47)	22(16.18)	36(25.42)	94(69.12)	55(40.44)	60(44.11)	136(60.2)			
Total	**132(67.69)**	**117(57.14)**	**94(48.21)**	**42(21.54)**	**51(26.15)**	**130(66.67)**	**75(38.46)**	**97(49.74)**	**195(65.0)**			
Family Type												
Nuclear family	80(70.80)	64(56.64)	48(42.48)	31(27.43)	35(30.97)	95(84.07)	43(38.05)	58(51.33)	113(66.5)	18.47	7	0.001 (S)
Joint family	52(63.41)	53(64.63)	46(56.10)	11(13.41)	16(19.51)	35(42.68)	32(39.02)	39(47.56)	82(63.1)			
Total	**132(67.69)**	**117(60)**	**94(48.21)**	**42(21.54)**	**51(26.15)**	**130(66.67)**	**75(38.46)**	**97(49.74)**	**195(65.0)**			
Education												
Illiterate	10(83.33)	10(83.33)	10(83.33)	3(25.00)	4(33.33)	7(58.33)	6(50.00)	6(50)	12(42.9)	21.17	42	0.99
Primary	27(65.85)	28(68.29)	25(60.98)	6(14.63)	11(26.83)	26(63.41)	15(36.59)	20(48.78)	41(57.7)			
Middle	19(57.58)	18(54.55)	16(48.48)	6(18.18))	8(24.24)	22(66.67)	15(45.45)	18(54.55)	33(60.0)			
High school	41(77.36)	38(71.70)	23(43.40)	13(24.53)	13(24.53)	38(71.70)	20(37.74)	29(54.72)	53(67.9)			
Hr. Secondary	11(61.11)	11(61.11)	10(55.56)	5(27.78)	6(33.33)	13(72.22)	5(27.78)	11(61.11)	18(72.0)			

(Contd...)

Graduate	20(62.5)	9(28.13)	10(31.25)	8(25.00)	8(25)	22(68.75)	12(37.50)	10(31.25)	32(86.5)			
Professional	4(66.67)	3(50)	0(0)	1(16.67)	1(16.67)	2(33.33)	2(33.33)	3(50)	06(100.0)			
Total	**132(67.69)**	**17(60)**	**94(48.21)**	**42(21.54)**	**51(26.15)**	**130(66.67)**	**75(38.46)**	**97(49.74)**	**195(65.0)**			
Present Age												
≤19	22(78.57)	16(57.14)	13(46.43)	7(25.00)	7(25)	19(67.86)	10(35.71)	18(64.29)	28(80.0)	19.23	28	0.89
20-24	38(63.33)	35(58.33)	29(53.06)	6(10.00)	15(25)	46(76.67)	30(50.00)	32(53.33)	60(62.5)			
25-29	29(59.18)	29(59.18)	26(53.06)	16(32.65)	13(26.53)	35(71.43)	17(34.69)	26(53.06)	49(70.0)			
30-34	19(73.08)	17(65.38)	12(46.15)	8(30.77)	9(34.62)	14(53.85)	8(30.77)	9(34.62)	26(54.2)			
Above 35	24 (75)	20(62.38)	14(43.75)	5(15.63)	7(21.88)	16(50)	10(31.25)	12(37.5)	32(62.7)			
Total	**132(67.69)**	**117(60)**	**94(48.21)**	**42(21.54)**	**51(26.15)**	**130(66.67)**	**75(38.46)**	**97(49.74)**	**195(65.0)**			
Age at Menarche												
≤12	13(86.67)	4(26.67)	11(73.33)	4(26.67)	2(13.33)	9(60)	6(40.00)	11(73.33)	15(75.0)	19.24	28	0.89
13	18(66.67)	11(40.74)	10(37.04)	8(29.63)	6(22.22)	20(74.07)	10(37.04)	13(48.15)	27(79.4)			
14	19(73.08)	19(73.08)	12(46.15)	7(26.92)	9(34.62)	17(65.38)	12(46.15)	19(73.08)	26(66.7)			
15	35(61.40)	34(59.65)	28(49.12)	9(15.79)	12(21.05))	38(66.67)	23(40.35)	27(47.37)	57(62.0)			
Above 16	47(67.14)	49(70)	33(47.14)	14(20.00)	22(34.62)	46(65.71)	24(34.29)	27(38.57)	70(60.9)			
Total	**132(67.69)**	**117(60)**	**9(48.21)**	**42(21.54)**	**51(26.15)**	**130(66.67)**	**75(38.46)**	**97(49.74)**	**195(65.0)**			
Occupation												
Agriculture	43(64.18	47(70.15)	44(65.67)	16(23.88)	26(38.81)	51(76.12)	25(37.31)	36(53.73)	67(61.5)	18.95	21	0.58
Coolies/wages	44(66.67)	41(62.12)	27(40.91)	15(22.73)	15(22.73)	43(65.15)	26(39.39)	37(56.06)	66(63.5)			
Business/Trade	17(80.95)	15(71.43)	13(61.90)	4(19.05)	2(9.52)	15(71.43)	7(33.33)	8(38.10)	21(67.7)			
Employed	28(68.29)	14(34.15)	10(24.39)	7(17.07)	8(19.51)	21(51.22)	17(41.46)	16(39.02)	41(73.2)			
Total	**132(67.69)**	**117(60)**	**94(48.21)**	**42(21.54)**	**51(26.15)**	**130(66.67)**	**75(38.46)**	**97(49.74)**	**195(65.0)**			

(Contd...)

Annual Household Income												
≤10,000	45(64.29	56(80)	34(48.57)	1724.29)	21(30)	50(71.43)	24(34.29)	35(50)	70(62.5)	55.76	42	0.05 (S)
10,001-20,000	45(65.22)	43(62.32)	39(56.52)	12(17.39)	20(28.99)	47(68.12)	27(39.13)	38(55.07)	69(63.9)			
20,001-30,000	11(78.57)	4(28.57)	8(57.14)	4(28.57)	4(28.57)	11(78.57)	4(28.57)	7(50)	14(56.0)			
30,001-40,000	7(77.78)	2(22.22)	4(44.44)	3(33.33)	2(22.22)	7(77.78)	6(66.67)	4(44.44)	9(75.0)			
40,001-50,000	4(66.67)	1(16.67)	1(16.67)	1(16.67)	1(16.67)	2(33.33)	4(66.67)	5(83.33)	6(66.7)			
50,001-60,000	6(66.67)	3(33.33)	4(44.44)	3(33.33)	2(22.22)	4(44.44)	3(33.33)	3(33.33)	9(90.0)			
Above 60,001	14(77.78)	8(44.44)	4(22.22)	2(11.11)	1(5.56)	3(16.67)	7(38.39)	5(27.78)	18(75.0)			
Total	**132(67.69)**	**117(60)**	**94(48.21)**	**42(21.54)**	**51(26.15)**	**130(66.67)**	**75(38.46)**	**97(49.74)**	**195(65.0)**			
Medical Expenditure												
<=500	56(66.67)	64(76.19)	44(52.38)	20(23.81)	28(33.33)	56(66.67)	28(33.33)	39(46.43)	84(64.6)	31.32	35	0.64
501-1000	33(70.21)	28(59.57)	25(53.19)	11(23.40)	17(36.17)	32(68.09)	23(48.94)	23(48.94)	47(58.0)			
1001-1500	15(78.95)	8(42.11)	10(52.63)	3(15.79)	0(00.00)	13(68.42)	5(26.32)	10(52.63)	19(65.5)			
1501-2000	7(53.85)	4(30.77)	4(30.77)	1(7.69)	1(7.69)	9(69.23)	6(46.15)	7(53.85)	13(76.5)			
2001-2500	5(62.50)	6(75)	4(50)	3(37.5)	1(12.50)	4(50.00)	1(12.5)	4(50.00)	8(66.7)			
Above 2501	16(66.67)	7(29.17)	7(29.17)	4(16.67)	4(16.67)	16(66.67)	12(50)	14(58.33)	24(77.4)			
Total	**132(67.69)**	**117(60)**	**94(48.21**	**42(21.54**	**51(26.15)**	**130(66.67)**	**75(38.46)**	**97(49.74)**	**195(65.0)**			

5.1.10 Treatment Taken for their Problems Before Marriage

Of the total of 195 women reported reproductive health problems, only 62 (31.3 per cent) women sought treatment for their problems. Other 68.7 per cent were not sought any treatment. Among the women sought healthcare for their problems, the women belong to nuclear families were higher than the women belong to joint families. The percentage of women sought medical treatment for their illness increases with their educational status. It shows that there is a positive relation between the percentages of women sought treatment for their problems and their present age. The treatment seeking behaviour of younger age women was higher than that of older women. The menarcheal age of the women also have an indirect relation with the treatment seeking behaviour. More number of women in the low age at menarche groups sought healthcare than their counterparts in the higher age at menarche groups. Further the analysis shows that there was no significant relationship between occupation, annual household income and medical expenses of the families with the percentages of women sought healthcare for their problems.

Table-5.3: Distribution of Respondents by the Treatment Taken for their Reproductive Health Problems Before Marriage by their Socio-economic and Demographic Background

SED/Sub-variables	*Yes*	*No*	*Total*	*Chi-Square*	*df*	*P value*
Religion						
Hindu	60 (31.9)	128 (68.09)	188	0.35	1	0.85
Christian	2 (28.57)	5 (71.43)	7			
Total	**62 (31.8)**	**133 (68.21)**	**195**			
Caste						
SC/ST	24 (41.4)	34 (58.62)	58	3.49	1	0.06
Others	38 (27.7)	99 (72.26)	137			
Total	**62 (31.8)**	**133 (68.21)**	**195**			
Family Type						
Nuclear family	37 (32.7)	76 (67.3)	113	0.11	1	0.73
Joint family	25 (30.52)	57 (69.05)	82			
Total	**62 (31.8)**	**133(68.21)**	**195**			

(Contd...)

Education						
Illiterate	3 (25)	9 (75)	12	9.04	6	0.17
Primary	14 (34.1)	27 (65.85)	41			
Middle	6 (18.18)	27 (81.82)	33			
High school	23(44.23)	29 (55.77)	52			
Hr. Secondary	6 (30)	14 (70)	20			
Graduate	7 (22.58)	24 (77.42)	31			
Professional	3 (50)	3 (50)	6			
Total	**62 (31.8)**	**133(68.21)**	**195**			
Present Age						
≤19	11 (39.29)	17 (60.71)	28	2.37	4	0.66
20-24	22 (36.67)	38 (63.33)	60			
25-29	15 (30.61)	34 (69.39)	49			
30-34	6 (23.07)	20 (76.92)	26			
Above 35	8 (25)	24 (75)	32			
Total	**62 (31.8)**	**133(68.21)**	**195**			
Age at Menarche						
≤12	7 (46.67)	8 (53.33)	15	2.66	4	0.61
13	9 (33.33)	18 (66.67)	27			
14	9 (34.62)	17 (65.38)	26			
15	15 (26.32)	42 (73.68)	57			
Above 16	22 (31.43)	48 (68.57)	70			
Total	**62 (31.8)**	**133(68.21)**	**195**			
Occupation						
Agriculture	18 (26.87)	49 (73.13)	67	1.40	3	0.70
Coolies/wages	24 (36.36)	42 (63.64)	66			
Business/Trade	7 (33.33)	14 (66.67)	21			
Employed	13 (31.71)	28 (68.29)	41			
Total	**62 (31.8)**	**133 68.21)**	**195**			
Household Income						
≤10,000	18 (25.71)	52 (74.29)	70	6.54	6	0.36
10,001-20,000	28 (40.58)	41 (59.42)	69			
20,001-30,000	6 (42.86)	8 (57.14)	14			
30,001-40,000	3 (33.33)	6 (66.67)	9			
40,001-50,000	2 (33.33)	4 (66.67)	6			
50,001-60,000	2 (22.22)	7 (77.78)	9			
Above 60,001	3 (16.67)	15 (83.3)	18			
Total	**62 (31.8)**	**133(68.21)**	**195**			

(Contd...)

Medical Expenditure						
≤500	25 (29.76)	59 (70.24)	84	2.82	5	0.72
501-1000	19 (40.43)	28 (59.57)	47			
1001-1500	6 (31.58)	13 (68.42)	19			
1501-2000	4 (30.77)	9 (69.23)	13			
2001-2500	2 (25)	6 (75)	8			
Above 2501	6 (25)	18 (75)	24			
Total	**62 (31.8)**	**133(68.21)**	**195**			

It is inferred from the above table there is no significant association between the treatment taking behaviour of the women for their problems during pre-marital period and the socio-economic and demographic characteristic of the women in the sample area since the $p>0.05$.

5.1.11 Place of Treatment Taken Before Marriage and Background Characteristics

The analysis of the place of treatment taken by the respondents with their socio-economic and demographic characteristics shows that, majority of respondents (64.5 per cent) sought treatment in private hospitals. Only 19.4 and 16.1 percentages of women sought treatment in government health facilities and traditional practices respectively. The same trend can also be inferred, while cross-classifying the socio-economic and demographic characteristics of the respondents sought treatment for their reproductive health problem with the place of treatment.

Table-5.4: Distribution of Respondents by the Place of Treatment Taken for their Reproductive Health Problems Before Marriage by their Socio-economic and Demographic Background

SED/Sub-variables	*Government Hospital*	*Private Hospital*	*Traditional Practice*	*Total*	*Chi-Square*	*df*	*P Value*
Religion							
Hindu	12(20.34)	39(66.10)	9(15.25)	60	1.87	2	0.39
Christian	0(00.00)	1(50.00)	1(50.00)	2			
Total	**12(19.35)**	**40(64.52)**	**10(16.13)**	**62**			
Caste							
SC/ST	7 (29.17)	12(50.00)	5 (20.80)	24	4.65	2	0.09

(Contd...)

Others	5 (13.16)	28(73.68)	5 (13.16)	38			
Total	**12(19.35)**	**40(64.52)**	**10(16.13)**	**62**			
Family type							
Nuclear family	5 (13.16)	23(60.53)	7 (18.42)	38	0.35	2	0.83
Joint family	4 (16.00)	16(64.00)	3 (12.00)	25			
Total	**12(19.35)**	**40(64.52)**	**10(16.13)**	**62**			
Education							
Illiterate	2 (66.67)	1 (33.33)	0(00.00)	3	11.24	12	0.50
Primary	2 (14.29)	9 (64.29)	3 (21.43)	14			
Middle	1 (16.67)	4 (66.67)	1 (16.67)	6			
High school	7 (30.43)	11(47.83)	5 (21.74)	23			
Hr. Secondary	0 (00.00)	6(100.00)	0 (00.00)	6			
Graduate	0 (00.00)	6 (85.70)	1 (14.30)	7			
Professional	0 (00.00)	3(100.00)	0 (00.00)	3			
Total	**12(19.35)**	**40(64.52)**	**10(16.13)**	**62**			
Present Age							
≤19	3 (27.27)	8 (72.73)	0 (00.00)	11	8.23	8	0.41
20-24	2 (09.09)	16(72.73)	4 (18.18)	22			
25-29	4 (26.67)	8 (53.33)	3 (20.00	15			
30-34	0 (00.00)	4 (66.67)	2 (33.33)	6			
Above 35	3 (37.50)	4 (50.00)	1 (12.50)	8			
Total	**12(19.35)**	**40(64.52)**	**10(16.13)**	**62**			
Age at Menarche							
≤12	3 (42.86)	3 (42.86)	1 (14.29)	7	11.43	8	0.17
13	1 (11.11)	6 (66.67)	2 (22.22)	9			
14	1 (11.11)	7 (77.78)	1 (11.11)	9			
15	4 (26.67)	8 (53.33)	3 (20.00)	15			
Above 16	3 (13.64)	16(72.73)	3 (13.04)	22			
Total	**12(19.35)**	**40(64.52)**	**10(16.13)**	**62**			
Occupation							
Agriculture	0 (00.00)	14(77.78)	4 (22.22)	18	14.66	6	0.02
Coolies/wages	9 (37.50)	12(50.00)	3 (12.50)	24			(S)
Business/Trade	2 (28.57)	5 (71.43)	0 (00.00)	7			
Employed	1 (7.69)	9 (69.23)	3 (23.08)	13			
Total	**12(19.35)**	**40(64.52)**	**10(16.13)**	**62**			
Household Income							
≤10,000	5 (27.78)	11(61.11)	2 (11.11)	18	9.17	12	0.68
10,001-20,000	6 (21.43)	15(53.57)	7 (25.00)	28			

(Contd...)

20,001-30,000	1 (16.67)	5(83.33)	0 (00.00)	6			
30,001-40,000	0 (00.00)	3(100.0)	0 (00.00)	3			
40,001-50,000	0 (00.00)	2(100.0)	0 (00.00)	2			
50,001-60,000	0 (00.00)	2(100.0)	0 (00.00)	2			
Above 60,001	0 (00.00)	2(66.67)	1 (33.33)	3			
Total	**12(19.35)**	**40(64.52)**	**10(16.13)**	**62**			
Medical Expenses							
≤ 500	4 (16.00)	19(76.00)	2 (08.00)	25	13.52	10	0.19
501-1000	5 (26.32)	10(52.63)	4 (21.05)	19			
1001-1500	2 (33.33)	2(33.33)	2 (33.33)	6			
1501-2000	0 (00.00)	2(50.00)	2 (50.00)	4			
2001-2500	1 (50.00)	1(50.00)	0 (00.00)	2			
Above 2501	0 (00.00)	6(100.0)	0 (00.00)	6			
Total	**12(19.35)**	**40(64.52)**	**10(16.13)**	**62**			

5.2 Reproductive Health Problems during Pregnancy and Socio-economic and Demographic Background

In this section, the reproductive health problems reported by the respondents in the study area were analysed with the socio-economic and demographic characteristics of the women. Pregnancy Induced Hypertension, Swelling of Feet/Face, Paleness/anemia, Fetal movement, White discharge, and Nausea/vomiting were the major problems reported by the women in the study area. Out of 300 respondents, only 260 respondents were married. Hence, to assess the reproductive health problems of the women in the antenatal, intranatal and postnatal periods these 260 married women were taken in to account for further analysis. The following table depicts the percentage of women reported reproductive health problems and their socio-economic and demographic background.

Table-5.5: Distribution of Respondents by Reproductive Health Problems during Pregnancy and their Background Characteristics

Sub-variables	*Yes*	*No*	*Total*	*Chi-Square*	*df*	*P value*
Religion						
Hindu	245(97.22)	7(2.78)	252(100)	0.22	1	0.63
Christian	8(100)	0(0.00)	8(100)			
Total	**253(97.31)**	**7(2.69)**	**260(100)**			

(Contd...)

Caste						
SC/ST	51(96.23)	2(3.77)	53(100)	0.29	1	0.58
Others	202(97.58)	5(2.42)	207(100)			
Total	**253(97.31)**	**7(2.69)**	**260(100)**			
Family Type						
Nuclear family	139(97.89)	3(2.11)	142(100)	0.40	1	0.52
Joint family	114(96.61)	4(3.39)	118(100)			
Total	**253(97.31)**	**7(2.69)**	**260(100)**			
Educational Status						
Illiterate	27(96.43)	1(3.57)	28(100)	4.07	6	6.66
Primary	68(98.55)	1(1.45)	69(100)			
Middle	49(94.25)	3(5.75)	52(100)			
High school	60(98.36)	1(1.64)	61(100)			
Hr. Secondary	17(94.44)	1(5.56)	18(100)			
Graduate	30(100.0)	0(0.00)	30(100)			
Professional	2(100.0)	0(0.00)	2(100)			
Total	**253(97.31)**	**7(2.69)**	**260(100)**			
Present Age						
≤19	17(94.44)	1(5.56)	18(100)	2.26	4	0.68
20-24	78(96.30)	3(3.70)	81(100)			
25-29	63(96.92)	2(3.08)	65(100)			
30-34	45(100)	0(000)	45(100)			
Above 35	50(98.04)	1(1.96)	51(100)			
Total	**253(97.31)**	**7(2.69)**	**260(100)**			
Age at Menarche						
<=12	14(100.0)	0(0.00)	14(100)	1.27	4	0.86
13	23(100.0)	0(0.00)	23(100)			
14	26(96.30)	1(3.70)	27(100)			
15	87(96.67)	3(3.33)	90(100)			
Above 16	103(97.17)	3(2.83)	106(100)			
Total	**253(97.31)**	**7(2.69)**	**260(100)**			
Age at Marriage						
Below 18	38(97.44)	1(2.56)	39(100)	0.81	3	0.84
18-20	107(97.27)	3(2.73)	110(100)			
21-23	85(96.59)	3(3.41)	88(100)			
above 24	23(100.0)	0(000)	23(100)			
Total	**253(97.31)**	**7(2.69)**	**260(100)**			

(Contd...)

Age at First Birth						
≤20	32(100)	0(00)	32(100)	5.88	4	0.20
21-22	29(96.67)	1(3.33)	30(100)			
23-24	87(96.67)	3(3.33)	90(100)			
25-26	42(97.67)	1(2.33)	43(100)			
Above 27	63(96.93)	2(3.17)	65(100)			
Total	**253(97.31)**	**7(2.69)**	**260(100)**			
Children Ever born						
1	60(93.75)	4(6.25)	64(100)	4.56	4	0.33
2	77(98.72)	1(1.28)	78(100)			
3	66(98.51)	1(1.49)	67(100)			
4	32(96.97)	1(3.03)	33(100)			
5 and above	18(100.0)	0(0.00)	18(100)			
Total	**253(97.31)**	**7(2.69)**	**260(100)**			
Family Size						
1	103(97.17)	3(2.83)	06(100)	0.178	4	0.99
2	103(97.17)	3(2.83)	106(100)			
Above 3	47(97.92)	1(2.08)	48(100)			
Total	**253(97.31)**	**7(2.69)**	**260(100)**			
Occupation						
Agriculture	95(97.94)	2(2.06)	97(100)	2.05	3	0.56
Coolies/wages	85(95.51)	4(4.49)	89(100)			
Business/ Trade	27(91.00)	0(0.00)	27(100)			
Employed	46(97.87)	1(2.13)	47(100)			
Total	**253(97.31)**	**7(2.69)**	**260(100)**			
Annual Household Income						
≤10,000	98(98.00)	2(2.00)	100(100)	4.59	6	0.59
10,001-20,000	88(94.62)	5(5.38)	93(100)			
20,001-30,000	21(100.0)	0(0.00)	21(100)			
30,001-40,000	10(100.0)	0(0.00)	10(100)			
40,001-50,000	8(100.0)	0(0.00)	8(100)			
50,001-60,000	8(100.0)	0(0.00)	8(100)			
Above 60,000	20(100.0)	0(0.00)	20(100)			
Total	**253(97.31)**	**7(2.69)**	**260(100)**			
Annual Medical Expenditure						
≤500	109(96.46)	4(3.54)	113(100)	3.32	5	0.65
501-1000	69(98.57)	1(1.43)	70(100)			

(Contd...)

1001-1500	24(96.00)	1(4.00)	25(100)			
1501-2000	16(94.18)	1(5.88)	11(100)			
2001-2500	11(100.0)	0. (0.00)	24(100)			
Above 2501	24(100.0)	0. (0.00)	24(100.0)			
Total	**253(97.31)**	**7(2.69)**	**260(100)**			

The above table discusses the percentage of women reported reproductive health problems and their socio-economic and demographic background. Religion, Caste, Family type, educational status, present age, age at marriage, age at menarche, age at first birth, children ever born, family size, occupation, household annual income and annual medical expenditure are the variables correlated with the women reported reproductive health problems during their pregnancy. The above discussion reveals that, out of 260 married women, 97.3 percent of them reported one or more reproductive health problems during their pregnancy. While cross-classifying the women reported reproductive health problems with their background characteristics, it was found that there is no significant relation between the variables and women with reproductive health problems.

Table-5.6: Reproductive Health Problems During Pregnancy and Background Characteristics

(N=253)

SED/Sub-variables	*Hyper-tension*	*Swelling of Feet/Face*	*Paleness/ Anemia*	*Foetal movement*	*White Discharge*	*Nausea/ Vomiting*	*Other Problems*	*Total*	*Chi-Square*	*df*	*P-value*
Religion											
Hindu	58 (23.7)	180 (73.7)	14 (5.7)	66 (26.4)	124 (50.6)	101 (41.2)	62 (25.3)	245 (97.22)			
Christian	2 (25.0)	5 (62.5)	0 (0.0)	1 (12.5)	4 (50.0)	7 (87.5)	1 (12.5)	8 (100.0)	5.53	6	0.47
Total	**60 (23.7)**	**185 (73.1)**	**14 (5.5)**	**67 (26.5)**	**128 (50.6)**	**108 (42.6)**	**63 (24.9)**	**253 (97.31)**			
Caste											
SC/ST	9 (17.6)	36 (70.6)	8 (15.7)	13 (25.5)	32 (62.8)	25 (49.0)	20 (39.2)	51 (96.23)			
Others	51 (25.3)	149 (73.8)	6 (2.97)	54 (26.7)	96 (47.5)	83 (41.1)	43 (21.3)	202 (97.58)	16.25	6	0.01 (S)
Total	**60 (23.7)**	**185 (73.1)**	**14 (5.5)**	**67 (26.5)**	**128 (50.6)**	**108 (42.7)**	**63 (24.9)**	**253 (97.31)**			
Family Type											
Nuclear family	30 (21.6)	102 (73.4)	11 (7.9)	33 (24.7)	67 (48.2)	59 (42.5)	38 (27.4)	139 (97.89)			
Joint family	30 (26.3)	83 (72.8)	3 (2.6)	34 (29.8)	61 (53.5)	49 (42.9)	25 (21.9)	114 (96.61)	5.63	6	0.46
Total	**60 (23.7)**	**185 (73.1)**	**14 (5.5)**	**67 (26.5)**	**128 (50.6)**	**108 (42.7)**	**63 (24.9)**	**253 (97.31)**			
Education											
Illiterate	6 (22.2)	17 (62.9)	2 (7.4)	9(33.3)	16 (59.3)	14(51.9)	6(22.2)	27 (96.43)			
Primary	15 (22.1)	53 (77.9)	4 (5.9)	16 (23.5)	39 (57.4)	25 (36.8)	14 (20.6)	68 (98.55)			
Middle	12 (24.5)	34 (69.4)	3 (6.1)	14 (28.6)	20 (40.8)	25 (51.0)	11 (22.5)	49 (94.25)			
High school	10 (16.7)	42 (70.0)	3 (5.0)	16 (26.7)	29 (48.3)	23 (38.3)	15 (25.0)	60 (98.36)	15.38	36	0.99

(Contd...)

Hr. Secondary	5 (29.4)	11 (64.7)	1 (5.9)	4 (23.5)	10 (58.8)	7 (41.2)	6 (35.3)	17 (94.44)			
Graduate	12 (40.0)	27 (90.0)	1 (3.3)	8 (26.7)	13 (43.3)	14 (46.7)	10 (33.3)	30 (100.0)			
Professional	0 (0.00)	1 (50.0)	0 (0.00)	0 (00.0)	1 (50.0)	0 (0.00)	1 (50.0)	2 (100.0)			
Total	**60 (23.7)**	**185 (73.1)**	**14 (5.5)**	**67 (26.5)**	**128 (50.5)**	**108 (42.7)**	**63 (24.9)**	**253 (97.31)**			
Present Age											
≤19	4 (23.5)	10 (58.8)	0 (0.00)	8 (47.1)	8 (47.1)	5 (29.4)	3 (17.7)	17 (94.44)			
20-24	15 (19.2)	54 (69.2)	2 (2.6)	21 (26.9)	43 (55.1)	23 (29.5)	17(21.7)	78 (96.30)			
25-29	17 (26.9)	41 (65.1)	4 (6.4)	16 (25.4)	34 (53.9)	30 (47.6)	20 (31.8)	63 (96.92)			
30-34	10 (22.2)	36 (80.0)	2 (4.4)	12 (26.7)	19 (42.2)	21 (46.7)	7 (15.6)	45 (100)	18.42	20	0.55
Above 35	14 (28.0)	44 (88.0)	6 (12.0)	10 (20.0)	24 (48.0)	29 (58.0)	16 (32.0)	50 (98.04)			
Total	**60 (23.7)**	**185 (73.1)**	**14 (5.53)**	**67 (26.5)**	**128 (50.5)**	**108 (42.7)**	**63 (24.9)**	**253 (97.31)**			
Age at Menarche											
≤12	1 (7.1)	9 (64.3)	2 (14.3)	3 (21.4)	9 (64.3)	6 (42.9)	1 (7.1)	14 (100)			
13	4 (17.4)	3 (56.5)	0 (00.0)	8 (34.8)	12 (52.2)	8 (34.8)	4 (17.4)	23 (100)			
14	12 (46.2)	19 (73.1)	1 (3.9)	15 (57.7)	11 (42.3)	9 (34.6)	3 (11.5)	26 (96.30)			
15	16 (18.4)	62 (71.3)	5 (5.8)	22 (25.3)	47 (52.0)	37 (42.5)	28 (32.2)	87 (96.67)	32.76	24	0.10
16 and above	27 (26.2)	82 (79.6)	6 (5.8)	19 (18.5)	49 (47.6)	48 (46.6)	27 (26.2)	103 (97.17)			
Total	**60 (23.7)**	**185 (73.1)**	**14 (5.5)**	**67 (26.5)**	**128 (50.5)**	**108 (42.7)**	**63 (24.9)**	**253 (97.31)**			
Age at Marriage											
Below 18	7 (18.4)	24 (63.2)	3 (7.9)	11 (28.9)	20 (52.6)	17 (44.7)	5 (13.2)	38 (97.44)			
18-20	23 (21.5)	74 (69.2)	5 (4.7)	33 (30.8)	59 (55.1)	43 (40.2)	34 (31.8)	107 (97.27)			
21-23	24 (28.2)	66 (77.7)	6 (7.1)	21 (24.7)	39 (45.9)	37 (43.5)	18 (21.2)	85 (96.59)	14.92	18	0.66
above 24	6 (26.1)	21 (91.3)	0 (0.0)	2 (8.7)	10 (43.5)	11 (47.8)	6 (26.1)	23 (100)			
Total	**60 (23.7)**	**185(73.1)**	**14(5.5)**	**67(26.5)**	**128(50.5)**	**108(42.7)**	**63(24.9)**	253 (97.31)			

(Contd...)

Age at Marriage											
Below 18	7 (18.4)	24 (63.2)	3 (7.9)	11 (28.9)	20 (52.6)	17 (44.7)	5 (13.2)	38 (97.44)	14.92	18	0.66
18-20	23 (21.5)	74 (69.2)	5 (4.7)	33 (30.8)	59 (55.1)	43 (40.2)	34 (31.8)	107 (97.27)			
21-23	24 (28.2)	66 (77.7)	6 (7.1)	21 (24.7)	39 (45.9)	37 (43.5)	18 (21.2)	85 (96.59)			
above 24	6 (26.1)	21 (91.3)	0 (0.0)	2 (8.7)	10 (43.5)	11 (47.8)	6 (26.1)	23 (100)			
Total	**60 (23.7)**	**185(73.1)**	**14(5.5)**	**67(26.5)**	**128(50.5)**	**108(42.7)**	**63(24.9)**	253 (97.31)			
Age at First Birth											
≤20	0 (0.00)	20 (62.5)	2 (6.3)	15 (46.9)	15 (46.9)	10 (31.3)	5 (15.6)	32 (100)	48.59	24	0.001 (S)
21-22	6 20.7)	17 (58.6)	0 (0.0)	9 (31.0)	16 (55.2)	12 (41. 4)	4 (13.8)	29 (96.67)			
23-24	8 09.2)	62 (71.3)	1 (1.2)	22 (25.3)	46 (52.9)	39 (44.8)	25 (28.8)	87 (96.67)			
25-26	18 (42.9)	31 (73.8)	5 (11.9)	11 (26.2)	22 (52.4)	21 (50. 0)	10 (23.8)	42 (97.67)			
Above 26	28 (44.4)	55 (87.3)	6 (9.5)	10 (15.9)	29 (46.0)	26 (41.3)	19 (30.2)	63 (96.93)			
Total	**60 (23.7)**	**185 (73.1)**	**14 (5.5)**	**67 (26.5)**	**128 (50.5)**	**108 (42.7)**	**63 (24.9)**	**253 (97.31)**			
Children Ever Born											
1	11 (18.3)	37 (61.7)	0 (0.0)	21 (35.0)	27 (45.0)	20 (33.3)	11 (18.3)	60 (93.75)	17.40	24	0.83
2	21 (27.3)	58 (75.3)	7 (9.1)	16 (20.8)	42 (54.6)	32 (41.6)	20 (25.9)	77 (98.72)			
3	14 (21.2)	54 (81.8)	3 (4.6)	20 (30.3)	30 (45.5)	33 (50.0)	18 (27.3)	66 (98.51)			
4	7 (21.9)	21 (65.6)	2 (6.3)	4 (12.50)	18 (56.3)	13 (40.6)	6 (18.8)	32 (96.97)			
Above 5	7 (38.9)	15 (83.3)	2 (11.1)	6 (33.33)	11 (61.1)	10 (55.6)	8 (44.4)	18 (100)			
Total	**60 (23.7)**	**185 (73.2)**	**14 (5.5)**	**67 (26.5)**	**128 (50.5)**	**108 (42.7)**	**63 (24.9)**	**253 (97.31)**			
Family Size											
1	29 (28.2)	76 (73.8)	7 (6.8)	29 (28.2)	48 (46.6)	39 (37.9)	28 (27.2)	103 (97.17)	7.63	12	0.81
2	19 (18.5)	77 (74.8)	4 (3.9)	29 (28.2)	57 (55.3)	47 (45.6)	21 (20.4)	103 (97.17)			
Above 3	12 (25.5)	32 (68.1)	3 (6.4)	9 (19.2)	23 (48.9)	22 (46.8)	14 (29.8)	47 (97.92)			
Total	**60 (23.7)**	**185 (73.1)**	**14 (5.5)**	**67 (26.5)**	**128 (50.5)**	**108 (42.7)**	**63 (24.9)**	**253 (97.31)**			

(Contd...)

Occupation											
Agriculture	24 (25.3)	67 (70.5)	5 (5.3)	31 (32.6)	49 (51.6)	32 (33.7)	17 (17.9)	95 (97.94)			
Coolies/Daily wages	19 (22.4)	58 (68.2)	6 (7.1)	21 (24.7)	47 (55.3)	38 (44.7)	29 (34.1)	85 (95.51)			
Business/Trade	5 (18.5)	22 (81.5)	1 (3.7)	7 (25.9)	14 (51.9)	14 (51.9)	5 (18.5)	27 (100.0)	14.82	18	0.67
Employed	12 (26.1)	38 (82.6)	2 (4.4)	8 (17.4)	18 (39.1)	24 (52.2)	12 (26.1)	46 (97.87)			
Total	**60 (23.7)**	**185 (73.1)**	**14 (5.5)**	**67 (26.5)**	**128 (50.5)**	**108 (42.7)**	**63 (24.9)**	**253 (97.31)**			
Household Income											
≤ 10,000	20 (20.4)	72 (73.5)	4 (4.1)	26 (26.5)	55 (55.1)	36 (36.7)	26 (26.5)	98 (98.0)			
10,001-20,000	19 (21.6)	68 (77.3)	7 (7.9)	29 (32.9)	41 (46.6)	39 (44.3)	20 (22.7)	88 (100.0)			
20,001-30,000	9 (42.9)	11 (52.4)	1 (4.8)	4 (19.1)	12 (57.1)	10 (47.6)	5 (23.8)	21 (100.0)			
30,001-40,000	4 (40.0)	7 (70.0)	0 (0.00)	1 (10.0)	6 (60.0)	5 (50.0)	1 (10.0)	10 (100.0)	25.19	36	0.91
40,001-50,000	1 (12.5)	6 (75.0)	0 (0.00)	0 (0.0)	4(50.0)	3(37.5)	1(12.5)	8 (100.0)			
50,001-60,000	2 (25.0)	5 (62.5)	0 (0.00)	1 (12.5)	5 (62.5)	4 (50.0)	4 (50.0)	8 (100.0)			
60,000+	5 (25.0)	6 (80.0)	2(10.0)	6 (30.0)	5(25.0)	11(55.0)	6(30.0)	20 (100)			
Total	**60 (23.7)**	**185 (73.1)**	**14 (5.5)**	**67 (26.5)**	**185 (50.5)**	**108 (42.7)**	**63 (24.9)**	**253 (97.31)**			
Medical Expenditure											
≤500	19 (17.4)	80 (73.4)	3 (2.8)	34 (31.2)	57 (52.3)	43 (39.5)	25 (22.9)	109 (96.46)			
501-1000	20 (28.9)	47 (68.2)	5 (7.3)	21 (30.4)	33 (47.8)	30 (43.5)	19 (27.5)	69 (98.57)			
1001-1500	12 (50.0)	16 (66.7)	2 (8.3)	2 (8.3)	13 (54.2)	12 (50.0)	5 (20.8)	24 (96.00)	28.58	30	0.53
1501-2000	3 (18.8)	13 (81.3)	3 (18.8)	2 (12.5)	9 (56.2)	7 (43.8)	6 (37.5)	16 (94.18)			
2001-2500	2 (18.2)	9 (81.8)	0 (0.0)	5 (45.5)	6 (54.6)	6 (54.6)	3 (27.3)	11 (100)			
2500+	4 (16.7)	20 (83.3)	1 (4.2)	3 (12.5)	10 (41.7)	10 (41.7)	5 (20.8)	24 (100)			
Total	**60 (23.7)**	**185 (73.1)**	**14 (5.5)**	**67 (26.5)**	**128 (50.5)**	**108 (42.7)**	**63 (24.9)**	**253 (97.31)**			

From the table it can be found that, hypertension, swelling of feet/Face, Paleness/Aneamia, Foetal movement, White discharge, Nausea/Vomiting was the major reproductive health problems reported by the women in the study area. The percentages of women reported each health problem was cross-classified with their socio-economic and demographic characteristics. Out of 253 women reported reproductive health problems in the study area, 185(73.1 per cent) and 128(50.5 per cent) women reported that they have suffered by the problem of Swelling of Feet/Face and White discharge respectively. The analysis of women reported problem of Swelling of Feet/Face and their socio-economic and demographic characteristics revealed that majority of women reported swelling of Feet/Face were belong to non-SC/ST, nuclear family, women belong to higher age, women with higher age at menarche, women with higher age at first birth, women with lower number of children ever born, women with lower family size, women occupied in agriculture and as coolies/daily wagers, women in the families of families of lower income groups and spent less money for their medical expenditures. The second reproductive health problem reported by more number of women was white discharge during their pregnancy. More than 50.5 per cent of the women reported that they have experienced this problem during their pregnancy period. While these women were cross-classified with their socio-economic and demographic characteristics, the analysis shows that the same trend has been inferred as in the case of swelling of feet/face. As far as the educational status is concerned, it has no significant relation with the percentage of women reported reproductive health problems. The overall discussion of the above table reveals that the percentage of women reported reproductive health problems were higher among the women belong to the categories of non-SC/ST, nuclear family, higher age group, higher menarcheal age, higher age at first birth, agriculture and coolies/daily wagers, families of low income groups and spending less money for their medical expenses irrespective of the problems. Hence special efforts should be made to safeguard the women in these categories in order to prevent them from contracting these reproductive health problems.

5.3 Place of Healthcare Treatment after Marriage

The following table analyses the place of treatment for their reproductive health problems before marriage with their socio-economic and demographic characteristics. Place of treatment sought by the women in rural areas is an important indicator of their treatment seeking behaviour as well as the reproductive health status of the women. In the following analysis the place of treatment for the health problems of 260 married women in the study area have been analysed with their socio-economic and demographic characteristics. The analysis shows that majority of the women (64.2 per cent) sought healthcare for their health problems from private health facility. Only 29.23 per cent of the women sought healthcare from government health facilities such as government hospitals and Primary Health Centres. A considerable proportion of women sought traditional medicines also. While the socio-economic and demographic characteristics of the respondents sought healthcare for their health problems before marriage correlated with the place of healthcare treatment, Out of 53 SC/ST women, more than 52 per cent of them sought healthcare from the government health facilities such as government hospitals and Primary Health Centres in the study area. Whereas the family type is concerned, there is no significant relation between the family type and the place of healthcare treatment. Surprisingly, the women sought healthcare treatment for their health problems from private health facilities were higher than the women sought healthcare treatment irrespective of their educational status. Present age of the women is also an important variable to be taken into consideration while assessing the reproductive health status and treatment seeking behaviour. In the study area, higher percentage of women in the higher age groups sought healthcare from government health facilities. Women with younger ages prefer private health facility for their health problems. Hence, there is an urgent need to create an awareness among young women about health services rendered by the government health facilities at free and low cost and the quality of healthcare services of the government healthcare facilities have to be improved so as to enable the young rural women to make use of the healthcare services. The age at menarche of the respondents in the study area has also been cross-classified with the place of treatment sought by them. The analysis shows that, there is no significant association between the age at menarche of the respondents and the place of healthcare treatment. The same trend can also be inferred while analysing the age at marriage with the place of healthcare treatment of the women in the sample area. The percentage of women sought healthcare treatment from private healthcare facility has increased with their age at first birth. Hence, it can be inferred that a positive association is exist between the ages at first birth and the percentage of women sought healthcare treatment in private health facility.

Table-5.7: Distribution of Respondents by the Place of Health-care Treatment for the Health Problems after Marriage and their Background Characteristics

SED/Sub-variables	*Govt. Hospital*	*Private Hospital*	*PHC/Sub-Centre*	*Traditional Method*	*Total*	*Chi-Square*	*df*	*P value*
Religion								
Hindu	42(16.7)	161(63.9)	33(13.1)	16(6.4)	252(100)	1.72	3	0.63
Christian	1 (12.5)	6(75.0)	0 (0)	1(12.5)	8(100)			
Total	**43(16.5)**	**167(64.2)**	**33 (12.7)**	**17(6.5)**	**260(100)**			
Caste								
SC/ST	17(32.1)	20 (37.4)	11(20.8)	5(9.4)	53 (100)	21.25	3	0.001
Others	26(12.6)	147(51.2)	22(10.6)	12(5.8)	207(100)			
Total	**43(16.5)**	**167(64.2)**	**33(12.7)**	**17(6.5)**	**260(100)**			
Family Type								
Nuclear family	35(24.7)	84 (59.2)	15 (1.6)	8 (5.6)	142(100)	15.20	3	0.002
Joint family	8 (6.8)	83 (70.3)	18 (15.3)	9(7.6)	118(100)			
Total	**43(16.5)**	**167(64.2)**	**33 (12.7)**	**17(6.5)**	**260(100)**			
Education								
Illiterate	2 (7.1)	17 (60.7)	7 (24.9)	2(7.14)	28 (100)	19.38	18	0.369
Primary	12(17.4)	40 (57.9)	12(17.4)	5(7.3)	69 (100)			
Middle	12(23.1)	30 (57.7)	7(13.5)	3(5.8)	52 (100)			
High School	7 (11.5)	43 (70.5)	5 (8.2)	6(9.8)	61 (100)			
Hr. Secondary	3 (16.7)	13 (72.2)	1(5.6)	1(5.6)	18 (100)			
Graduate	6 (20.0)	23 (76.7)	1(3.3)	0(0)	30 (100)			
Professional	1 (50.0)	1 (50.0)	0(0)	(0)	2 (100)			
Total	**43(16.5)**	**167(64.2)**	**33(12.7)**	**17(6.5)**	**260(100)**			

(Contd...)

Present Age								
≤19	1 (5.6)	12 (66.7)	3 (16.7)	2(11.1)	18 (100)			
20-24	7 (8.6)	61 (75.3)	7(8.6)	6(7.4)	81(100)			
25-29	13(20.0)	37 (56.9)	9 (13.9)	6(9.2)	65 (100)	16.61	12	0.165
30-34	8 (17.8)	28 (62.2)	8(17.8)	1(2.2)	45 (100)			
Above 35	14(27.5)	29 (56.7)	6(11.6)	2(3.9)	51 (100)			
Total	**43(16.5)**	**167(64.2)**	**33(12.7)**	**17(6.5)**	**260(100)**			
Age at Menarche								
<12	2(14.3)	10(71.4)	2(14.3)	0(0)	14(100)			
13	2 (8.7)	14 (60.9)	4 (17.4)	3(13.0)	23(100)			
14	4 (14.8)	17 (62.9)	3(11.1)	3(11.1)	27 (100)	8.59	12	0.73
15	15(16.7)	54 (60.0)	14 (15.6)	7(7.8)	90 (100)			
Above 16	20(18.9)	72 (67.7)	10 (9.4)	4(3.8)	106(100)			
Total	**43(16.5)**	**167(64.2)**	**33(12.7)**	**17(6.5)**	**260(100)**			
Age at Marriage								
≤18	6 (15.4)	27 (69.2)	3 (7.7)	3(7.7)	39 (100)			
18-20	20(18.2)	72 (65.5)	14 12.7)	4(3.6)	110(100)			
21-23	15(17.1)	54 (72.7)	12(13.6)	7(7.9)	88 (100)	9.77	9	0.36
24+	2 (8.7)	14 (60.9)	4 (17.4)	3(13.0)	23 (100)			
Total	**43(16.5)**	**167(64.2)**	**33(12.7)**	**17(6.5)**	**260(100)**			
Age at First Birth								
≤20	5(15.6)	2(65.6)	4(12.5)	2(6.3)	32(100)			
21-22	5 (16.7)	18 (60.0)	3(10.0)	4(13.3)	30(100)			
23-24	14(15.6)	55 (61.1)	15(16.7)	6(6.7)	90 (100)	11.12	12	0.51
25-26	8 (18.6)	26 (60.5)	4(1.7)	5(11.6)	43 (100)			
26+	11(16.9)	47 (72.3)	7(10.8)	0(0)	65 (100)			
Total	**43(16.5)**	**167(64.2)**	**33(12.7)**	**17(6.5)**	**260(100)**			
Children Ever Born								
1	5(7.8)	46(71.9)	5(7.8)	8(12.5)	64(100)			
2	6(7.7)	55 (70.5)	15(19.2)	2(2.6)	78 (100)			
3 (S)	17(25.4)	43 (64.2)	3 (4.5)	4(5.9)	67 (100)	34.74	12	0.001
4	11(33.3)	14 (42.4)	6 (18.2)	2(6.1)	33 (100)			
4+	4 (22.2)	9 (50.0)	4(2.2)	1(5.6)	18(100)			
Total	**43(16.5)**	**167(64.2)**	**33(12.7)**	**17(6.5)**	**260(100)**			
Family Size								
1	8(7.6)	75 (70.8)	18(16.9)	5 (4.7)	106(100)			
2	20(18.9)	71(66.9)	6 (5.7)	9(8.5)	106(100)	25.37	12	0.01
3 and above	15(31.3)	21 (43.8)	9(18.8)	3(6.3)	48 (100)			
Total	**43(16.5)**	**167(64.2)**	**33(12.7)**	**17(6.5)**	**260(100)**			

(Contd...)

Occupation								
Agriculture	7(7.2)	73 (75.3)	11(11.3)	6(6.2)	97 (100)	26.98	9	.001
Coolies/wages	23(25.8)	43 (48.3)	14(15.7)	9(10.1)	89 (100)			
Business/Trade	1(3.7)	20 (74.1)	5(6.4)	1(3.7)	27 (100)			
Employed	12(25.5)	31 (65.9)	3(6.4)	1(2.1)	47 (100)			
Total	**43(16.5)**	**167(64.2)**	**33(12.7)**	**17(6.5)**	**260(100)**			
Annual Household Income								
≤10,000	16(16.0)	64 (64.0)	14(14.0)	6(6.0)	100(100)	13.83	18	.740
10,001-20,000	15(16.1)	54 (58.1)	14 (15.1)	10(10.8)	93 (100)			
20,001-30,000	5(23.8)	12 (57.1)	3(14.3)	1(4.8)	21 (100)			
30,001-40,000	1(10.0)	8 (80.0)	1(10.0)	0(0)	10 (100)			
40,001-50,000	1(12.5)	6 (75.0)	1(12.5)	0(0)	8 (100)			
50,001-60,000	1(12.5)	7(87.5)	0(0)	0(0)	8 (100)			
Above 60,001	4(20.0)	16 (80.0)	0(0)	0(0)	20 (100)			
Total	**43(16.5)**	**167(64.2)**	**33(12.7)**	**17 (6.5)**	**260(100)**			
Medical Expenditure								
≤500	16(14.2)	71 (62.8)	17(15.0)	9(7.9)	113(100)	16.85	15	0.32
501-1000	12(17.1)	42 (60.0)	11(15.7)	5(7.1)	70 (100)			
1001-1500	7(28.0)	14 (56.0)	2(08.0)	2(8.0)	25 (100)			
1501-2000	1(05.9)	13 (76.5)	2(11.8)	1(5.9)	17 (100)			
2001-2500	4(36.4)	6 (54.6)	1(09.1)	0(0.0)	11 (100)			
Above 2501	3(12.5)	21 (87.5)	0(00.0)	0(0.0)	24 (100)			
Total	**43(16.5)**	**167(64.2)**	**33(12.7)**	**17(6.5)**	**260(100)**			

Among the women sought healthcare treatment in private health facility, the women with lesser number of children ever born were higher in proportion than women with higher number of ever born children. The percentage of women seeking healthcare treatment from private health facility is decreasing with the increase in the family size. Hence, an indirect association is being exists between the family size and the number of women sought healthcare treatment from private healthcare facility. The higher cost for medical treatment in private health facilities is the major reason for the decrease in the treatment seekers from the private health facilities. Hence, stringent efforts should be taken to streamline the fees collected by the private health facilities and reformative measures should also be accelerated to enrich the quality as well as quantity of the healthcare services rendered by the government health facilities. Surprisingly, higher percentage of women engaged in agricultural occupation and engaged as coolies/daily wagers sought private health facility than government health facilities for their reproductive health problems. Higher percentage of women from the families of higher income groups sought healthcare treatment from the private health facility than the women in the lower income group families. Similarly, the higher percentage of women in the families spending more money for their medical expenditure sought healthcare from private healthcare facilities. Higher the money spent on medical expenses higher the percentage of women sought medicalcare from private health facility.

5.4 Ante Natal Care and Background Characteristics

Antenatal care allows for the management of pregnancy, detection and treatment of complications, and promotion of good health. However, women rarely perceive child bearing as problematic and therefore do not seek healthcare. This affects the utilisations of maternal health services in regions of the country where poverty and illiteracy are widespread. But the possibility of complications occurring is there and routine checks are highly desirable. In this section the respondents were probed regarding to their number of antenatal care visits, confirmation of pregnancy test, services received by the respondents were cross-classified with the socio-economic and demographic characteristics of the respondents.

5.5 Number of Antenatal Care Visits

Through antenatal care visits, women benefits from various interventions, including counselling about healthy life styles, the provision of iron and folic acid supplements, and tetanus toxoid vaccinations reported to protect new-borns against neonatal deaths. The minimum standard services provided include the measurement of body weight, blood pressure, symphysis-fundus height, Tetanus Toxiod vaccination, and iron and folic acid supplements. In the following section the number of antenatal care visits made by the respondents was cross-classified with their socio-economic and demographic characteristics.

Table-5.8: Distribution of Respondents by Number of ANC Visits and their Background Characteristics

SED/Sub-variables	*< 3*	*4*	*5*	*6*	*7*	*8*	*9*	*10+*	*Total*	*Chi-Square*	*df*	*P-value*
Religion												
Hindu	25 (9.92)	25 (9.92)	67 (26.59)	23 (9.13)	53 (21.03)	14 (5.56)	34 (13.49)	11 (4.37)	252 (100)	11.79	8	0.16
Christian	3 (37.5)	0(0.00)	1 (12.50)	0 (0)	1 (12.5)	0(0.00)	3 (37.5)	0 (0.00)	8 (100)			
Total	**28 (10.77)**	**25(9.62)**	**68 (26.15)**	**23 (8.85)**	**54 (20.77)**	**14 (5.38)**	**37 (14.23)**	**11 (4.23)**	**260 (100)**			
Caste												
SC/ST	9 (16.98)	6 (11.32)	16 (30.19)	3 (5.66)	7 (13.21)	3 (5.66)	6 (11.32)	3 (5.66)	53 (100)	6.62	8	0.57
Others	19 (9.18)	19 (9.18)	52 (25.12)	20 (9.66)	47 (22.71)	11 (5.31)	31 (14.98)	8 (3.86)	207 (100)			
Total	**28 (10.77)**	**25 (9.62)**	**68 (26.15)**	**23 (8.85)**	**54 (20.77)**	**14 (5.38)**	**37 (14.23)**	**11 (4.23)**	**260 (100)**			
Family Type												
Nuclear family	12 (8.45)	11 (7.75)	44 (30.99)	11 (7.75)	29 (20.42)	6 (4.12)	20 (14.08)	9 (6.34)	142 (100)	11.42	8	0.17
Joint family	16 (13.26)	14 (11.86)	24 (20.34)	12 (10.67)	25 (21.17)	8 (6.78)	17 (14.41)	2 (1.69)	118 (100)			
Total	**28 (10.77)**	**25 (9.62)**	**68 (26.15)**	**23 (8.85)**	**54 (20.77)**	**14 (5.38)**	**37 (14.23)**	**11 (4.23)**	**260 (100)**			
Education												
Illiterate	3 (10.71)	4 (14.29)	9 (32.14)	1 (3.57)	7 (25.00)	1 (3.57)	3 (10.71)	0 (0.00)	28 (100)	51.36	48	0.34
Primary	5 (7.25)	11 (15.94)	19 (27.54)	5 (7.25)	13 (18.84)	5 (7.25)	7 (10.14)	4 (5.80)	69 (100)			
Middle	7 (13.46)	4 (7.69)	15 (28.85)	4 (7.69)	10 (19.23)	2 (3.84)	7 (13.46)	3 (5.77)	52 (100)			
High school	8 (13.11)	4 (56.00)	15 (24.60)	7 (11.46)	16 (26.23)	5 (8.20)	4 (6.56)	2 (3.28)	61 (100)			
Hr. Secondary	3 (16.67)	2 (11.11)	4 (22.22)	3 (16.67)	3 (16.67)	0 (0.00)	2 (11.11)	1 (5.56)	18 (100)			
Graduate	2 (6.67)	0(0.00)	5 (16.67)	3 (10.00)	5 (16.67)	1 (3.33)	13 (43.33)	1 (3.33)	30 (100)			

(Contd...)

Professional	0 (0.00)	0(0.00)	1 (50.00)	0 (0.00)	0 (0.00)	0 (0.00)	1 (50.00)	0 (0.00)	2 (100)			
Total	**28 (10.77)**	**25 (9.62)**	**68 (26.15)**	**23 (8.85)**	**54 (20.77)**	**14 (5.38)**	**37 (14.23)**	**11 (4.23)**	**260 (100)**			
Present Age												
≤19	2 (11.11)	3 (16.67)	4 (22.22)	3 (16.67)	2 (11.11)	2 (11.11)	1 (5.56)	1 (5.56)	18 (100)	33.81	32	0.38
20-24	12 (14.81)	10 (12.35)	19 (23.46)	8 (9.88)	17 (20.99)	6 (6.17)	5 (6.77)	4 (4.94)	81 (100)			
25-29	2 (3.08)	6 (9.23)	18 (27.69)	6 (9.23)	15 (23.08)	2 (3.08)	11 (16.92)	5 (7.69)	65 (100)			
30-34	4 (8.89)	3 (6.67)	12 (26.67)	3 (6.67)	10 (22.22)	4 (8.89)	8 (17.78)	1 (2.22)	45 (100)			
Above 35	8 (15.67)	3 (5.88)	15 (29.41)	3 (5.88)	10 (19.61)	0 (0.00)	12 (23.53)	0 (0.00)	51 (100)			
Total	**28 (10.77)**	**25 (9.62)**	**68 (26.15)**	**23 (8.85)**	**54 (20.77)**	**14 (5.38)**	**37 (14.23)**	**11 (4.23)**	**260 (100)**			
Age at Menarche												
<12	3 (21.43)	2 (14.29)	5 (35.71)	1 (7.14)	1 (7.14)	0 (0.00)	1 (7.14)	1 (7.14)	14 (100)	61.25	32	0.001 (S)
13	3 (13.04)	8 (34.78)	3 (13.04)	1 (4.35)	3 (13.04)	1 (4.35)	1 (4.35)	3 (13.04)	23 (100)			
14	2 (7.41)	0(0.00)	7 (25.93)	5 (18.52)	3 (11.11)	4 (14.81)	3 (11.11)	3 (11.11)	27 (100)			
15	10 (11.11)	9 (10.00)	21 (23.35)	6 (6.67)	28 (31.11)	3 (3.33)	10 (11.11)	3 (3.33)	90 (100)			
Above 16	10 (9.43)	6 (5.66)	32 (30.19)	10 (9.43)	19 (17.92)	6 (5.66)	22 (20.75)	1 (0.94)	106 (100)			
Total	**28 (10.77)**	**25 (9.62)**	**68 (26.15)**	**23 (8.85)**	**54 (20.77)**	**14 (5.38)**	**37 (14.23)**	**11 (4.23)**	**260 (100)**			
Age at Marriage												
Below 18	4 (10.26)	8 (20.51)	10 (25.64)	6 (15.38)	1 (2.56)	4 (10.26)	4 (10.26)	2 (5.13)	39 (100)	22.65	24	0.54
18-20	10 (9.09)	6 (5.45)	32 (20.09)	10 (9.09)	23 (20.91)	6 (5.46)	22 (20.00)	1 (0.91)	110 (100)			
21-23	11 (12.50)	6 (6.82)	22 (25.00)	6 (6.82)	25 (28.41)	3 (3.41)	10 (11.36)	5 (5.68)	88 (100)			
Above 24	3 (13.04)	5 (21.74)	4 (17.39)	1 (4.35)	5 (21.74)	1 (4.35)	1 (4.35)	3 (13.04)	23 (100)			
Total	**28 (10.77)**	**25 (9.62)**	**68 (26.15)**	**23 (8.85)**	**54 (20.77)**	**14 (5.38)**	**37 914.23)**	**11 (4.23)**	**260 (100)**			

(Contd...)

Age at First Birth												
≤20	5 (15.63)	5 (15.63)	8 (25.00)	3 (9.38)	4 (12.5)	3 (9.38)	0 (0.00)	4 (12.5)	32 (100)	48.92	32	0.02 (S)
21-22	3 (4.00)	4 (13.33)	7 (23.33)	3 (4.00)	2 (6.67)	2 (6.67)	5 (16.67)	4 (13.33)	30 (100)			
23-24	9 (10.00)	9 (10.00)	20 (22.22)	8 (8.89)	28 (31.11)	3 (3.33)	11 (12.22)	2 (2.22)	90 (100)			
25-26	7 (16.28)	3 (6.98)	15 (34.88)	3 (6.98)	5 (11.63)	2 (4.66)	7 (16.28)	1 (2.33)	43 (100)			
Above 27	4 (6.15)	4 (6.15)	18 (27.69)	6 (9.23)	15 (23.08)	4 (6.15)	14 (21.54)	0 (0.00)	65 (100)			
Total	**28 (10.77)**	**25 (9.62)**	**68 (26.15)**	**23 (8.85)**	**54 (20.77)**	**14 (5.38)**	**37 (14.23)**	**11 (4.23)**	**260 (100)**			
Children Ever Born (Total)												
1	8 (12.50)	12 (18.75)	17 (26.56)	6 (9.38)	6 (9.38)	3 (4.69)	2 (3.13)	10 (15.63)	64 (100)	71.12	32	0.001 (S)
2	7 (8.97)	4 (5.13)	16 (20.51)	9 (11.54)	20 (25.64)	6 (7.70)	16 (20.51)	0 (0.00)	78 (100)			
3	6 (8.96)	1 (1.49)	18 (26.87)	6 (8.96)	21 (31.34)	4 (5.97)	11 (16.42)	0 (0.00)	67 (100)			
4	5 (15.15)	4 (12.12)	10 (30.30)	1 (3.03)	6 (18.18)	1 (3.03)	5 (15.15)	1 (3.03)	33 (100)			
Above 5	2 (11.11)	4 (22.22)	7 (38.89)	1 (5.56)	1 (5.56)	0 (0.00)	3 (16.67)	0 (0.00)	18 (100)			
Total	**28 (10.77)**	**25 (9.62)**	**68 (26.15)**	**23 (8.85)**	**54 (20.77)**	**14 (5.38)**	**37 (14.23)**	**11 (4.23)**	**260 (100)**			
Family Size												
1	8 (7.55)	10 (9.43)	27 (25.47)	11 (10.38)	20 (18.87)	10 (9.43)	17 (16.04)	3 (2.83)	106 (100)	56.14	32	0.005 (S)
2	13 (12.26)	7 (6.60)	24 (22.64)	10 (9.43)	28 (26.42)	3 (2.81)	14 (13.21)	7 (6.60)	106 (100)			
Above 3	7 (14.58)	8 (16.67)	17 (35.42)	2 (24.17)	6 (12.50)	1 (2.08)	6 (12.50)	1 (2.08)	48 (100)			
Total	**28 (10.77)**	**25 (9.62)**	**68 (26.15)**	**23 (8.85)**	**54 (20.77)**	**14 (5.38)**	**37 (14.23)**	**11 (4.23)**	**260 (100)**			
Occupation												
Agriculture	10 (10.31)	8 (8.25)	26 (21.65)	5 (5.15)	24 (24.74)	9 (9.28)	9 (9.28)	6 (6.19)	97 (100)	36.93	24	0.04
Coolies/wages	12 (13.48)	14 (15.73)	21 (23.59)	11 (12.36)	14 (15.73)	5 (5.62)	9 (10.11)	3 (3.37)	89 (100)			
Business/Trade	0(0.00)	1 (3.70)	11 (40.74)	3 (11.11)	6 (12.50)	0 (0.00)	6 (22.22)	0 (0.00)	27 (100)			

(Contd...)

Employed	6 (12.77)	2 (4.26)	10 (21.28)	4 (8.51)	10 (21.28)	0 (0.00)	13 (27.66)	2 (4.262)	47 (100)			
Total	**28 (10.77)**	**25 (9.62)**	**68 (26.15)**	**23 (8.85)**	**54 (20.77)**	**14 (5.38)**	**37 (14.23)**	**11 (4.23)**	**260 (100)**			
Annual Household Income												
<10,000	9 (9.00)	8 (8.00)	30 (30.00)	10 (10.00)	19 (19.00)	9 (9.00)	9 (9.00)	6 (6.00)	100 (100)	39.51	48	0.80
10,001-20,000	12 (12.90)	11 (11.83)	24 (25.81)	8 (8.60)	21 (22.58)	4 (4.30)	10 (10.75)	3 (3.23)	93 (100)			
20,001-30,000	4 (19.05)	4 (19.05)	4 (19..05)	0 (0.00)	5 (23.81)	0 (0.00)	3 (14.29)	1 (4.76)	21 (100)			
30,001-40,000	1 (10.00)	1 (10.00)	2 (20.00)	1 (10.00)	2 (20.00)	1 (10.00)	2 (20.00)	0 (0.00)	10 (100)			
40,001-50,000	1 (12.50)	1 (12.5)	2 (25.00)	1 (12.5)	1 (12.5)	0 (0.00)	2 (25.00)	0 (0.00)	8 (100)			
50,001-60,000	0 (0.00)	0(0.00)	1 (12.50)	1 (12.5)	2 (25.00)	0 (0.00)	4 (50.00)	0 (0.00)	8 (100)			
Above 60,001	1(5.00)	0(0.00)	5 (25.00)	2 (10.00)	4 (20.00)	0 (0.00)	7 (35.00)	1 (5.00)	20 (100)			
Total	**28 (10.77)**	**25 (9.62)**	**68 (26.15)**	**23 (8.85))**	**54 (20.77)**	**14 (5.38)**	**37 (14.23)**	**11 (4.23)**	**260 (100)**			
Medical Expenditure												
≤500	10 (8.85)	10 (8.85)	34 (30.09)	12 (10.62)	21 (18.58)	8 (7.08)	12 (10.62)	6 (5.31)	113 (100)	46.54	40	0.22
501-1000	8 (11.43)	8 (11.43)	20 (28.57)	3 (4.29)	20 (28.57)	4 (5.72)	5 (7.14)_	2 (2.86)	70 (100)			
1001-1500	5 (20.00)	2 (8.00)	6 (24.00)	1 (4.00)	4 (16.00)	2 (8.00)	4 (16.00)	1 (4.00)	25 (100)			
1501-2000	1 (5.88)	1 (5.88)	2 (11.76)	3 (17.63)	4 (23.53)	0 (0.00)	5 (29.41)	1 (5.88)	17 (100)			
2001-2500	1 (9.09)	1 (9.09)	3 (27.27)	1 (9.09)	4 (36.36)	0 (0.00)	1 (9.09)	0 (0.00)	11 (100)			
Above 2501	3 (12.50)	3 (12.50)	3 (12.50)	3 (12.5)	1 (4.16)	0 (0.00)	10 (41.67)	1 (4.16)	24 (100)			
Total	**28 (10.77)**	**25 (9.62)**	**68 (26.15)**	**23 (8.85)**	**54 (20.77)**	**14 (5.38)**	**37 (14.23)**	**11 (4.23)**	**260 (100)**			

The table shows the percentage distribution of respondents by the number of antenatal care check up and their background characteristics. From the table it can be inferred that, the average number of antenatal check up made by the women in the study area was seven during their pregnancy. But the average number of antenatal check up was lower for the women belong to the category of SC/ST, Joint families, illiterate and lower educational status, with lower age groups and low age at menarche, women with low age at first birth, women with higher family size, and the families of low income groups than their counterparts.

5.6 TT Injection and IFA Supplements Received and Background Characteristics

Tetanus Toxoid (TT injection) injections are given during pregnancy for the prevention of tetanus among new born. Tetanus is a life-threatening bacterial disease that is caused by the toxin of a bacterium called *Clostridium tetani*. Tetanus bacteria enter the body through an open wound. It could well be a tiny prick or scratch on the skin, although Tetanus infection is more common when there is a deep puncture wound such as a bite, cut, burn or an ulcer. Tetanus affects a person's nervous system and can be fatal if left untreated. It is preventable through immunisation. The Tetanus Toxoid (TT) vaccine is given during pregnancy to prevent tetanus to you as well as your baby. Antibodies formed in women's body, after the vaccination, are passed on to the baby and protect her for a few months after birth. It also helps prevent premature delivery.

In the first pregnancy, doctor will recommend at least two doses of the TT vaccine. The first vaccination is given in the first trimester soon after the pregnancy tests are confirmed and after the first antenatal appointment. The second dose of the TT vaccine is given at least four to eight weeks after the first. Some experts recommend that the second dose of the vaccine should be given four weeks prior to the expected date of delivery. The WHO also recommends that a third vaccine be given six months after the second one to provide protection for at least five years. If this is the second pregnancy and it has been less than two years since the last pregnancy, when a woman had received both TT vaccines, then only a booster dose is recommended. In many countries such as the US, the TD or tetanus-diphtheria vaccine is recommended for pregnant women. This vaccine is now available in India also.

Prevalence of Aneamia in India is among the highest in the world. Anaemia is higher among pregnant women and preschool children. Even among higher income educated segments of population 50 per cent of children, adolescent girls and pregnant women are anaemic. Worried about the estimated high prevalence of anaemia in the country, five major surveys National Family Health Survey (NFHS), District Level Household Facility Survey (DLHS), Indian Council of Medical Research's (ICMR), Micronutrient survey, Micro nutrient survey conducted by National Nutrition Monitoring Bureau (NNMB), were undertaken to estimate the prevalence of anaemia in the country. The findings of all these surveys showed that over 70 per cent of preschool children were anaemic. NNMB, DLHS and ICMR surveys showed that over 70 per cent of pregnant women and adolescent girls in the country were anaemic. Studies carried out in India and elsewhere have shown that iron deficiency is the major cause of anaemia followed by folate deficiency. Data from NNMB surveys showed that iron and folic acid intake in the country in all the age groups was very low. In this study, the percentage of women received TT injection and IFA supplements were cross-classified with their socio-economic and demographic characteristics as poverty, ignorance, illiteracy and other variables are having close relationship with the level of utilisation of available health facilities. The following table analyses the women received TT injection and IFA supplements during their pregnancy with their socio-economic and demographic background. In the study area, more than 90 per cent of the women received TT injection and IFA supplements. More than 94 per cent of the women received TT injection irrespective of their caste category. While analysing percentage of women received TT injection and IFA supplementary with their family type, it can be found that there was no significant association between these two variables. Interestingly, even educational status of the women in the study area does not have any bearing on the number of women received TT injection and IFA tablets.

Table-5.9: Distribution of Respondents by TT Injection and IFA Supplement Received and their Background Characteristics

SED/Sub-variables	*TT*			*IFA*		
	No	*Yes*	*Total*	*No*	*Yes*	*Total*
Religion						
Hindu	14 (5.56)	238(94.44)	252 (100)	24(9.52)	228(90.8)	252 (100)
Christian	0 (0.0)	8 (100.0)	8 (100)	1 (12.5)	7 (87.5)	8 (100)
Total	**14(5.38)**	**246(94.62)**	**260 (100)**	**25 (9.62)**	**235(90.38)**	**260(100)**
Caste						
SC/ST	3 (5.66)	50 (94.34)	53 (100)	4(7.55)	49(92.45)	53 (100)
Others	11 (5.31)	196 (94.69)	207 (100)	21(10.14)	186(89.86)	207 (100)
Total	**14(5.38)**	**246(94.62)**	**260 (100)**	**25(9.62)**	**235(90.38)**	**260(100)**
Family Type						
Nuclear family	10 (7.04)	132 (92.96)	142 (100)	9(6.34)	133(93.66)	142 (100)
Joint family	4 (3.39)	114 (96.61)	118 (100)	16(13.56)	102(86.44)	118 (100)
Total	**14(5.38)**	**246(94.62)**	**260 (100)**	**25 (9.62)**	**235(90.38)**	**260(100)**
Education						
Illiterate	0 (0.00)	28 (100.00)	28 (100)	1 (3.57)	27(96.43)	28 (100)
Primary	3 (4.35)	66 (95.65)	69 (100)	5 (7.25)	64(92.75)	69 (100)
Middle	4 (7.69)	48 (92.31)	52 (100)	9(17.31)	43(82.69)	52 (100)
High school	3 (4.92)	58 (95.08)	61 (100)	7 (11.48)	54(88.52)	61 (100)
Hr. Secondary	2 (11.11)	16 (88.89)	18 (100)	2 (11.11)	16(88.89)	18 (100)
Graduate	2 (6.67)	28 (93.33)	30 (100)	1 (3.33)	29(96.67)	30 (100)
Professional	0(0.00)	2 (100.00)	2 (100)	0(100)	2(100.00)	2 (100)
Total	**14(5.38)**	**246(94.62)**	**260 (100)**	**25 (9.62)**	**235 (90.38)**	**260(100)**
Present Age						
≤19	2 (11.11)	16 (88.89)	18 (100)	4 (22.22)	14(77.78)	18 (100)
20-24	6 (7.41)	75 (92.59)	81 (100)	13(16.05)	68(83.95)	81 (100)
25-29	5 (7.69)	60 (92.31)	65 (100)	6 (9.23)	59(90.77)	65 (100)
30-34	1 (2.22)	44 (97.78)	45 (100)	0 (0.00)	45(100.00)	45 (100)
Above 35	0 (0.00)	51 (100.00)	51 (100)	2 (3.92)	49(96.08)	51 (100)
Total	**14(5.38)**	**246(94.62)**	**260 (100)**	**25 (9.62)**	**235(90.38)**	**260 (100)**
Age at Menarche						
≤12	2 (14.29)	12 (85.71)	14 (100)	2 (14.29)	12(85.71)	14 (100)
13	4 (17.39)	19 (82.01)	23 (100)	5 (21.74)	18(78.26)	23 (100)
14	3 (11.11)	24 (88.89)	27 (100)	3 (11.11)	24(88.89)	27 (100)
15	3 (3.33)	87 (96.67)	90 (100)	7(7.78)	83(92.22)	90 (100)
Above 16	3 (2.83)	103 (97.17)	106 (100)	8 (7.55)	98(92.45)	106 (100)
Total	**14(5.38)**	**246(94.62)**	**260 (100)**	**25(9.62)**	**235(90.38)**	**260(100)**

(Contd...)

Age at Marriage						
≤18	3 (7.69)	36 (92.31)	39 (100)	5 (12.82)	34(87.18)	39 (100)
18-20	4 (3.64)	106 (96.36)	110 (100)	12(10.91)	98(89.09)	110 (100)
21-23	5 (5.68)	83 (94.32)	88 (100)	7 (7.95)	81(92.05)	88 (100)
Above 24	2 (8.70)	21 (91.30)	23 (100)	1(4.35)	22(95.65)	23 (100)
Total	**14(5.38)**	**246(94.62)**	**260 (100)**	**25 (9.62)**	**235(90.38)**	**260(100)**
Age at First Birth						
≤20	4 (12.50)	28 (87.50)	32 (100)	6 (18.75)	26(81.25)	32 (100)
21-22	5 (16.67)	25 (83.33)	30 (100)	5(16.67)	25(83.33)	30 (100)
23-24	1 (1.11)	89 (98.89)	90 (100)	6 (6.67)	84(93.33)	90 (100)
25-26	3 (6.98)	40 (93.02)	43 (100)	7 (16.28)	36(83.72)	43 (100)
Above 27	1 (1.54)	64 (98.46)	65 (100)	1 (1.54)	64(98.46)	65 (100)
Total	**14(5.38)**	**246(94.62)**	**260 (100)**	**25(9.62)**	**235(90.38)**	**260(100)**
Children Ever Born						
1	14(21.87)	50 (78.13)	64 (100)	17(26.56)	47(73.44)	64 (100)
2	0 (0.00)	78 (100.00)	78 (100)	4(5.13)	74(94.87)	78 (100)
3	0 (0.00)	67 (100.00)	67 (100)	2 (2.99)	65(97.01)	67 (100)
4	0 (0.00)	33 (100.00)	33 (100)	2(6.06)	31(93.94)	33 (100)
Above 5	0 (0.00)	18 (100.00)	18 (100)	0 (0.00)	18(100.00)	18 (100)
Total	**14 (5.38)**	**246(94.62)**	**260 (100)**	**25(9.62)**	**235(90.38)**	**260(100)**
Family Size						
1	3 (2.83)	103 (97.17)	106 (100)	7 (6.60)	99(93.40)	106 (100)
2	11(10.38)	95 (89.62)	106 (100)	16(15.09)	90(89.25)	106 (100)
Above 3	0 (0.00)	48 (100.00)	48 (100)	2 (4.17)	46(100.00)	48 (100)
Total	**14 (5.38)**	**246(94.62)**	**260 (100)**	**25(9.62)**	**235(90.38)**	**260(100)**
Occupation						
Agriculture	8 (8.25)	89 (91.75)	97 (100)	15(15.46)	82(84.54)	97 (100)
Coolies/wages	4 (4.49)	85 (95.51)	89 (100)	7 (7.87)	82(92.13)	89 (100)
Business/Trade	0 (0.00)	27 (100.00)	27 (100)	0 (0.00)	27(100.00)	27 (100)
Employed	2 (4.26)	45 (95.74)	47 (100)	3 (6.38)	44(93.62)	47 (100)
Total	**14 (5.38)**	**246(94.62)**	**26 (100)**	**25(9.62)**	**235(90.38)**	**260(100)**
Annual Household Income						
≤10,000	6 (6.00)	94 (94.00)	100 (100)	10(10.00)	90(90.00)	100 (100)
10,001-20,000	5 (5.38)	88 (94.62)	93 (100)	10(10.75)	83(89.25)	93 (100)
20,001-30,000	1 (4.76)	20 (95.24)	21 (100)	0 (0.00)	21(100.00)	21 (100)
30,001-40,000	1 (10.00)	9 (90.00)	10 (100)	2 (20.00)	8 (80.00)	10 (100)
40,001-50,000	0 (0.00)	8 (100.00)	8 (100)	2 (25.00)	6 (75.00)	8 (100)
50,001-60,000	0 (0.00)	8 (100.00)	8 (100)	0 (0.00)	8(100.00)	8 (100)
Above 60,000	1 (5.00)	19 (95.00)	20 (100)	1 (5.00)	19(95.00)	20 (100)

(Contd...)

Total	**14 (5.38)**	**246(94.62)**	**260(100)**	**25(9.62)**	**235(90.38)**	**260(100)**
Medical Expenditure						
≤500	6 (5.31)	107 (94.59)	113 (100)	12(10.62)	101(89.38)	113 (100)
501-1000	3 (4.29)	67 (95.71)	70 (100)	5 (7.14)	65(92.86)	70 (100)
1001-1500	1 (4.00)	24 (96.00)	25 (100)	2 (8.00)	23(92.00)	25 (100)
1501-2000	1 (5.88)	16 (94.12)	17 (100)	2 (11.76)	15(88.24)	17 (100)
2001-2500	1 (9.09)	10 (90.91)	11 (100)	0 (0.00)	11(100.00)	11 (100)
Above 2500	2 (8.33)	22 (91.67)	24 (100)	4 (20.00)	20(80.00)	24 (100)
Total	**14(5.38)**	**246(94.62)**	**260 (100)**	**25(9.62)**	**235(90.38)**	**260(100)**

From the above analysis, it can be revealed that the percentage of illiterate women received TT injection and IFA Tablets was higher than the women with higher educational status. It can also be inferred that, the percentage of women received TT injection and IFA supplements is increases with the present age of the women in the study area. Hence, there is a direct association between the present age and the percentage of women received these vaccines and supplements. The same trend is prevailing while analysing the age at menarche of the women and the percentage of women received TT injections and IFA supplements. The analysis of women received TT injection and IFA supplements with their age at marriage shows that, the percentages of women with lower age at marriage (below 18 years) and higher age at marriage (24+years) received TT injection were lower than the women with age at marriage of 18-23 years. Whereas in receiving the IFA supplements, the percentage women increase with the increase in the age at marriage. The same trend can also be found that the percentage of women received TT injection and IFA supplements increase with their age at first birth. The family size of the respondents has an inverse relation with the percentage of women received IFA supplements. Lower the family size higher the percentage of women received IFA supplements. The percentage of women received TT injection and IFA supplements were lower among the women engaged in agricultural occupation and as daily wagers than the women engaged in other occupations. The percentages of women received TT injection and IFA supplementary were high among all the women in the study area irrespective of their annual household income and the amount spent for medical expenses. Though the overall percentage of women received TT injection and IFA supplementary were high, there were some special groups like higher educational status, lower age group women, women with lower age at menarche, women with lower and higher age at marriages, women with lower age at first birth and women with higher family size need to be taken special care in order to achieve an equity in receiving TT injection and IFA supplementary.

5.7 Health Advices Received During Antenatal Visits

Antenatal care is systematic medical supervision including examination and advice to a pregnant woman with the aim to ensure that every wanted pregnancy culminates in the delivery of a healthy baby without impairing the health of the mother. Ideally this care should begin soon after conception and continue throughout the pregnancy.

The District Level Household Survey (2007-08) was used to compute rich-poor ratios and concentration indices. Binary logistic regressions were used to investigate inequalities in advice provided by public health workers. The dependent variables comprised the advice provided on seven essential components of maternal and child healthcare. A significant proportion of pregnant women who attended at least four ANC sessions were not advised on these components during their antenatal sessions. Only 51 per cent-72 per cent of the pregnant women were advised on at least one of the components. Moreover, socioeconomic inequalities in providing advice were significant and the provision of advice concentrated disproportionately among the rich. Inequalities were highest in the case of advice on family planning methods. Advice on breastfeeding was least unequal. Public health workers working in lower level health facilities were significantly less likely than their counterparts in the higher level health facilities to provide specific advice. A significant proportion of women were not advised on recommended components of maternal and child health in rural India. Moreover, there were enormous socioeconomic inequalities. The findings of this study raise questions about the capacity of the public healthcare system in providing equitable services in India. The Government of India must focus on training and capacity building of the public health workers in communication skills so that they can deliver appropriate and recommended advice to all clients, irrespective of their socioeconomic status.

Table-5.10: Distribution of Respondents by Advices Received During their Ante Natal Visits and their Background Characteristics

SED/Sub-variables	*Advices Received*			*Special food items taken during pregnancy*		
	Nutrition	*Health Care Advice*	*Family Planning*	*Milk*	*Green Leafy Vegetables*	*Fruits*
Religion						
Hindu	198(78.57)	206(81.75)	174(69.05)	187(74.21)	211(83.73)	183(72.61)
Christian	5(62.50)	8(100.00)	7(87.50)	5(62.50)	5(62.50)	7(87.50)
Total	**203(78.08)**	**214(82.31)**	**181(69.62)**	**192(73.85)**	**219(84.23)**	**190(73.08)**
Caste						
SC/ST	35(66.04)	42(79.25)	37(69.81)	28(52.83)	47(88.68)	43(81.13)
Others	168(81.16)	172(83.09)	144(69.57)	164(79.22)	169(81.64)	147(71.01)
Total	**203(78.08)**	**214(82.31)**	**181(69.62)**	**192(73.85)**	**219(84.23)**	**190(73.08)**
Family Type						
Nuclear family	105(73.94)	112(78.87)	101(71.12)	98(69.01)	117(82.39)	106(74.65)
Joint family	98(83.05)	102(86.44)	80(67.80)	94(79.66)	99(83.90)	84(71.19)
Total	**203(78.08)**	**214(82.31)**	**181(69.62)**	**192(73.85)**	**219(84.23)**	**190(73.08)**
Education						
Illiterate	21(75.00)	23(82.14)	17(60.71)	21(75.00)	26(92.86)	21(75.00)
Primary	56(81.16)	55(79.71)	51(73.91)	46(66.67)	62(89.86)	49(71.01)
Middle	34(65.380	42(80.77)	39(82.69)	36(69.23)	41(78.85)	41(78.85)
High school	51(83.61)	52(85.25)	42(68.85)	49(80.33)	50(81.97)	45(73.77)
Hr. Secondary	14(77.78)	14(77.78)	14(77.78)	15(83.33)	15(83.33)	9(50.00)
Graduate	25(83.33)	26(86.67)	17(56.67)	24(80.00)	20(66.67)	23(76.67)
Professional	2(100.00)	2(100.00)	1(50.00)	1(50.00)	2(100.00)	2(100.00)
Total	**203(78.08)**	**214(82.31)**	**181(69.62)**	**192(73.85)**	**219(84.23)**	**190(73.08)**
Present Age						
≤19	16(88.89)	15(83.33)	14(77.78)	15(83.33)	18(100.0)	11(61.11)
20-24	70(86.42)	66(81.48)	58(71.60)	66(81.48)	65(80.25)	52(64.20)
25-29	48(73.85)	57(87.69)	48(73.85)	48(73.85)	53(81.54)	52(80.01)
30-34	34(75.56)	34(75.56)	31(68.89)	30(66.67)	38(84.44)	34(75.56)
Above 35	35(68.63)	42(82.35)	34(66.67)	33(64.71)	42(82.35)	41(66.67)
Total	**203(78.08)**	**214(82.31)**	**181(69.62)**	**192(73.85)**	**219(84.23)**	**190(73.08)**
Age at Menarche						
≤12	12(85.71)	12(85.71)	10(71.43)	7(50.00)	12(85.71)	12(85.71)
13	19(82.61)	19(82.61)	12(52.17)	18(78.26)	17(73.91)	15(65.22)
14	18(66.67)	21(77.78)	20(74.07)	21(77.78)	23(85.19)	18(66.67)
15	68(75.56)	71(78.89)	66(73.33)	63(70.00)	80(88.89)	64(71.11)

(Contd...)

Above 16	86(81.13)	91(85.85)	73(68.87)	83(78.30)	84(79.25)	81(76.42)
Total	**203(78.08)**	**214(82.31)**	**181(69.62)**	**192(73.85)**	**219(84.23)**	**190(73.08)**
Age at Marriage						
≤18	26(66.67)	31(79.49)	27(69.23)	26(66.67)	35(89.74)	27(69.23)
18-20	85(77.27)	91(82.73)	75(68.18)	80(72.73)	95(86.36)	79(71.82)
21-23	72(81.82)	71(80.68)	63(71.59)	69(78.41)	72(81.82)	64(72.73)
Above 24	20(86.96)	21(91.30)	16(69.57)	17(73.91)	14(60.87)	20(86.96)
Total	**203(78.08)**	**214(82.31)**	**181(69.62)**	**192(73.85)**	**219(84.23)**	**190(73.08)**
Age at First Birth						
≤20	26(81.25)	29(90.63)	19(59.38)	24(75.00)	26(81.25)	22(68.75)
21-22	20(66.67)	19(63.33)	24(80.00)	22(73.33)	23(76.67)	18(60.00)
23-24	70(77.78)	73(81.11)	66(73.33)	65(72.22)	80(88.89)	67(74.44)
25-26	34(79.07)	39(90.70)	27(62.79)	30(69.77)	35(81.40)	31(72.09)
Above 27	53(81.54)	54(83.08)	45(69.23)	51(78.46)	52(80.00)	52(80.00)
Total	**203(78.08)**	**214(82.31)**	**181(69.62)**	**192(73.85)**	**219(84.23)**	**190(73.08)**
Children Ever Born						
1	53(82.81)	52(81.25)	45(70.31)	52(81.25)	50(78.13)	51(79.69)
2	69(88.46)	66(84.62)	52(66.67)	70(89.74)	67(85.90)	70(89.74)
3	47(70.15)	56(83.58)	45(67.16)	45(67.16)	57(85.07)	44(65.67)
4	20(60.61)	27(81.82)	25(75.76)	17(51.52)	25(75.76)	17(51.52)
Above 5	14(77.78)	13(72.22)	14(77.78)	8(44.44)	16(88.89)	8(44.44)
Total	**203(78.08)**	**214(82.31)**	**181(69.62)**	**192(73.85)**	**219(84.23)**	**190(73.08)**
Family Size						
1	94(88.68)	90(84.91)	73(68.87)	94(88.68)	90(81.13)	92(86.79)
2	79(74.53)	87(82.08)	72(67.92)	75(70.75)	86(83.33)	75(70.75)
Above 3	30(65.50)	37(77.08)	36(75.00)	23(47.92)	40(86.60)	23(47.92)
Total	**203(78.08)**	**214(82.31)**	**181(69.62)**	**192(73.85)**	**219(84.23)**	**190(73.08)**
Occupation						
Agriculture	77(79.38)	76(78.35)	71(73.20)	81(83.51)	84(86.60)	63(64.95)
Coolies/wagers	64(71.91)	72(80.90)	62(69.66)	57(64.04)	80(89.89)	68(76.40)
Business/Trade	22(81.48)	24(88.89)	20(74.07)	19(70.37)	20(74.07)	21(77.78)
Employed	40(85.11)	42(89.36)	28(59.57)	35(74.47)	32(68.09)	38(80.85)
Total	**203(78.08)**	**214(82.31)**	**181(69.62)**	**192(73.85)**	**219(84.23)**	**190(73.08)**
Annual Household Income						
≤10,000	78(78.00)	83(83.00)	68(68.00)	73(73.00)	89(89.00)	69(69.00)
10,001-20,000	70(75.27)	73(78.49)	70(75.27)	69(74.19)	78(83.87)	68(73.12)
20,001-30,000	15(71.43)	17(80.95)	15(71.43)	17(80.95)	15(71.43)	17(80.95)
30,001-40,000	9(90.00)	9(90.00)	8(80.00)	6(60.00)	8(80.00)	6(60.00)
40,001-50,000	7(87.50)	6(75.00)	3(37.50)	7(87.50)	7(87.50)	5(62.50)
50,001-60,000	8(100.00)	8(100.00)	5(62.50)	7(87.50)	6(75.00)	7(87.50)

(Contd...)

Above 60,001	16(80.00)	18(90.00)	12(60.00)	13(65.00)	13(65.00)	18(90.00)
Total	**203(78.08)**	**214(82.31)**	**181(69.62)**	**192(73.85)**	**219(84.23)**	**190(73.08)**
Medical Expenditure						
≤500	88(77.88)	93(82.30)	83(73.45)	82(72.57)	97(85.84)	82(72.57)
501-1000	53(81.77)	52(80.23)	48(74.06)	52(80.23)	56(86.40)	52(80.23)
1001-1500	21(84.00)	24(96.00)	15(60.00)	19(76.00)	22(88.00)	19(76.00)
1501-2000	14(82.35)	12(70.59)	13(76.47)	14(82.35)	16(94.12)	12(70.59)
2001-2500	7(63.64)	10(90.91)	6(54.55)	9(81.82)	7(63.64)	9(81.82)
Above 2501	20(83.33)	23(95.83)	16(66.67)	16(66.67)	21(87.50)	15(62.50)
Total	**203(78.08)**	**214(82.31)**	**181(69.62)**	**192(73.85)**	**219(84.23)**	**190(73.08)**

Note: Percentage adds to more than 100 due to multiple responses.

In this study, information relating to the advices received by the women during their antenatal visits was obtained and tabulated in the following table. The analysis of the table shows that, information relating to nutrition, the healthcare measures to be taken during pregnancy and advices relating to Family Planning were the important advices given by the health personal in the health facilities. Women belong to SC/ST were less provided (66.04 per cent) about Nutrition advices than other category women (81.16 per cent). But the advices provided regarding family planning to SC/ST and other category women were equal. The percentage of women belong to joint families received advice regarding nutrition and healthcare measures to be taken during pregnancy was higher than the women belong to Nuclear families. In contrary, the family planning advice was provided to higher percentage of women belong to nuclear families than the joint families. The health personal in the health facilities have some fear over the elders in the joint families to provide family planning advices. While educational status of the respondents correlated with the health advices received, it can be inferred that, higher proportion of women with higher education received health advices than the women with less educated and illiterates. Similarly, the women with higher education were not provided advice regarding family planning by the health workers. This may be because of the fear over the educated women. Only 50-56 per cent of the educated women were provided advices relating to family planning. At the same time higher proportion of younger age women were provided advices regarding to Nutrition and Family Planning. Equal proportion of women in the study area received advice relating to healthcare to be taken during pregnancy irrespective of their age group. It can also be inferred that there was no significant relationship between the age at menarche of the women and the health advices received. The age at marriage of the respondents is an important variable to be correlated with the percentage of women received healthcare advices. In the study area, lesser proportion of women with low age at marriage received nutrition and family planning advices than the women with higher age at marriage. Higher the age at marriage higher the percentage of women received health advices during antenatal period. The proportion of women received healthcare advices decreases with the increase in the family size. At the same time, the proportion of women received family planning advice increases with the family size. Higher percentage of employed women and women engaged in business were received advices regarding nutrition and antenatal healthcare measures than the women occupied in agriculture and as daily wagers. At the same time, the family planning advice provided to lesser proportion of employed women (59.57 per cent) than the women engaged in agriculture and as daily wagers (73.20 per cent). Similarly, lesser proportion of women in the higher income group and the women belong to the families spent more on medical expenses were provided advices relating to family planning. Hence, the above discussion reveals that, a significant proportion of women were not advised on recommended components of maternal and child health in the study area. Moreover, there were enormous socioeconomic inequalities. The findings of this study raise questions about the capacity of the public healthcare system in providing equitable services. The government must focus on training and capacity building of the public health workers in communication skills so that they can deliver appropriate and recommended advice to all clients, irrespective of their socio-economic status.

5.8 Special Food Items Taken During Pregnancy

The respondents in the study area were probed regarding the special food items taken during pregnancy so as to assess the knowledge of consuming nutritional food during pregnancy. More than 85 per cent of the women in the study area responded that they have taken some special food items during pregnancy as they have to feed two persons. From the table, it is also inferred that milk, green leafy vegetables and fruits were the special foods taken by the mothers in the study area. Though 74 per cent of the respondents reported that they took milk as special food during pregnancy, only 52.8 per cent of the women belong to SC/ST reported that they have taken milk during pregnancy. Further, only a lesser proportion of women with low age at menarche (50.0 per cent), low age at marriage (66.7 per cent) were taken milk during pregnancy compared with the women belong to higher age at menarche and higher age at marriage. Only 64.04 per cent of the respondents engaged as coolies/wagers have taken milk during pregnancy. Green leafy vegetables were consumed by majority of the respondents irrespective of the socio-economic and demographic background as it was easily available at low cost in the study area. As far as the fruits are concerned, though, more than 73 per cent of the respondents in general took more fruits during pregnancy, the percentages of women took fruits belong to lower (<24 years) and higher age groups (35+ years), women with higher number of ever born children, women with higher family size and women belong to the occupation of agriculture were lesser compared with their counterparts. Hence, the above discussion shows that there was a significant association between the socio-economic and demographic background and the special food taken during pregnancy.

5.9 Problems at the Time of Delivery

The delivery of a baby, called the second stage of labour, begins as soon as the mother's cervix has fully dilated to 10 cm (4 inch) and ends when the baby is born. About 4 in 10 mothers experience problems during delivery, and the risk is higher for a first pregnancy. With careful management, it may be possible to carry out a normal vaginal delivery, but if the second stage of labour is long, and the fetus's oxygen supply becomes insufficient, there is an increased risk of fetal distress. The doctor may then carry out an assisted delivery, using vacuum suction or forceps, or a caesarean section.

5.9.1 Prevalence of Reproductive Health Problems During Delivery

In the study area, the respondents were probed about the problems faced by them during their pregnancy. More than 51 per cent of the women assessed, reported health problems during their delivery. While the caste is correlated with the prevalence of reproductive health problems, interestingly lower proportion of women reported reproductive health problems than the women belong to other category. Similarly, higher percentage of women reported reproductive health problems were belong to nuclear families, higher educated women, women of higher age groups, women with higher age at menarche, women with higher number of children ever born, women with higher family size, women engaged in agricultural occupation and as coolies/ daily wages, women with lower household income, and the women belong to the families spent lesser amount for their medical expenses. A lower proportion of women among illiterates reported reproductive health problems than other higher educated women. The overall discussion of the above table shows that there were some socio-economic inequalities exist in the prevalence of reproductive health problems among the women in the study area.

Table-5.11: Distribution of Respondents Experienced Problems of Women During Delivery and their Background Characteristics

SED/sub-variables	*No*	*Yes*	*Total*	*Chi-Square*	*df*	*P value*
Religion						
Hindu	123(48.80)	129(51.19)	252 (100)	0.004	1	0.94
Christian	4(50.00)	4 (50.00)	8 (100)			
Total	**127(48.84)**	**133(51.15)**	**260(100)**			
Caste						
SC/ST	27 (50.94)	26(49.06)	53 (100)	0.11	1	0.73
Others	100 (48.31)	107(51.69)	207(100)			
Total	**127(48.84)**	**133(51.15)**	**260(100)**			
Family Type						
Nuclear family	65 (45.77)	77 (54.23)	142 (100)	1.18	1	0.27
Joint family	62 (52.54)	56 (47.46)	118 (100)			
Total	**127(48.84)**	**133(51.15)**	**260(100)**			
Education						
Illiterate	18 (64.29)	10 (35.71)	28 (100)	9.51	6	0.14
Primary	28 (40.58)	41 (59.42)	69 (100)			

(Contd...)

Middle	23 (44.23)	29 (55.77)	52 (100)			
High school	34 (55.74)	27 (47.40)	61 (100)			
Hr. Secondary	11 (61.11)	7 (38.89)	18 (100)			
Graduate	13 (43.33)	17 (56.67)	30 (100)			
Professional	0 (0.00)	2 (100.00)	2 (100)			
Total	**127(48.84)**	**133(51.15)**	**260(100)**			
Present Age						
≤19	13 (72.22)	5 (27.78)	18 (100)	7.50	4	0.11
20-24	40 (49.38)	41 (50.62)	81 (100)			
25-29	34 (52.31)	31 (47.69)	65 (100)			
30-34	16 (35.56)	29 (64.44)	45 (100)			
Above 35	24 (47.06)	27 (56.87)	51 (100)			
Total	**127(48.84)**	**133(51.15)**	**260(100)**			
Age at Menarche						
≤12	10 (71.43)	4 (28.57)	14 (100)	5.80	4	0.21
13	13 (56.62)	10 (43.48)	23 (100)			
14	16 (59.26)	11 (40.74)	27 (100)			
15	40 (44.44)	50 (55.56)	90 (100)			
Above 16	48 (45.28)	58 (54.72)	106 (100)			
Total	**127(48.84)**	**133(51.15)**	**260(100)**			
Age at Marriage						
<18	22 (56.41)	17 (43.59)	39 (100)	1.47	3	0.68
18-20	51 (46.36)	59 (53.63)	110 (100)			
21-23	44 (50.00)	44 (50.00)	88 (100)			
Above 24	10 (43.48)	13 (56.62)	23 (100)			
Total	**127(48.84)**	**133(51.15)**	**260(100)**			
Age at First Birth						
≤20	22 (68.75)	10 (31.25)	32 (100)	17.33	5	0.004
21-22	16 (53.33)	14 (46.67)	30 (100)			
23-24	42 (46.67)	48 (53.33)	90 (100)			
25-26	27 (62.79)	16 (37.21)	43 (100)			
Above 27	20 (30.77)	45 (69.23)	65 (100)			
Total	**127(48.84)**	**133(51.15)**	**260(100)**			
Children Ever Born						
1	43 (68.25)	20 (31.75)	63 (100)	21.22	5	0.001
2	21 (61.76)	13 (38.24)	34 (100)			
3	30 (34.89)	56 (65.17)	86 (100)			

(Contd...)

Above 4	33 (42.86)	44 (57.14)	77 (100)			
Total	**127(48.84)**	**133(51.15)**	**260(100)**			
Family Size						
1	51 (48.11)	55 (51.89)	106 (100)			
2	58 (54.72)	48 (45.28)	106 (100)			
Above 3	18 (37.50)	30 (62.50)	48 (100)			
Total	**127(48.84)**	**133(51.15)**	**260(100)**			
Occupation						
Agriculture	54 (55.67)	43 (44.33)	97 (100)	3.86	3	0.27
Coolies/wages	43 (48.31)	46 (51.69)	89 (100)			
Business/Trade	11 (40.74)	16 (59.26)	27 (100)			
Employed	19 (40.43)	28 (59.57)	47 (100)			
Total	**127(48.84)**	**133(51.15)**	**260(100)**			
Annual Household Income						
≤10,000	51 (51.00)	49 (49.00)	100 (100)	3.42	6	7.55
10,001-20,000	49 (52.69)	44 (47.31)	93 (100)			
20,001-30,000	10 (47.62)	11 (52.38)	21 (100)			
30,001-40,000	4 (40.00)	6 (60.00)	10 (100)			
40,001-50,000	3 (37.50)	5 (62.50)	8 (100)			
50,001-60,000	3 (37.50)	5 (62.50)	8 (100)			
Above 60,000	7 (35.00)	13 (65.00)	20 (100)			
Total	**127(48.84)**	**133(51.15)**	**260(100)**			
Medical Expenditure						
<=500	56 (49.56)	57 (50.44)	113 (100)			
501-1000	35 (50.00)	35 (50.00)	70 (100)			
1001-1500	12 (48.00)	13 (52.00)	25 (100)			
1501-2000	8 (47.06)	9 (52.94)	17 (100)			
2001-2500	5 (45.45)	6 (54.55)	11 (100)			
Above 2501	11 (45.83)	13 (54.17)	24 (100)			
Total	**127(48.84)**	**133(51.15)**	**260(100)**			

5.9.2 Reproductive Health Problems Experienced by Women During Delivery

Delivery occurs normally after nine months of pregnancy. If delivery is before time special care for baby may be needed. As far as possible a pregnant women should have delivery in a health centre or a hospital even if pregnancy is normal. This is mainly because during delivery, labour complications may suddenly occur which can threaten the life of the mother, baby or both. During delivery the time between starting of a problem to death of mother, baby or both is so short that it may not be possible to save the life of mother or baby, if pregnant mother is not already in a well-equipped health centre or hospital.

The respondents in the study area were quizzed about their reproductive health problems during delivery and the data obtained from them were cross-classified with their socio-economic and demographic background. The analysis from the cross-classification shows that prolonged labour, Excessive bleeding, Malpresentation, Episiotomy/Perineal tears and retained placenta was the problems reported by the women in the study area.

Foetal malpresentation refers to foetal presenting part other than vertex, and includes breech, transverse, face, brow and sinciput. It may be identified late in pregnancy, or may not be discovered until the initial assessment during labour. Presentation of a part of a foetus other than the back of the head during parturition is mal-presentation.

An **episiotomy** is a cut the doctor or midwife makes in the perineum, which is the area between the vagina and anus. It is done to help deliver the baby or to help prevent the muscles and skin from tearing. The cut is made just before the baby's head comes out of the birth canal. It is stitched up after the birth. An episiotomy also known as perineotomy, is a surgically planned incision on the perineum and the posterior vaginal wall during second stage of labour. The incision, which can be midline or at an angle from the posterior end of the vulva, is performed under local anesthetic (pudendal anesthesia), and is sutured closed after delivery. It is one of the most common medical procedures performed on women, and although its routine use in childbirth has steadily declined in recent decades, it is still widely practiced in many parts of the world including India. There are times when an episiotomy is needed-for example, if the baby's heart rate drops too much during pushing or if the baby's position is causing problems. The decision cannot be made until delivery. Episiotomies are more common with first-time deliveries.

The **retained placenta** is a significant cause of maternal mortality and morbidity throughout the developing world. It complicates two per cent of all deliveries and has a case mortality rate of nearly ten per cent in rural areas. Retained placenta means that all or part of the placenta or membranes is left behind in your uterus (womb) during the third stage of labour. The third stage is when you deliver the placenta and membranes. You'll be treated for retained placenta if the third stage takes longer than usual, or if there are signs that any of the placenta or membrane is still attached to your uterus. The third stage takes about five to ten minutes. Just as your baby is being born, you'll be given an injection in your thigh. This injection causes your uterus to contract and your placenta to come away. Your doctor will gently pull on your umbilical cord to deliver your placenta. Managing the third stage reduces the risk of your experiencing heavy bleeding. A 'natural' third stage takes longer and can mean that you bleed more. You'll be treated for retained placenta if you have not completely delivered the placenta within 30 minutes of your baby's birth.

Labour is said to be prolonged when the combined duration of both the first stage and second stages of labour is more than 18 hours. It is more common in a first pregnancy and in women over the age of 35 years. Sometimes, labour stalls or occurs much too slowly. Prolonged labour may also be referred to as "failure to progress." Prolonged labour can be determined by labour stage and whether the cervix has thinned and opened appropriately during labour. If your baby is not born after approximately 20 hours of regular contractions, you are likely to be in prolonged labour. Some health experts may say it occurs after 18 to 24 hours.

After the baby is delivered, **excessive bleeding** from the uterus is a major concern. Ordinarily, the woman loses about one pint of blood after delivery. Blood is lost because some blood vessels are opened when the placenta detaches from the uterus. The contractions of the uterus help close these vessels until the vessels can heal. Loss of more than about one pint of blood during or after the third stage of labour (when the placenta is delivered) is considered excessive. Severe blood loss usually occurs soon after delivery but may occur as late as one month afterward. Excessive bleeding may result when the contractions of the uterus after delivery are impaired. Then, the blood vessels that were opened when the placenta detached continue to bleed.

Excessive bleeding after one delivery may increase the risk of excessive bleeding after subsequent deliveries. Fibroids in the uterus may also increase the risk.

Despite these complications, some other complications of pregnancy also cause problems during labour or delivery. For example, Preeclampsia, which involves high blood pressure accompanied by protein in the urine, can develop at any time from the twentieth week of pregnancy through the six weeks after delivery. Preeclampsia may lead to premature detachment of the placenta from the uterus (placental abruption) and problems in the newborn. Other complications develop only after labour and delivery occur.

Amniotic Fluid Embolis very rarely, a volume of amniotic fluid—the fluid that surrounds the foetus in the uterus—enters the woman's bloodstream, usually during a particularly difficult labour. The fluid can cause a serious reaction that involves a rapid heart rate, irregular heart rhythm, collapse, shock, or even cardiac arrest and death (in about one-fifth of women). Widespread blood clotting (disseminated intravascular coagulation), sometimes also with bleeding, is a common complication, requiring emergency care.

The following table shows the distribution of respondents by their reproductive health problems during their delivery with their socio-economic and demographic characteristics. This analysis shows that majority of the respondents (53.4 per cent) respondents reported that they have experienced the complication of malpresentation during delivery. Forty-six per cent of the respondents reported that they have experienced the complication of excessive bleeding during their delivery. The third most problem reported by the respondents in the study area was the prolonged labour. Episiotomy/Perineal tears and retained placenta were also the problems reported by a considerable proportion of the women in the study area. Further, the analysis examined the relationship of the socio-economic and demographic variables with the prevalence of the problems. It shows that, higher percentage of women belong to joint family, higher age group women, women with higher age at menarche, women with higher age at first birth, higher number of children ever born, and higher family size, were reported the problem of foetal malpresentation. The analysis also shows that there was no significant association between the variables such as caste, educational status, age at marriage, occupation, household income and money spent for medical expenses. While analysing the prevalence of the problem of excessive bleeding during delivery with the socio-economic and demographic characteristics

Table-5.12: Distribution of Respondents by Problems of Women Experienced During Delivery and their Background Characteristics

SED/Sub-variables	*Prolonged Labour*	*Excessive Bleeding*	*Malpres-entation*	*Episiotomy/ Perineal Tears*	*Retained Placenta*	*Total*	*df*	*P Value*
Religion								
Hindu	38(29.5)	60(46.5)	67(51.9)	18(13.9)	7(5.4)	2.82	4	0.58
Christian	1(25.0)	1(25.0)	4(100.0)	0 (0.0)	0 (0.0)			
Total	**39(29.3)**	**61(45.9)**	**71(53.4)**	**18(13.5)**	**7 (5.3)**			
Caste								
SC/ST	8 (30.8)	10(38.5)	14(53.9)	1 (3.3)	0 (0.0)	3.85	4	0.42
Others	31 (8.9)	51(47.7)	57(53.3)	17(15.9)	7 (6.5)			
Total	**39(29.3)**	**61(45.9)**	**71(53.4)**	**18(13.5)**	**7 (5.3)**			
Family Type								
Nuclear family	19(24.7)	40(51.9)	39(50.7)	8 (10.4)	5(6.5)	4.77	4	0.311
Joint family	20(35.7)	21(37.5)	32(57.1)	10(17.9)	2 (3.6)			
Total	**39(29.3)**	**61(45.9)**	**71(53.4)**	**18(13.5)**	**7 (5.3)**			
Education								
Illiterate	1(10.00)	3(30.00)	4(40.00)	1(10.00)	0(0.00)	8.55	24	0.99
Primary	13(31.7)	20(48.8)	22(53.7)	5 (12.2)	2 (4.9)			
Middle	8 (27.6)	16(55.2)	15(51.7)	4 (13.8)	1 (3.5)			
High school	9 (33.3)	9 (33.3)	16(59.3)	3 (11.1)	3(11.1)			
Hr. Secondary	2 (28.6)	3 (42.9)	3 (42.9)	1 (14.3)	0 (0.0)			
Graduate	6 (35.3)	6 (35.3)	10(58.8)	4 (23.5)	1 (5.9)			
Professional	0 (0.0)	0 (0.0)	1 (50.0)	0 (0.0)	0 (0.0)			
Total	**39(29.3)**	**61(45.9)**	**71(53.4)**	**18(13.5)**	**7 (5.3)**			
Present Age								
≤19	1(20.0)	3 (60.0)	2 (40.0)	1 (20.0)	1(20.0)	15.16	16	0.51
20-24	14(34.2)	18(43.9)	20(48.8)	7 (17.1)	2 (4.9)			
25-29	9 (29.0)	14(45.2)	19(61.3)	2 (6.5)	1 (3.2)			
30-34	6 (20.7)	20(68.9)	12(41.4)	5 (17.2)	1 (3.4)			
Above 35	9 (33.3)	6 (22.2)	18(66.7)	3 (11.1)	2 (7.4)			
Total	**39(29.3)**	**61(45.9)**	**71(53.4)**	**18(13.5)**	**7 (5.3)**			

(Contd...)

Age at Menarche								
≤12	0 (0.0)	4(100.0)	0 (0.0)	0 (0.0)	0 (0.0)	13.91	16	0.60
13	2 (20.0)	4 (40.0)	4 (40.0)	1 (10.0)	0 (0.0)			
14	2 (18.2)	7 (63.6)	5 (45.5)	1 (9.1)	1 (9.1)			
15	17(34.0)	18(36.0)	31(62.0)	9 (18.0)	3 (6.0)			
Above 16	18(31.0)	28(48.3)	31(53.5)	7 (12.1)	3 (5.2)			
Total	**39(29.3)**	**61(45.9)**	**71(53.4)**	**18(13.5)**	**7 (5.3)**			
Age at Marriage								
≤18	4 (23.5)	10(58.8)	6 (35.3)	2 (11.8)	0 (0.0)	7.29	12	0.83
18-20	20(33.9)	23(38.9)	33(55.9)	10(16.9)	4 (6.8)			
21-23	11(25.0)	22(50.0)	25(56.8)	3 (6.8)	2 (4.6)			
24+	4 (30.8)	6 (46.2)	7 (53.9)	3 (23.1)	1 (7.7)			
Total	**39(29.3)**	**61(45.9)**	**71(53.4)**	**18(13.5)**	**7(5.3)**			
Age at First Birth								
≤20	1 (10.0)	6 (60.0)	3 (30.0)	1 (10.0)	1(10.0)	19.73	16	0.23
21-22	5 (35.7)	7 (50.0)	6 (42.9)	1 (7.1)	0 (0.0)			
23-24	15(31.3)	18(37.5)	31(64.6)	9 (18.8)	3 (6.3)			
25-26	3 (18.8)	7 (43.8)	8 (50.0)	0 (0.0)	0 (0.0)			
Above 27	15(33.3)	23(51.1)	23(80.0)	7 (15.6)	3 (6.7)			
Total	**39(29.3)**	**61(45.9)**	**71(53.4)**	**18(13.5)**	**7 (5.3)**			
Child Ever Born								
1	3 (14.3)	7 (33.3)	8 (38.1)	3 (14.3)	0(0.0)	45.01	16	0.001 (S)
2	14(36.8)	13(34.2)	18(47.4)	6(15.8)	4(10.5)			
3	13(28.3)	22(47.8)	23(50.0)	5 (10.9)	3(6.5)			
4	5 (25.0)	13(65.0)	16(80.0)	2 (10.0)	0 (0.0)			
5+	4 (50.0)	6 (75.0)	6 (66.7)	2 (25.0)	0 (0.0)			
Total	**39(29.3)**	**61(45.9)**	**71(53.4)**	**18(13.5)**	**7 (5.3)**			
Family Size								
1	16(29.1)	28(50.9)	26(47.3)	9 (16.4)	4(7.3)	13.61	8	0.09
2	14(29.2)	22(45.8)	25(52.1)	5 (10.4)	2 (4.2)			
3+	9 (30.0)	11(36.7)	20(66.7)	4 (13.3)	1 (3.3)			
Total	**39(29.3)**	**61(45.9)**	**71(53.4)**	**18(13.5)**	**7 (5.3)**			
Occupation								
Agriculture	10(23.3)	24(24.7)	24(55.8)	8 (18.6)	2 (4.7)	17.78	12	0.12
Coolies/wages	14(30.4)	20(22.5)	25(54.4)	3 (6.5)	3(6.5)			
Business/Trade	4 (25.0)	8 (29.6)	7 (43.8)	3 (18.8)	0(0.0)			
Employed	11(39.2)	9 (19.2)	15(53.6)	4 (14.3)	2(7.1)			
Total	**39(29.3)**	**61(45.9)**	**71(53.4)**	**18(13.6)**	**7 (5.3)**			
Household Income								
≤10000	16(32.7)	25(51.0)	26(58.1)	4 (8.2)	3 (6.1)	50.52	24	0.001 (S)
10,001-20,000	11(25.0)	21(47.7)	25(56.8)	9 (20.5)	2 (4.6)			

(Contd...)

20,001-30,000	3(27.3)	4 (36.4)	6 (54.6)	0 (0.0)	0(0.0)			
30,001-40,000	3 (50.0)	3 (50.0)	0 (0.0)	1 (16.7)	1(16.7)			
40,001-50,000	1 (20.0)	3 (60.0)	0 (0.0)	2 (40.0)	0 (0.0)			
50,001-60,000	1 (20.0)	3 (60.0)	4 (80.0)	1 (20.0)	0 (7.7)			
Above 60,001	4 (30.8)	2 (10.0)	10(76.9)	2 (15.4)	1(7.7)			
Total	**39(29.3)**	**61(45.9)**	**71(53.4)**	**18(13.5)**	**7 (5.3)**			
Medical Expenditure								
≤500	16(28.1)	23(40.4)	33(57.9)	6(10.5)	2 (5.5)	29.85	20	0.07
501-1000	9 (25.7)	18(51.4)	17(48.6)	4 (11.4)	2 (5.7)			
1001-1500	5 (38.5)	5 (38.5)	8 (61.5)	3 (23.1)	1(7.7)			
1501-2000	3 (33.3)	5 (55.6)	4 (44.4)	2 (22.2)	1(7.7)			
2001-2500	2 (33.3)	3 (50.0)	3 (50.0)	1 (16.7)	0(0.0)			
Above 2501	4 (30.8)	7 (53.9)	6 (46.2)	1 (7.7)	1 (7.7)			
Total	**39(29.3)**	**61(45.9)**	**71(53.4)**	**18(13.5)**	**7 (5.3)**			

Note: Percentage adds to More Than 100 due to Multiple Responses.

of the women in the study area, higher proportion of women belong to other than SC/ST, nuclear family, married below the age of 18 years, women with higher number of children ever born, and higher family size reported the problem of excessive bleeding during delivery. The analysis also shows that there was no significant association between the variables such as, educational status, age at menarche, age at first birth, occupation, household income and money spent for medical expenses. As far as the other diseases such as prolonged labour, Episiotomy/Perineal tears and retained placenta were concerned the same trend has been witnessed.

5.9.3 Place of Delivery and Socio-economic and Demographic Background

Appropriate delivery care is crucial for both maternal and perinatal health and increasing skilled attendance at birth is a central goal of the safe motherhood and child survival movements. Skilled attendance at delivery is an important indicator in monitoring progress towards Millennium Development Goal 5 to reduce the maternal mortality ratio by three quarters between 1990 and 2015. In addition to professional attention, it is important that mothers deliver their babies in an appropriate setting, where life saving equipment and hygienic conditions can also help reduce the risk of complications that may cause death or illness to mother and child. Over the past decade interest has grown in examining influences on care-seeking behaviour. As cited in the "three delays" model, three main inhibitors to healthcare service utilisation exist: the delay in deciding to seek care, the delay in reaching an adequate healthcare facility and the delay in receiving adequate care at that facility. The first delay may be due to a lack of understanding of danger signs, the absence of the decision-maker from the household, the low status of the woman, cost, previous unsatisfactory experience with the healthcare system and perceived low quality of care. Phase 2, delays may be due to distance from facility, lack of transportation, difficult terrain and the high cost of travel.

Research consistently shows that high cost is an important constraint to service utilisation particularly for the poor. In India, studies show a very high out of pocket expenditure on delivery care, and, although the private sector is more expensive, the cost of public sector inpatient care services has increased since the 1990s. Hence, income is a major determinant of care seeking. Recent analysis of the third National Family Health Survey (2005/6) shows 13 per cent of women in the lowest wealth quintile accessing institutional delivery care compared with 84 per cent in the highest. In this study, to assess the percentage of women accessing institutional delivery, respondents were quizzed to obtain information relating to the place of delivery. Irrespective of the socio-economic and demographic background of the mothers in the study area, nearly 5.4 per cent of the respondents delivered their babies in their home itself. More than 54 per cent of

Table-5.13: Distribution of Respondents by Place of Delivery and their Background Characteristics

SED/Sub-variables	*Govt. Hospital*	*Private Hospital*	*Maternity Home*	*Home*	*Total*	*Chi-Square*	*df*	*P value*
Religion								
Hindu	101(40.1)	135(53.6)	2(0.8)	14(5.6)	252(100)	1.61	3	0.657
Christian	2(25.0)	6(75.0)	0 (0.0)	0 (0.0)	8(100)			
Total	**103(39.6)**	**141(54.2)**	**2(0.8)**	**14(5.4)**	**260(100)**			
Caste								
SC/ST	34 (64.2)	15 (28.3)	0 (0.0)	4 (7.6)	53(100)	19.459	3	0.001(S)

(Contd...)

Others	69 (33.3)	126(60.9)	2 (0.9)	10(4.8)	207(100)			
Total	**103(39.6)**	**141(54.2)**	**2(0.8)**	**14(5.4)**	**260(100)**			
Family Type								
Nuclear family	61 (42.9)	70 (49.3)	0 (0.0)	11(7.8)	142(100)	7.936	3	.047(S)
Joint family	42 (35.6)	71 (60.2)	2 (1.7)	3(2.5)	118(100)			
Total	**103(39.6)**	**141(54.2)**	**2(0.8)**	**14(5.4)**	**260(100)**			
Education								
Illiterate	12(42.9)	13(46.4)	0(0.0)	3(10.7)	28(100)	16.910	18	.529
Primary	34(49.3)	32(46.4)	0 (0.0)	3(4.4)	69(100)			
Middle	19 (34.4)	30 (49.2)	0 (0.0)	3 (4.9)	52 (100)			
High school	21 (34.4)	37 (60.7)	2 (3.3)	1 (1.6)	61(100)			
Hr. Secondary	8 (44.4)	9 (50.0)	0 (0.0)	1 (5.6)	18(100)			
Graduate	8 (26.7)	19 (63.3)	0 (0.0)	3(10.0)	30(100)			
Professional	1(50.0)	1(50.0)	0(0.0)	0(0.0)	2(100)			
Total	**103(39.6)**	**141(54.2)**	**2(0.8)**	**14(5.4)**	**260(100)**			
Present Age								
≤19	7(38.9)	11(61.1)	0(0.0)	0(0.0)	18(100)	18.19	12	0.11
20-24	29(35.8)	51(62.9)	1(1.2)	0(0.0)	81(100)			
25-29	25(38.5)	35(53.9)	1(1.5)	4(6.2)	65 (100)			
30-34	18 (40.0)	24 (53.3)	0(0.0)	3 (6.7)	45 (100)			
Above 35	24(47.1)	20(39.2)	0(0.0)	7(13.7)	51(100)			
Total	**103(39.6)**	**141(54.2)**	**2(0.8)**	**14(5.4)**	**260(100)**			
Age at Menarche								
≤12	10 (71.4)	4 (28.6)	0 (0.0)	0 (0.0)	14(100)	14.057	12	.297
13	11 (47.8)	12 (52.2)	0 (0.0)	0 (0.0)	23(100)			
14	8 (29.6)	16 (59.3)	1 (3.7)	2 (7.4)	27(100)			
15	34 (37.8)	49 (54.4)	0 (0.0)	7 (7.8)	90(100)			
Above 16	40 (37.7)	60 (56.6)	1 (0.9)	5 (4.7)	106(100)			
Total	**103(39.6)**	**141(54.2)**	**2(0.8)**	**14(5.4)**	**260(100)**			
Age at Marriage								
≤18	18 (46.2)	19 (48.7)	0 (0.0)	2 (5.1)	39(100)	18.19	12	0.11
18-20	41 (37.3)	62 (56.4)	1 (0.9)	6 (5.5)	110(100)			
21-23	37 (42.1)	46 (52.3)	1 (1.1)	4 (4.6)	88(100)			
Above 24	7 (30.4)	14 (60.9)	0 (0.0)	2 (8.7)	23(100)			
Total	**103(39.6)**	**141(54.2)**	**2(0.8)**	**14(5.4)**	**260(100)**			
Age at First Birth								
≤ 20	15 (46.9)	17 (53.1)	0 (0.0)	0 (0.0)	32 (100)	9.34	12	0.67
21-22	11 (36.7)	16 (53.3)	1 (3.3)	2 (6.7)	30 (100)			
23-24	36 (40.0)	47 (52.2)	0 (0.0)	7 (7.8)	90 (100)			
25-26	18 (41.9)	22 (51.2)	0 (0.0)	3 (6.9)	43 (100)			
Above 27	23 (35.4)	39 (60.0)	1 (1.5)	2 (3.1)	65 (100)			
Total	**103(39.6)**	**141(54.2)**	**2(0.8)**	**14(5.4)**	**260(100)**			

(Contd...)

Child Ever Born								
1	34 (53.1)	30 (46.9)	0 (0.0)	0 (0.0)	64 (100)	36.90	12	0.01(S)
2	15 (19.2)	60 (76.9)	2 (2.6)	1 (1.3)	78 (100)			
3	30 (44.8)	32 (47.8)	0 (0.0)	5 (7.5)	67 (100)			
4	18 (54.6)	12 (36.4)	0 (0.0)	3 (9.1)	33 (100)			
Above 5	6 (33.3)	7 (38.9)	0 (0.0)	5(27.8)	18 (100)			
Total	**103(39.6)**	**141(54.2)**	**2(0.8)**	**14(5.4)**	**260(100)**			
Family Size								
1	37 (34.9)	66 (62.3)	2 (1.9)	1 (0.9)	106(100)			
2	56 (52.8)	46 (43.4)	0 (0.0)	4 (3.8)	106(100)			
Above 3	10 (20.8)	29 (60.4)	0 (0.0)	9(18.8)	48 (100)			
Total	**103(39.6)**	**141(54.2)**	**2(0.8)**	**14(5.4)**	**260(100)**			
Occupation								
Agriculture	33 (34.0)	63 (64.9)	0 (0.0)	1 (1.0)	97(100)	23.76	9	0.005(S)
Coolies/wages	47 (52.8)	35 (39.3)	0 (0.0)	7 (7.9)	89(100)			
Business/Trade	8 (29.6)	15 (55.6)	1 (3.7)	3(11.1)	27(100)			
Employed	15 (31.9)	28 (59.6)	1 (2.1)	3 (6.4)	47(100)			
Total	**103(39.6)**	**141(54.2)**	**2(0.8)**	**14(5.4)**	**260(100)**			
Household Income								
≤10,000	37 (37.0)	59 (59.0)	0 (0.0)	4 (4.0)	100(100)	41.91	18	0.001(S)
10,001-20,000	39 (41.9)	49 (52.7)	0 (0.0)	5 (5.4)	93(100)			
20,001-30,000	13 (61.9)	6 (28.6)	1 (4.8)	1 (4.8)	21(100)			
30,001-40,000	7 (70.0)	2(20.0)	0 (0.0)	1(10.0)	10(100)			
40,001-50,000	2 (25.0)	5 (62.50	1(12.5)	0 (0.0)	8(100)			
50,001-60,000	1 (12.5)	7 (87.5)	0 (0.0)	0 (0.0)	8(100)			
Above 60,001	4 (20.0)	13 (65.0)	0 (0.0)	3(15.0)	20(100)			
Total	**103(39.6)**	**141(54.2)**	**2 (0.8)**	**14(5.4)**	**260(100)**			
Medical Expenditure								
≤500	38 (33.6)	67 (59.3)	0 (0.0)	8 (7.1)	113(100)	21.44	15	0.12
501-1000	27 (38.6)	39 (55.7)	0 (0.0)	4 (5.7)	70 (100)			
1001-1500	13(52.0)	10(40.0)	1(4.0)	1(4.0)	25(100)			
1501-2000	9 (52.9)	6 (35.3)	1 (5.9)	1 (5.9)	17(100)			
2001-2500	7 (63.6)	4 (36.4)	0 (0.0)	0 (0.0)	11(100)			
Above 2501	9 (37.5)	15 (62.5)	0 (0.0)	0 (0.0)	24(100)			
Total	**103(39.6)**	**141(54.2)**	**2 (0.8)**	**14(5.4)**	**260(100)**			

the respondents accessing private hospitals, nearly 40 per cent of the respondents accessing government health facilities for delivery, and a meager of 0.8 per cent of the respondents delivered in maternity homes. Though the number of respondents delivered children in their homes (14), the higher percentages were among Nuclear families, belong to SC/ST, Illiterate women, higher age group women

(35+ years), women with higher number of children ever born, women with higher family size and women of the families spending less amount for their medical expenses.

It is inferred from the above table that, regarding place of delivery the Chi-square result proves that there is no association between the religion, respondent's education, respondent's present age and age at menarche are not significant (P>0.05). But the caste, family type, respondent's annual household income is significantly associated with the place of delivery (P<0.05). Also the child ever born, family size, occupation are significantly associated (P<0.05), whereas the other variables respondents age at marriage, age at first birth, and respondent's expenditure on medical are also not significantly associated (P>0.05).

5.10 Reproductive Health Problems of Women during Post Partum Period

The first few weeks after pregnancy are important for the health of babies and mothers. The National Committee for Quality Assurance (NCQA) recommends that women have a postpartum care visit 21 to 56 days after giving birth. In Indian culture, mothers are traditionally forbidden to touch the ground for six weeks after birth. Other female members of the family take turns with the housework, caring for the newborn as well as preparing special foods. The mother eats only fresh, non-processed foods that have warming spices to restore heat to her body. The postpartum mother also experiences daily massages, bringing comfort and easing the pain accumulated from pregnancy and labour.

A postpartum visit is important to make sure that the mother's body has recovered from pregnancy and birth and that there are not any problems. Postpartum care visits provide important opportunities to check the physical and mental well-being of the mother. It is also an opportunity to get information about family planning, and referrals for any chronic conditions such as diabetes, high blood pressure, or obesity. PNC use has been unacceptably low in India given the risks of mortality for mothers and babies shortly after birth. However, there is evidence to suggest that effective use of pregnancy and childbirth care in health facilities led to better PNC. There are also significant socio-economic inequalities in access to PNC even for those accessing facility-based care. The coverage of essential PNC is inadequate, especially for mothers from economically disadvantaged households. The findings suggest the need for strengthening PNC services to keep pace with advances in coverage for care at birth and prenatal services in India through targeted policy interventions. A continuum of care throughout pregnancy and the postpartum period is critically important in India where both mothers and children are vulnerable to a range of health risks resulting from the vicious cycle of malnutrition and poverty. Moreover, despite a recent decline in infant mortality rates, there is little subsequent improvement in most Indian states. The infant mortality rate was around 57 per 1000 live births in 2005–06 and ranged between as low as 15 in Kerala to as high as 73 in Uttar Pradesh. Maternal mortality rates were also high at 212 deaths per 100,000 live births, which varied widely across Indian states. The Government of India introduced several policy measures and interventions to tackle the burden of infant and maternal mortality by reorienting the National Population Policy (2000), the National Health Policy (2002), the Reproductive and Child Health Programme (Phase I–1997–2004, Phase II–2005–2010), and the National Rural Health Mission (2005–2012)–wherein improving postnatal coverage was envisaged as one of the key intervention strategies to reduce infant and maternal mortality rates. Unfortunately, although the policies have rightly emphasised on components such as skilled attendance and antenatal and institutional care at birth, they have overlooked the need to strengthen postnatal care within the reproductive health services.

To assess the prevalence of reproductive health problems during postnatal period of the women in the study area, respondents were probed to obtain information on the experience of reproductive health problems and type of health problem, treatment taken, and place of treatment. This information was cross-classified with the socio-economic and demographic characteristics of the women in the study area and tabulated in the following section. The analysis shows that more than 71 per cent of the respondents reported that they had one or more reproductive health problems during their post partum period. The percentage of women experienced problems in this period was higher among the women belong to other than SC/ST, Nuclear families, higher age group, higher menarcheal age group, higher age at first birth, women with lower number of children ever born, lower family size, and women with higher income groups. The analysis further shows that there was no significant association between religion, educational status, and age at marriage.

Table-5.14: Distribution of Respondents by Prevalence of Reproductive Health Problems During Post Natal Period and their Background Characteristics

SED/Sub-variables	*No*	*Yes*	*Total*	*Chi-Square*	*df*	*P value*
Religion						
Hindu	73(28.97)	179(71.03)	252(100)	0.59	1	0.80
Christian	2(25.00)	6(75.00)	8(100)			
Total	**75(28.85)**	**185(71.15)**	**260(100)**			
Caste						
SC/ST	16(30.19)	37(69.81)	53 (100)	0.58	1	0.80
Others	59(28.50)	148(71.50)	207 (100)			
Total	**75(28.85)**	**185(71.15)**	**260(100)**			
Family Type						
Nuclear family	36(25.35)	106(74.64)	142 (100)	1.86	1	0.17
Joint family	39(33.05)	79(66.94)	118 (100)			
Total	**75(28.85)**	**185(71.15)**	**260(100)**			
Education						
Illiterate	12(42.85)	16(57.14)	28(100)	8.15	6	0.22
Primary	24(34.78)	45(65.21)	69(100)			
Middle	9(17.30)	43(82.69)	52(100)			
High school	17(27.86)	44(72.13)	61(100)			
Hr. Secondary	5(27.78)	13(72.23)	18(100)			
Graduate	8(26.67)	22(73.34)	30(100)			
Professional	0(0.00)	2(100.0)	2(100)			
Total	**75(28.85)**	**185(71.15)**	**260(100)**			
Present Age						
≤19	9(50.00)	9(50.00)	18(100)	13.54	4	0.001(S)
20-24	32(39.51)	49(60.49)	81(100)			
25-29	15(23.08)	50(76.92)	65(100)			

(Contd...)

30-34	10(22.22)	35(77.78)	45(100)			
Above 35	9(17.65)	42(82.35)	51(100)			
Total	**75(28.85)**	**185(71.15)**	**260(100)**			
Age at Menarche						
≤12	8(57.14)	6(42.86)	14(100)	18.98	4	0.001(S)
13	13(56.52)	10(43.48)	23(100)			
14	10(37.34)	17(62.96)	27(100)			
15	19(21.11)	71(78.89)	90(100)			
Above 16	25(23.58)	81(76.42)	106(100)			
Total	**75(28.85)**	**185(71.15)**	**260(100)**			
Age at Marriage						
≤18	13(33.33)	26(66.67)	39 (100)	2.58	3	0.45
18-20	26(23.64)	84(76.36)	110 (100)			
21-23	29(32.95)	59(67.05)	88 (100)			
Above 24	7(30.43)	16(69.57)	23 (100)			
Total	**75(28.85)**	**185(71.15)**	**260(100)**			
Age at First Birth						
≤20	18(56.25)	14(43.75)	32 (100)	17.99	4	0.001 (S)
21-22	11(36.67)	19(63.33)	30 (100)			
23-24	19(21.11)	71(78.89)	90 (100)			
25-26	14(32.56)	29(67.44)	43 (100)			
Above 27	13(20.00)	52(80.00)	65 (100)			
Total	**75(28.85)**	**185(71.15)**	**260(100)**			
Child Ever Born						
1	16(25.00)	48(75.00)	64 (100)	43.67	4	0.001 (S)
2	23(29.49)	55(70.51)	78 (100)			
3	20(29.85)	47(70.15)	67 (100)			
4	10(30.30)	23(69.70)	33 (100)			
Above 5	6(33.33)	12(66.67)	18 (100)			
Total	**75(28.85)**	**185(71.15)**	**260(100)**			
Family Size						
1	28(26.42)	78(73.58)	106 (100)	5.57	4	0.23
2	32(30.19)	74(69.81)	106 (100)			
Above 3	15(31.25)	33(68.75)	48 (100)			
Total	**75(28.85)**	**185(71.15)**	**260(100)**			
Occupation						
Agriculture	31(31.96)	66(68.04)	97 (100)	1.16	3	0.76

(Contd...)

Coolies/wages	25(28.09)	64(71.91)	89 (100)			
Business/Trade	8(29.62)	19(70.37)	27 (100)			
Employed	11(23.40)	36(76.60)	47 (100)			
Total	**75(28.85)**	**185(71.15)**	**260(100)**			
Annual Household Income						
≤10,000	32(32.00)	68(68.00)	100 (100)	5.39	6	0.49
10,001-20,000	26(27.96)	67(72.04)	93 (100)			
20,001-30,000	7(33.33)	14(66.67)	21 (100)			
30,001-40,000	4(40.00)	6(60.00)	10 (100)			
40,001-50,000	0(0.00)	8(100.0)	8 (100)			
50,001-60,000	2(25.00)	6(75.00)	8 (100)			
Above 60,001	4(20.00)	16(80.00)	20 (100)			
Total	**75(28.85)**	**185(71.15)**	**260(100)**			
Medical Expenditure						
≤500	41(36.28)	72(63.72)	113 (100)	4.87	5	0.43
501-1000	15(21.43)	55(78.57)	70 (100)			
1001-1500	5(20.00)	20(80.00)	25 (100)			
1501-2000	3(17.65)	14(82.35)	17 (100)			
2001-2500	1(9.09)	10(90.91)	11 (100)			
Above2501	10(41.67)	14(58.33)	24 (100)			
Total	**75(28.85)**	**185(71.15)**	**260(100)**			

It is inferred from the above table that regarding distribution of respondent's by problems immediately after delivery across SED variables, the religion, caste, family type, respondent's education, respondent's present age, respondent's age at marriage, children ever born, is not significantly associated $p>0.05$. The age at menarche, age at first birth, family size, respondent's annual household income, respondent medical expenditure, occupation is significantly associated with Distribution of Respondent's by Problems immediately after delivery across SED variables $P<0.05$.

5.10.1 Types of Reproductive Health Problems and Socio-economic and Demographic Background

Delivering a baby in itself is a very difficult process for mother. After this, to care of the baby in the immediate period after the birth of the child can be very stressful. With so many problems that, the mother faces immediately after the delivery, she needs all the support from the family and healthcare providers.

Lochia is the name given to postpartum bleeding. Every woman who delivers a child, either vaginally or through cesarean section, will experience this type of bleeding. It is the way in which your body expels excess mucus, placental tissue, and blood after giving birth. Postpartum bleeding, which is a natural process, is called Lochia and usually takes between two and four weeks to clear. However, many women bleed for up to six week or more. It begins with a heavy flow, often requiring heavy duty protection, and then gradually tapers off over the days and weeks. It does take time for menses to begin again and sometimes menstrual cycles may not be the same in terms of intervals or longevity as they were before you became pregnant. There may also be some changes in the menstrual flow-lighter or heavier- and sometimes delayed postpartum bleeding occurs, which is not menses and can be disconcerting. Sometimes postpartum bleeding lasts only for a few days and then disappears, only to come back with a fury several weeks later. This could indicate that part of the placenta or uterine lining may not have passed out of your body after the birth. It could also point to the presence of a uterine infection. If you are passing clots or if the bleeding is soaking one sanitary pad per hour you could be hemorrhaging and should receive immediate medical attention.

After a baby arrives, the mother's body must recover from pregnancy and childbirth. Abdominal muscles, including the uterus, need time to get back to a normal, non-pregnant size. These changes can cause intense abdominal pain for the first few days after birth. After birth pains, sometimes called after-pains, can be quite debilitating. After the placenta is delivered, the site where it was attached is like an open wound requiring pressure to stop bleeding. The contractions that come after birth help close off the wound by squeezing the uterus. Pain is caused by contraction and relaxation of the uterus.

The following table shows the distribution of respondents by their reproductive health problems during their postnatal period with their socio-economic and demographic characteristics. This analysis shows that majority of the respondents (60.1 per cent) respondents reported that they have experienced the problem of lower abdominal pain

Table-5.15: Distribution of Respondents by Type of Reproductive Health Problems During Post Natal Period and their Background Characteristics

SED/Sub-variables	*Excessive Bleeding Pain*	*Lower Abdomen*	*Fainted more than 15 Minutes*	*Foul Smelling Discharge*	*Pus Formation*	*Fever*	*Total*	*Chi-Square*	*df*	*P-value*
Religion										
Hindu	83 (46.4)	110(61.5)	28(15.6)	7(3.9)	5(2.8)	34(18.2)	179(71.03)	2.379	5	0.79
Christian	5 (83.3)	3 (50.0)	2 (33.3)	0(0.0)	0(0.0)	1(16.7)	6(75.00)			
Total	**88 (47.6)**	**113(61.1)**	**30(16.2)**	**7(3.8)**	**5(2.7)**	**35(18.9)**	**185(71.15)**			
Caste										
SC/ST	19 (51.4)	20(54.1)	4 (10.8)	1(2.7)	0(0.0)	6(16.22)	37(69.81)	2.40	5	0.79
Others	69 (46.6)	93 (62.8)	26(17.6)	6(4.1)	5(3.4)	29(19.6)	148(71.50)			
Total	**88 (47.6)**	**113(61.1)**	**30(16.2)**	**7(3.8)**	**5(2.7)**	**35(18.9)**	**185(71.15)**			
Family Type										
Nuclear family	53 (50.0)	58 (54.7)	18(16.9)	5(4.7)	3(2.8)	17(18.9)	106(74.64)	3.27	5	0.65
Joint family	35 (44.3)	55 (69.6)	12(15.2)	2(2.5)	2(2.5)	18(22.8)	79(66.94)			
Total	**88 (47.6)**	**113(61.1)**	**30(16.2)**	**7(3.8)**	**5(2.7)**	**35(18.9)**	**185(71.15)**			
Education										
Illiterate	7 (43.8)	12 (75.0)	3 (18.8)	0(00)	1(6.3)	4 (25.0)	16(57.14)	20.80	30	0.89
Primary	19 (44.2)	25 (55.6)	9 (20.0)	4(8.9)	2(4.4)	9 (20.0)	45(65.21)			
Middle	19 (44.2)	25 (58.1)	9 (20.9)	2(4.7)	1(2.3)	8 (18.6)	43(82.69)			
High school	22 (50.0)	31 (70.5)	4 (9.1)	0(0)	1(2.3)	7 (15.9)	44(72.13)			
Hr. Secondary	4 (30.8)	10 (76.9)	2 (15.4)	0(00)	0(0.0)	4 (30.8)	13(72.23)			

(Contd...)

Graduate	15 (68.2)	9 (40.9)	3 (13.6)	1(4.6)	0(0.0)	3 (13.6)	22(73.34)			
Professional	2(100.0)	1(50.0)	0(0.0)	0(0)	0(0.0)	0 (0.0)	2(100.0)			
Total	**88 (47.6)**	**113(61.1)**	**30(16.2)**	**7(3.8)**	**5(2.7)**	**35(18.9)**	**185(71.15)**			
Present Age										
< 19	2 (22.2)	8 (88.9)	0(0.0)	1(11.1)	2(22.2)	5 (55.6)	9(50.00)	29.10	20	0.08
20-24	21 (42.9)	33 (67.4)	9(18.4)	1(2.0)	1(2.0)	11(22.5)	49(60.49)			
25-29	24 (48.0)	29 (58.0)	8 (16.0)	2(4.0)	(0.0)	8 (16.0)	50(76.92)			
30-34	13 (37.1)	23 (65.7)	6 (17.1)	1(2.9)	2(5.7)	6 (17.1)	35(77.78)			
Above 35	28 (66.7)	20 (47.6)	7 (16.7)	2(4.8)	0(0.0)	5 (11.9)	42(82.35)			
Total	**88 (47.6)**	**113(61.1)**	**30(16.2)**	**7(3.9)**	**5(2.7)**	**35(18.9)**	**185(71.15)**			
Age at Menarche										
< 12	2 (33.3)	5 (83.3)	0 (0.0)	0(0)	0(0.0)	3 (50.0)	6(42.86)	69.07	20	0.001 (S)
13	5 (50.0)	8 (80.0)	0 (0.0)	0(0)	2(20)	3 (30.0)	10(43.48)			
14	5 (29.4)	13 (76.5)	1 (5.9)	1(5.9)	1(5.9)	5 (29.4)	17(62.96)			
15	46 (64.8)	43 (60.6)	13(18.3)	1(1.4)	1(1.4)	9 (12.7)	71(78.89)			
Above 16	30 (37.0)	0 (0.0)	16(19.8)	5(6.2)	1(1.2)	15(18.5)	81(76.42)			
Total	**88 (47.6)**	**113(65.4)**	**30(16.2)**	**7(3.8)**	**5(2.7)**	**35(18.9)**	**185(71.15)**			
Age at Marriage										
<18	6 (23.1)	17 (65.4)	1 (3.9)	1(3.9)	2(7.7)	6 (23.1)	26(66.67)	17.19	15	0.30
18-20	42 (50.0)	56 (66.7)	14(16.7)	1(1.2)	2(2.4)	16(19.1)	84(76.36)			
21-23	33 (55.9)	32 (54.2)	12(20.3)	5(8.5)	1(1.7)	10(16.9)	59(67.05)			
24+	7 (43.8)	8 (50.0)	3 (18.8)	0(0)	0(0.0)	3 (18.8)	16(69.57)			
Total	**88 (47.6)**	**113(61.1)**	**30(16.2)**	**7(3.8)**	**5(2.7)**	**35(18.9)**	**185(71.15)**			

(Contd...)

Age at First Birth										
< 20	3(21.4)	6(42.9)	0(0.0)	0(0)	1(7.1)	8 (57.1)	14(43.75)	34.95	20	0.02 (S)
21-22	4((21.1)	16 (84.2)	1 (5.3)	1(5.3)	1(5.3)	4 (21.1)	19(63.33)			
23-24	35 (49.0)	47 (66.2)	12(16.9)	1(1.4)	2(2.8)	8 (11.3)	71(78.89)			
25-26	17 (58.6)	17 (58.6)	7 (24.1)	2(6.9)	0(0.0)	6 (20.7)	29(67.44)			
27+	29 (55.8)	27 (51.9)	9 (17.3)	3 (5.8)	1(1.9)	9 (17.3)	52(80.00)			
Total	**88 (47.6)**	**113(61.1)**	**30(16.2)**	**7(3.8)**	**5(2.7)**	**35(18.9)**	**185(71.15)**			
Children Ever Born										
1	22 (45.8)	33 (68.8)	4 (8.3)	2 (4.2)	1(2.1)	5 (10.4)	48(75.00)	10.58	20	0.95
2	25 (45.5)	33 (60.0)	11(20.0)	3 (5.5)	2(3.6)	15(27.3)	55(70.51)			
3	23 (48.9)	28 (59.5)	9 (19.2)	2 (4.3)	1(2.1)	8 (17.0)	47(70.15)			
4	11 (47.8)	13 (56.5)	5 (21.7)	0(0)	1(4.4)	5 (21.7)	23(69.70)			
5+	7 (58.3)	6 (50.1)	1 (8.3)	0(0)	0(0.0)	2 (16.7)	12(66.67)			
Total	**88 (47.6)**	**113(61.1)**	**30(16.2)**	**7(3.8)**	**5(2.7)**	**35(21.8)**	**185(71.15)**			
Family Size										
1	38 (48.7)	52 (66.7)	7 (8.9)	4(5.1)	3(3.9)	14(18.9)	78(73.58)	58.14	10	0.001 (S)
2	37 (50.0)	38 (51.4)	11(14.9)	2(2.7)	2(2.7)	4 (12.1)	74(69.81)			
3+	13 (39.4)	23 (69.7)	12(36.4)	1(3.0)	0(0.0)	35(18.9)	33(68.75)			
Total	**88 (47.6)**	**113(61.1)**	**30(16.2)**	**7(3.8)**	**5(2.7)**	**55(22.7)**	**185(71.15)**			
Occupation										
Agriculture	33 (50.0)	50 (75.8)	13(19.7)	2(3.0)	2(3.0)	12(18.7)	66(68.04)	87.56	15	0.001 (S)
Coolies/wages	30 (46.9)	36 (56.3)	8 (12.5)	1(1.6)	2(3.1)	2 (10.5)	64(71.91)			
Business/ Trade	8 (42.1)	10 (52.6)	4 (21.1)	3(15.8)	1(5.3)	6 (16.7)	19(70.37)			

(Contd...)

Employed	17 (47.2)	17 (47.2)	5 (13.9)	1(2.8)	0(0.0)	35(18.9)	36(76.60)			
Total	**88 (47.6)**	**113(61.1)**	**30(16.2)**	**7(3.8)**	**5(2.7)**	**55(22.1)**	**185(71.15)**			
Annual Household Income										
<10,000	25 (36.8)	44 (64.7)	14(20.6)	3(4.4)	3(4.4)	12(17.9)	68(68.00)	97.15	30	0.001 (S)
10,001-20,000	30 (44.8)	44 (65.7)	8 (11.9)	2(2.9)	2(2.9)	3 (21.4)	67(72.04)			
20,001-30,000	8 (57.1)	7 (50.0)	2 (14.3)	1(7.1)	0(0.0)	1 (16.7)	14(66.67)			
30,001-40,000	4 (66.7)	2 (33.3)	0 (0.0)	1(16.7)	0(0.0)	1 (12.5)	6(60.00)			
40,001-50,000	5(62.5)	5 (62.5)	1 (12.5)	0(00)	0(0.0)	1 (16.7)	8(100.0)			
50,001-60,000	2 (33.3)	3 (50.0)	0 (0.0)	0(0)	0(0.0)	2 (12.5)	6(75.00)			
Above 60,001	14 (87.5)	8 (50.0)	5 (31.3)	0(0)	0(0.0)	35(18.9)	16(80.00)			
Total	**88 (47.6)**	**113(61.1)**	**30(16.2)**	**7 (3.8)**	**5(2.7)**	**55(20.8)**	**185(71.15)**			
Medical Expenditure										
< 500	21 (29.2)	48 (66.7)	15(20.8)	2 (2.8)	4(5.6)	7 (12.7)	72(63.72)	106.4	25	0.001 (S)
501-1000	30 (54.6)	34 (61.8)	10(18.2)	4 (7.3)	1(1.8)	5 (25.0)	55(78.57)			
1001-1500	13 (65.0)	9 (45.0)	1 (5.0)	1 (5.0)	0(0.0)	3 (23.1)	20(80.00)			
1501-2000	9 (64.3)	7 (53.9)	1 (7.7)	0(0)	0(0.0)	2 (18.2)	14(82.35)			
2001-2500	4 (40.00)	4 (36.36)	1 (9.09)	0(00)	0(0.0)	3 (21.4)	10(90.91)			
Above 2501	11 (78.6)	11 (78.6)	2 (14.3)	0(0)	0(0.0)	35(18.9)	14(58.33)			
Total	**88 (47.6)**	**113(61.1)**	**30(16.2)**	**7(3.8)**	**5(2.7)**	**170**	**185(71.15)**			

Note: Percentage adds to more than 100 due to multiple responses.

during their postnatal period. Excessive bleeding was also a problem reported by 47.6 per cent of the respondents. Fever, fainted for more than 15 minutes, foul smelling discharge and pus formation were the other problems faced by a considerable proportion of the respondents in the study area. The percentage of women experienced lower abdominal pain during their post partum period was higher among the women belong to the category of non-SC/ST, joint families, illiterates, mothers of lower ages, mothers of low age at menarche, mothers of higher number of children ever born, mothers of lower family size, and mothers engaged in agriculture occupation. While analysing the second highest reported problem of heavy bleeding after birth with the socio economic and demographic background, it is inferred that, women belong to SC/ST, nuclear families, higher educated women, higher age group, women with higher ages at first birth, and women spending higher amount for medical expenses. The other variables like, religion, age at marriage, children ever born, family size, and income were not significantly associated with the prevalence of the problems.

It is inferred from the above table that regarding immediately after delivery all yes variables on the basis of SED variables, the religion, caste, family type, respondent's education, respondent's present age, respondent's age at marriage, children ever born is not significantly associated $p>0.05$. The age at menarche, age at first birth, occupation family size, respondent's annual household income, respondent medical expenditure, is significantly associated with immediately after delivery all yes variables SED variables $p<0.05$.

5.10.2 Treatment Taken for the Problems Immediately After Birth

Postpartum maternal healthcare is a neglected aspect of women's healthcare. In Asia, postpartum care is considered to be a very importance stage of a woman's life and this belief and practice is passed down through many generations. In Western countries, it is becoming more popular as the women weigh the vast health benefits more than anything else. Experts refer postpartum period as the first six weeks after childbirth. In real context, postpartum period can stretch up to 4-6 months with the mother herself coping and adapting physically and emotionally after childbirth. Postpartum care can be categorised to different categories such as external, internal and mental care. For a new mother, she has to make sure she takes good care of herself in these three aspects during the postpartum period.

External care refers to the physical body such as dealing with the change in body shape, coping with breastfeeding problems like engorgement or sore nipples, caesarean incision or even hair loss issues.

Internal care refers to things like physical fatigue, body aches, afterbirth cramps, perineal pain or constipation problems.

Mental care refer to emotions such as anxiety, impatient, confidence level or low self esteem due to hormonal changes that trigger us to be more sensitive during postpartum period.

Table-5.16: Distribution of Respondents by Treatment Taken for Reproductive Health Problems Immediately After Delivery and their Background Characteristics

SED/Sub-variables	*No*	*Yes*	*Total*	*Chi-Square*	*df*	*P value*
Religion						
Hindu	41 (22.9)	138(77.1)	179	0.84	1	0.77
Christian	1 (16.7)	5(83.3)	6			
Total	**42(22.7)**	**143(77.3)**	**185**			
Caste						
SC/ST	10 (27.0)	27 (72.9)	37	0.86	1	0.35
Others	32 (21.6)	116(78.4)	148			
Total	**42(22.70)**	**143(77.30)**	**185**			
Family Type						
Nuclear	29 (27.4)	77 (72.6)	106	4.04	1	0.04 (S)
Joint	13 (16.5)	66 (83.5)	79			
Total	**42 (22.7)**	**143 (77.3)**	**185**			
Education						
Illiterate	7 (43.7)	9 (56.3)	16	9.87	6	0.13
Primary	11(24.4)	34 (75.6)	45			
Middle	9 (20.9)	34 (79.1)	43			
High school	12 (27.3)	32 (72.7)	44			
Hr. Secondary	1 (7.7)	12 (92.3)	13			

(Contd...)

Graduate	2 (0.1)	20 (90.9)	22			
Professional	0 (0.0)	2 (100.0)	2			
Total	**42 (22.7)**	**143 (77.3)**	**185**			
Present Age						
≤19	2 (22.2)	7(77.8)	9	3.90	4	0.41
20-24	13 (26.5)	36 (73.5)	49			
25-29	13 (26.0)	37 (74.0)	50			
30-34	6 (17.1)	29 (82.9)	35			
Above 35	8 (29.1)	34 (80.9)	42			
Total	**42 (22.7)**	**143 (77.3)**	**185**			
Age at Menarche						
≤12	0 (0.0)	6 (100.0)	6	6.34	4	0.17
13	5 (50.0)	5 (50.0)	10			
14	6 (35.3)	11 (64.7)	17			
15	17 (23.9)	54 (76.1)	71			
Above 16	14 (17.3)	67(82.7)	81			
Total	**42 (22.7)**	**143 (77.3)**	**185**			
Age at Marriage						
≤18	6 (23.1)	20 (16.9)	26	1.17	3	0.76
18-20	19 (22.6)	65 (77.4)	84			
21-23	15 (25.4)	44 (74.6)	59			
Above 24	2 (12.5)	14 (87.5)	16			
Total	**42(22.70)**	**143(77.30)**	**185**			
Age at First Birth						
≤20	3 (21.43)	11 (78.57)	14	2.94	4	0.56
21-22	6 (31.58)	13 (68.42)	19			
23-24	19(26.76)	52 (73.24)	71			
25-26	7 (24.14)	22 (75.86)	29			
Above 27	7 (13.46)	45 (86.54)	52			
Total	**42 (22.7)**	**143(77.30)**	**185**			
Children Ever Born						
1	12 (25.0)	36 (75.0)	48	4.17	4	0.38
2	17 (30.9)	38 (69.1)	55			
3	7 (14.9)	40 (85.1)	47			
4	3 (13.0)	20 (86.9)	23			
5	3 (25.0)	9 (75.0)	12			
Total	**42 (22.7)**	**143 (77.3)**	**185**			

(Contd...)

Family Size						
1	18 (23.1)	60 (76.9)	78	6.67	4	0.15
2	16 (21.6)	58 (78.4)	74			
Above 3	8 (24.2)	25 (75.8)	33			
Total	**42 (22.7)**	**143 (77.3)**	**185**			
Occupation						
Agriculture	14 (21.2)	52 (78.8)	66	7.03	3	0.07
Coolies/wages	21 (32.8)	43 (67.2)	64			
Business/Trade	4 (21.1)	15 (78.9)	19			
Employed	3 (8.3)	33 (91.7)	36			
Total	**42 (22.7)**	**143 (77.3)**	**185**			
Annual Household Income						
≤10,000	20 (29.4)	48 (70.6)	68	7.27	6	0.29
10,001-20,000	16 (23.9)	51 (76.1)	67			
20,001-30,000	3 (21.4)	11 (78.6)	14			
30,001-40,000	1 (16.7)	5 (83.3)	6			
40,001-50,000	0 (0.0)	8 (100.0)	8			
50,001-60,000	0 (0.0)	6 (100.0)	6			
Above 60,001	2 (12.5)	14 (87.5)	16			
Total	**42 (22.7)**	**143 (77.3)**	**185**			
Medical Expenditure						
≤500	17 (23.6)	55 (76.4)	72	9.21	5	0.10
501-1000	12 (21.8)	43 (78.2)	55			
1001-1500	5 (25.0)	15 (75.0)	20			
1501-2000	3 (21.4)	11 (78.6)	14			
2001-2500	2 (20.0)	8 (80.0)	10			
Above 2501	3 (21.4)	11 (78.6)	14			
Total	**42 (22.7)**	**143 (77.3)**	**185**			

The above table shows the distribution of respondents by their treatment seeking behaviour for the problems reported during their post-partum period and their socio-economic and demographic background. It can be inferred from the table that more than three-fourth (77.3 per cent) of the women in the study area taken some treatment for their problems during postpartum period. The percentage of women taken treatment were high among the women belong to non-SC/ST, joint families, higher educated, higher age groups, higher age at marriage, higher age at first birth, and women employed with other than agricultural activities. The other variables such as religion, age at menarche, children ever born, family size, annual income and amount spent for medical expenses were not associated with the percentage of women taken treatment for their problems during post-partum period.

It is inferred from the above table that immediately after delivery treatment taken on the basis of SED variables, the religion, caste, respondent's education, respondent's present age, respondent's age at marriage, age at menarche, age at first birth, children ever born, family size, occupation, respondent's annual household income, respondent medical expenditure, is not significantly associated $p>0.05$. The family type is significantly associated with immediately after delivery treatment taken on the basis of SED variables $P<0.05$. Health programmes should invest to ensure that all women receive early postpartum visits after delivery at home and after discharge from institution to detect and manage maternal morbidity. Further, health programmes should also ensure that women are properly screened for complications before their discharge from hospitals after delivery.

5.10.3 Post Natal Care Treatment and their Background Characteristics

Postnatal care is one of the most important maternal health-care services for not only prevention of impairment and disabilities but also reduction of maternal mortality. The time when effective postnatal care can make the most difference to the health and life chances of mothers and newborns is in the early neonatal period, the time just after the delivery and through the first seven days of life. However, the whole of the neonatal period, from birth to the 28th day after the birth, is a time of increased risk. Deaths during the first 28 days of babies who were born alive is reported by all countries in the world as the neonatal mortality rate (the number of babies who die in the first 28 days) per 1,000 live births. Similarly, reports of maternal mortality include deaths of women from complications associated with postnatal problems, not just problems arising during the birth. Both these rates are important indicators of the effectiveness of postnatal care. Thirty-nine per cent of neonatal deaths in India occur on the first day of life, and 57 per cent during the first three days of births (DLHS-3).

So, the first reason why you need to focus more care and attention on the postnatal period is that this is a very critical time for the mother and her newborn baby.

The respondents in the study area were probed for obtaining information relating to the postnatal care received. The data obtained from the respondents were analysed and tabulated here. The table shows that 90.0 per cent of the women in the study area took some sort of postnatal care. While analysing the mothers who took post-natal care with their socio-economic and demographic background, it can be inferred that the percentage of mothers took postnatal care was higher among the mothers belong to joint families, with low age at menarche, low age at first birth, lesser number of children ever born, higher family size, of agriculture occupation and coolies/daily wagers, and spending more money for their medical expenses. The variables like religion, caste, educational status, present age, age at marriage were not significantly associated with the women took post-natal care.

Table-5.17: Distribution of Respondents by Post Natal Care Treatment and their Background Characteristics

SED Variables	*No*	*Yes*	*Total*	*Chi-Square*	*df*	*P value*
Religion						
Hindu	25 (9.9)	227(90.1)	252(100)	0.57	1	0.811
Christian	1 (1.3)	7(87.5)	8(100)			
Total	**26(10.0)**	**234(90.0)**	**260(100)**			
Caste						
SC/ST	6(11.3)	7(88.7)	53(100)	0.12	1	0.719
Others	20 (9.7)	187(90.3)	207(100)			
Total	**26(10.0)**	**234(90.0)**	**260(100)**			
Family Type						
Nuclear	21(14.8)	121(85.2)	142(100)	7.97	1	0.005 (S)
Joint	5 (4.2)	113(95.8)	118(100)			
Total	**26(10.0)**	**234(90.0)**	**260(100)**			
Education						
Illiterate	6 (21.4)	22 (78.6)	28 (100)	8.57	6	0.19
Primary	7 (10.1)	62 (82.9)	69 (100)			

(Contd...)

Middle	2 (3.8)	50 (96.2)	52 (100)			
High school	5 (8.2)	56 (91.8)	61 (100)			
Hr. Secondary	1 (5.6)	17 (94.4)	18 (100)			
Graduate	5 (16.7)	25 (83.3)	30 (100)			
Professional	0 (0.0)	2 (100.0)	2 (100)			
Total	**26(10.0)**	**234(90.0)**	**260(100)**			
Present Age						
≤19	2 (11.1)	16 (88.9)	18 (100)	14.26	4	0.001 (S)
20-24	0 (0.0)	81(100.0)	81 (100)			
25-29	8 (12.3)	57 (87.7)	65 (100)			
30-34	8 (17.8)	37 (88.2)	45 (100)			
Above 35	8 (15.7)	43 (84.3)	51 (100)			
Total	**26(10.0)**	**234(90.0)**	**260(100)**			
Age at Menarche						
≤12	0 (0.0)	14(100.0)	14 (100)	6.33	4	0.17
13	2 (8.7)	21 (91.3)	23 (100)			
14	1 (3.7)	26 (96.3)	27 (100)			
15	7 (7.8)	83 (92.2)	90 (100)			
Above 16	16(15.1)	90 (84.9)	106(100)			
Total	**26(10.0)**	**234(90.0)**	**260(100)**			
Age at Marriage						
≤18	5 (12.8)	34 (87.2)	39 (100)	2.65	3	0.44
18-20	8 (7.3)	102(92.7)	11(100)			
21-23	9 (10.2)	79 (89.8)	88 (100)			
Above 24	4 (17.4)	19 (82.6)	23 (100)			
Total	**26(10.0)**	**234(90.0)**	**260(100)**			
Age at First Birth						
≤20	3(9.38)	29 (90.6)	32 (100)	2.07	4	0.72
21-22	2 (6.7)	28 (93.3)	30 (100)			
23-24	7 (7.8)	83 (92.2)	90 (100)			
25-26	5 (11.6)	38 (88.4)	43 (100)			
Above 27	9 (13.9)	56 (86.2)	65 (100)			
Total	**26(10.0)**	**234(90.0)**	**260(100)**			
Child Ever Born						
1	6 (9.4)	58 (90.6)	64 (100)	9.77	4	0.04 (S)
2	5 (6.4)	73 (93.6)	78 (100)			
3	6 (8.9)	61 (91.0)	67 (100)			

(Contd...)

4	6 (18.2)	27 (81.8)	33 (100)			
Above 5	3 (16.7)	15 (83.3)	18 (100)			
Total	**26(10.0)**	**234(90.0)**	**260(100)**			
Family Size						
1	12(11.3)	94 (88.7)	106(100)	5.62	4	0.22
2	13(12.3)	93 (87.7)	106(100)			
Above 3	01 (2.1)	47 (97.9)	48 (100)			
Total	**26(10.0)**	**234(90.0)**	**260(100)**			
Occupation						
Agriculture	7 (7.2)	90 (92.8)	97 (100)	4.713	3	0.194
Coolies/wages	7 (7.9)	82 (92.3)	89 (100)			
Business/Trade	5 (81.5)	22 (81.5)	27 (100)			
Employed	7 (14.9)	40 (85.1)	47 (100)			
Total	**26(10.0)**	**234(90.0)**	**260(100)**			
Annual Household Income						
≤10,000	11(11.0)	89 (89.0)	100(100)	5.44	6	0.48
10,001-20,000	7 (7.5)	86 (92.5)	93 (100)			
20,001-30,000	3 (14.3)	18 (85.7)	21(100)			
30,001-40,000	0 (0.0)	0(100.0)	10(100)			
40,001-50,000	0 (0.0)	8(100.0)	8 (100)			
50,001-60,000	1 (12.5)	7(87.5)	8 (100)			
Above 60,001	4 (20.0)	6(80.0)	20 (100)			
Total	**26(10.0)**	**234(90.0)**	**260(100)**			
Medical Expenditure						
≤500	14(12.4)	99 (87.6)	113(100)	8.60	5	0.12
501-1000	8(11.4)	62 (88.6)	70 (100)			
1001-1500	2(8.0)	23 (92.0)	25 (100)			
1501-2000	1(5.9)	16 (94.1)	17 (100)			
2001-2500	1(9.1)	10 (90.9)	11(100)			
Above 2501	0(0.0)	24(100.0)	24 (100)			
Total	**26(10.0)**	**234(90.0)**	**260(100)**			

The above table shows the details about medical checkup after delivery. Considering the religion, the Chi-square result proves that there is no association between religion of the respondent and their complication. Similarly the caste, respondent's education, age at first birth, age at menarche, age at marriage, family size, expenditure on medical, occupation and annual income are not significant. Since the calculated Chi-Square values are not significant (P>0.05). Further, the Chi-square result proves that there is association between family type, children ever born, and respondent's present age are significant. Since the calculated Chi-square values are significant ($P<0.05$).

5.10.4 Place of Post Natal Care and Socio-economic and Demographic Background

In general, postnatal care uptake has been limited in South Asia and particularly in India. According to the 2005–06 National Family Health Survey (NFHS-3), only 42 per cent of women reported receiving postnatal check-up after their recent birth. Of these, only about a third received check-up within the first two days after birth. Unfortunately, the NFHS-3 collected data on postnatal care from only mothers who had given birth in a health facility. Postnatal care is under-researched in India at the national level, except a study conducted in the state of Madhya Pradesh, one conducted in southern India and another rural-based study. However, none of these studies explicitly addressed the socio-economic inequalities in postnatal care use.

PNC use has been unacceptably low in India given the risks of mortality for mothers and babies shortly after birth. However, there is evidence to suggest that effective use of pregnancy and childbirth care in health facilities led to better PNC. There are also significant socio-economic inequalities in access to PNC even for those accessing facility-based care. The coverage of essential PNC is inadequate, especially for mothers from economically disadvantaged households. Promoting antenatal care and skilled attendance at birth is clearly not enough for improving maternal and child health. The WHO guidelines on postnatal care recommend essential routine postnatal care for all mothers and their newborns, extra care for low birth weight and small babies, and early identification and referral or management of emergency conditions. The guidelines further recommend postnatal visits within six to twelve hours after birth, and follow-up visits from three to six days, at six weeks, and then at six months. Strategies aimed at promoting universal access to postnatal care have been recommended for several years and these interventions can have measurable and sustained impact in reducing neonatal and maternal mortality. Yet, despite governmental initiatives and policy efforts, there is a lack of follow-up after childbirth. Moreover, mothers often only seek postnatal care in the event of complications after birth. Poverty, lack of schooling, poor knowledge, and inadequate follow-up services in healthcare systems deter women from seeking postnatal care. To date, there has not been any systematic national level analysis of population data to understand the levels and socio-economic differentials in the use of postnatal care in India. Little evidence exists on the extent and timing of postnatal care and how these differ between women who received home and institutional care at birth.

Table-5.18: Distribution of Respondents by Place of Post Natal Care and their Background Characteristics

SED Variables	*Govt. Hospitals*	*Private Hospitals*	*Home Visit*	*Total*	*Chi-Square*	*df*	*P value*
Religion							
Hindu	74 (29.4)	170(67.5)	8(3.2)	252(100)	3.80	2	0.14
Christian	0(00.0)	8(100)	0(0.0)	8(100)			
Total	**74 (28.5)**	**178(68.5)**	**8 (3.1)**	**260(100)**			
Caste							
SC/ST	27 (50.9)	21(39.6)	5 (9.4)	53(100)	28.65	2	0.001 (S)
Others	47 (22.7)	157(75.9)	3(1.5)	207(100)			
Total	**74(28.5)**	**178(68.5)**	**8(3.1)**	**260(100)**			
Family Type							
Nuclear	48(33.8)	87(61.3)	7(4.9)	142(100)	8.99	2	0.01 (S)
Joint	26(22.0)	91(77.2)	1(0.9)	118(100)			
Total	**74(28.5)**	**178(68.5)**	**8(3.1)**	**260(100)**			
Education							
Illiterate	9(32.1)	17(60.7)	2(7.1)	28(100)	7.60	12	0.81
Primary	20(28.9)	46(66.7)	3(4.4)	69(100)			
Middle	13(25.0)	39(75.0)	0(00)	52(100)			
High school	18(29.5)	42(68.9)	1(1.6)	61(100)			
Hr. Secondary	6(16.7)	12(08.3)	0(00)	18(100)			
Graduate	7(23.3)	21(70.0)	2(6.7)	30(100)			
Professional	1(50.0)	1(50.0)	0(00)	2(100)			
Total	**74(28.5)**	**178(68.5)**	**8(3.0)**	**260(100)**			
Present Age							
≤19	5(27.8)	13(72.2)	0(00)	18(100)	34.03	8	0.001 (S)
20-24	10(12.4)	71(87.7)	0(00)	81(100)			

(Contd...)

25-29	18(27.7)	45(69.2)	2(3.1)	65(100)			
30-34	21(46.7)	23(51.1)	1(2.2)	45(100)			
Above 35	20(39.2)	26(50.9)	5(9.8)	51(100)			
Total	**74(28.5)**	**178(68.5)**	**8(3.0)**	**260(100)**			
Age at Menarche							
≤12	1(07.1)	12(85.7)	1(7.1)	14(100)	10.71	8	0.21
13	4(17.4)	18(78.3)	1(4.4)	23(100)			
14	6(22.2)	20(74.1)	1(3.7)	27(100)			
15	23(25.6)	65(72.2)	2(2.2)	90(100)			
Above 16	40(37.7)	63(59.4)	3(2.8)	106(100)			
Total	**74(28.5)**	**178(68.5)**	**8(3.0)**	**260(100)**			
Age at Marriage							
≤18	18(46.2)	19(48.7)	2(5.1)	39(100)	9.19	6	0.16
18-20	26(23.6)	81(73.6)	3(2.7)	110(100)			
21-23	25(28.4)	61(69.3)	2(2.3)	88(100)			
Above 24	5(21.7)	17(73.9)	1(4.4)	23(100)			
Total	**74(28.5)**	**178(68.5)**	**8(3.0)**	**260(100)**			
Age at First Birth							
≤20	7(21.9)	23(71.9)	2(6.3)	32(100)	4.41	8	0.81
21-22	8(26.7)	21(70.0)	1(3.3)	30(100)			
23-24	23(25.6)	65(72.2)	2(2.2)	90(100)			
25-26	14(32.6)	27(62.8)	2(4.7)	43(100)			
Above 27	22(33.9)	42(64.6)	1(1.5)	65(100)			
Total	**74(28.5)**	**178(68.5)**	**8(3.0)**	**260(100)**			
Children Ever Born							
1	12(18.8)	52(81.3)	0(00)	64(100)	33.02	8	0.001 (S)
2	16(20.5)	60(76.9)	2(2.6)	78(100)			
3	28(41.8)	38(56.8)	1(1.5)	67(100)			
4	15(45.5)	16(48.5)	2(6.1)	33(100)			
Above 5	3(16.7)	12(66.7)	3(16.7)	18(100)			
Total	**74(28.5)**	**178(68.5)**	**8(3.0)**	**260(100)**			
Family Size							
1	25(23.6)	79(74.5)	2(1.9)	106(100)	25.72	8	0.001 (S)
2	42(39.6)	62(58.5)	2(1.9)	106(100)			
Above 3	7(14.6)	37(77.1)	4(8.3)	48(100)			
Total	**74(28.5)**	**178(68.5)**	**8(3.0)**	**260(100)**			

(Contd...)

Occupation							
Agriculture	18(18.6)	78(80.4)	1(1.0)	97(100)	21.53	6	0.002 (S)
Coolies/wages	37(47.6)	47(52.8)	5(5.6)	89(100)			
Business/Trade	4(14.8)	23(85.2)	0(00)	27(100)			
Employed	15(31.9)	30(63.8)	2(4.3)	47(100)			
Total	**74(28.5)**	**178(68.5)**	**8(3.0)**	**260(100)**			
Annual Household Income							
≤10,000	24(24.0)	74(74.0)	2(2.0)	100(100)	8.69	12	0.72
10,001-20,000	30(32.3)	60(64.5)	3(3.2)	93(100)			
20,001-30,000	7(33.3)	13(61.9)	1(4.8)	21(100)			
30,001-40,000	3(30.0)	7(70.0)	0(0.0)	10(100)			
40,001-50,000	2(25.0)	6(75.0)	0(0.0)	8(100)			
50,001-60,000	1(12.5)	7(87.5)	0(0.0)	8(100)			
60,001+	7(35.0)	11(55.0)	2(10.0)	20(100)			
Total	**74(28.5)**	**178(68.5)**	**8(3.0)**	**260(100)**			
Medical Expenditure							
≤500	26(23.0)	84(74.3)	3(2.7)	113(100)	10.73	10	0.37
501-1000	21(30.0)	45(64.3)	4(5.7)	70(100)			
1001-1500	12(48.0)	13(52.0)	0(0.0)	25(100)			
1501-2000	5(29.4)	12(70.6)	0(0.0)	17(100)			
2001-2500	6(54.6)	4(36.4)	1(9.1)	11(100)			
2501+	4(16.7)	20(83.3)	0(0.0)	24(100)			
Total	**74(28.5)**	**178(68.5)**	**8(3.0)**	**260(100)**			

The above table shows that 68.5 per cent of the 260 women assessed, received postnatal care services from private hospitals. Only 28.5 per cent of the respondents received postnatal care services from government health facilities. Only 3.0 per cent of the respondents received postnatal care services from the health workers during their home visits. The percentage of women received postnatal care services from government health facility were higher among the women belong to SC/ST, higher age group, higher age at menarche, lower age at marriage, higher age at first birth, higher number of children ever born, and women engaged as coolies/daily wagers. While the women received postnatal care services from private hospitals were cross-classified with their socio-economic and demographic characteristics, the analysis showed that women belong to non-SC/ST, joint families, lower age group women, lower age at menarche, higher age at marriage, women with lower age at first birth, and women with fewer number of children ever born were higher in percentage than their counterparts.

It is inferred from the above table that, regarding post-partum care service across SED variables, the Chi-square result proves that there is no association between the religion, respondent's education and age at menarche are not significant ($P>0.05$). But the caste, family type, respondent's present age is significantly associated with the post-partum care service across SED variables ($P<0.05$). Also the child ever born, family size, occupation are significantly associated ($P<0.05$), whereas the other variables respondents age at marriage, age at first birth, respondent's annual household income and respondent's expenditure on medical are also not significantly associated ($P>0.05$). The findings suggest the need for strengthening PNC services to keep pace with advances in coverage for care at birth and prenatal services in India through targeted policy interventions.

5.11 Prevalence of Gynecological Problems Among Women and Socio-economic and Demographic Background

Gynecological morbidity has been defined as structural and functional disorders of the genital tract which are not directly related to pregnancy, delivery and puerperium. It includes menstrual disorders, reproductive tract infections, and cervical cell changes. The magnitude of gynecological morbidity was high with about 45 per cent of the women reporting at least one gynecological morbidity, the most common being menstrual disorders. However, the proportion of women reporting at least two gynecological morbidities was much lower with menstrual disorders and uterine prolapsed being the most frequent. The women in the study area were probed to obtain information on general gynecological morbidity experienced by them. Then the data obtained were cross-classified with the socio-economic and demographic characteristics of the respondents and tabulated in the above table. The above analysis shows that 45 per cent of the respondents in the study area reported

Table-5.19: Distribution of Respondents by Gynecological Problems and their Background Characteristics

SED/Sub-variables	*No*	*Yes*	*Total*	*Chi-Square*	*df*	*P value*
Religion						
Hindu	138(54.8)	114(45.2)	252(100)	0.18	1	0.66
Christian	5 (62.5)	3(37.5)	8(100)			
Total	**143(55.0)**	**117(45.0)**	**260(100)**			
Caste						
SC/ST	17 (32.1)	36 (67.9)	53 (100)	14.13	1	0.001 (S)
Others	126(60.9)	81 (39.2)	207(100)			
Total	**143(55.0)**	**117(45.0)**	**260(100)**			
Family Type						
Nuclear	60 (43.7)	82 (57.8)	142(100)	20.53	1	0.001 (S)
Joint	83 (70.3)	35 (29.7)	118(100)			
Total	**143(55.0)**	**117(45.0)**	**260(100)**			
Education						
Illiterate	15 (53.6)	13 (46.4)	28 (100)	4.18	6	0.65
Primary	40 (57.9)	29 (42.0)	69 (100)			
Middle	27 (51.9)	25 (48.1)	52 (100)			
High school	37 (60.7)	24 (39.3)	61 (100)			
Hr. Secondary	9 (50.0)	9 (50.0)	18 (100)			
Graduate	15 (50.0)	15 (50.0)	30 (100)			
Professional	0 (0.00)	2(100.0)	2 (100)			
Total	**143(55.0)**	**117(45.0)**	**260(100)**			
Present Age						
≤19	15 (83.3)	3 (16.7)	18 (100)	54.52	4	0.001 (S)
20-24	62 (76.5)	19 (23.5)	81 (100)			
25-29	39 (60.0)	26 (40.0)	65 (100)			
30-34	18 (40.0)	27 (60.0)	45 (100)			
Above 35	9 (17.7)	42 (82.4)	51 (100)			
Total	**143(55.0)**	**117(45.0)**	**260(100)**			
Age at Menarche						
≤12	9 (64.3)	5 (35.7)	14 (100)	1.85	4	0.76
13	15 (56.2)	8 (34.8)	23 (100)			
14	14 (51.9)	13 (48.2)	27 (100)			
15	47 (52.2)	43 (47.8)	90 (100)			

(Contd...)

Above 16	58 (54.7)	48 (45.3)	106(100)			
Total	**143(55.0)**	**117(45.0)**	**260(100)**			
Age at Marriage						
≤18	18 (46.2)	21 (53.9)	39 (100)	2.28	3	0.51
18-20	60 (54.6)	50 (45.5)	110(100)			
21-23	53 (60.2)	35 (39.8)	88 (100)			
Above 24	12 (52.2)	11 (47.8)	23 (100)			
Total	**143(55.0)**	**117(45.0)**	**260(100)**			
Age at First Birth						
≤20	21 (65.6)	11 (34.4)	32 (100)	4.24	4	0.37
21-22	20 (66.7)	10 (33.3)	30 (100)			
23-24	45 (50.0)	45 (50.0)	90 (100)			
25-26	23 (53.5)	20 (46.5)	43 (100)			
Above 27	34 (52.3)	31 (47.7)	65 (100)			
Total	**143(55.0)**	**117(45.0)**	**260(100)**			
Children Ever Born						
1	34 (53.1)	30 (46.9)	64 (100)	39.17	4	0.001 (S)
2	35 (44.9)	43 (55.1)	78 (100)			
3	47 (70.2)	20 (29.9)	67 (100)			
4	20 (60.6)	13 (39.4)	33 (100)			
Above 5	7 (38.9)	11 (61.1)	18 (100)			
Total	**143(55.0)**	**117(45.0)**	**260(100)**			
Family Size						
1	62 (58.5)	44 (41.5)	106(100)	22.59	4	0.001 (S)
2	66 (62.3)	40 (37.7)	106(100)			
Above 3	15 (31.3)	33 (68.8)	48 (100)			
Total	**143(55.0)**	**117(45.0)**	**260(100)**			
Occupation						
Agriculture	68 (70.1)	29 (29.9)	97 (100)	16.89	3	0.001 (S)
Coolies/wages	37 (41.6)	52 (58.4)	89 (100)			
Business/Trade	16 (59.3)	11 (40.7)	27 (100)			
Employed	22 (46.8)	25 (53.2)	47 (100)			
Total	**143(55.0)**	**117(45.0)**	**260(100)**			
Annual Household Income						
≤10,000	62 (62.0)	38 (38.0)	100(100)	8.24	6	0.22
10,001-20,000	51 (54.8)	42 (45.2)	93 (100)			
20,001-30,000	9 (42.9)	12 (57.1)	21 (100)			

(Contd...)

30,001-40,000	6 (60.0)	4 (40.0)	10 (100)			
40,001-50,000	2 (25.0)	6 (75.0)	8 (100)			
50,001-60,000	5 (62.5)	3 (37.5)	8 (100)			
Above 60,001	8 (40.0)	12 (60.0)	20 (100)			
Total	**143(55.0)**	**117(45.0)**	**260(100)**			
Medical Expenditure						
≤500	69 (61.1)	44 (38.9)	113(100)	2.98	5	0.74
501-1000	32 (45.7)	38 (54.3)	70 (100)			
1001-1500	15 (60.0)	10 (40.0)	25 (100)			
1501-2000	7 (41.2)	10 (58.8)	17 (100)			
2001-2500	6 (54.6)	5 (45.5)	11 (100)			
Above 2501	14 (58.3)	10 (41.7)	24 (100)			
Total	**143(55.0)**	**117(45.0)**	**260(100)**			

that they have experienced one or more gynecological problems. The prevalence of gynecological problems were high among the mothers belong to SC/ST, nuclear families, higher age group, higher age at menarche, low age at marriage, and higher family size. The characteristics like religion, education of the respondents, age at first birth of the mother, children ever born, household income and household expenditure on medical care were not significantly associated with the prevalence of gynecological morbidity. The percentage of women reported gynecological morbidity was higher among the mothers engaged as coolies/daily wagers.

The above findings were established with the help of statistical tools also. The above table shows the details about gynecological problem. Considering the religion, the Chi-square result proves that there is no association between religion of the respondent and their complication. Similarly the respondent's age at menarche, age at marriage, respondent's education, age at first birth, annual income and expenditure on medical are not significant. Since the calculated Chi-square values are not significant ($P>0.05$).

Further, the Chi-square test result proves that there is an association between castes; family type, respondent's present age, family size, children ever born, and occupation are significant. Since the calculated Chi-square values are significant ($P<0.05$).

Table-5.20: Distribution of Respondents by Gynecological Problems and their Background Characteristics

SED /Sub-Variables	Irregualr Periods	Excessive Bleeding	Painful Mensutrution	Foul smelling discharge	Itching During Menstruation	Scanty Bleeding	Passes Clots	Abdomen pain / Backache	Prolepse	Urinary trach Infection	Aneamic	White Discharge	Total	Chi-square	Df	P value
Religion																
Hindu	39 (34.21)	43 (37.72)	10 (8.77)	6 (5.26)	12 (10.53)	9 (7.89)	2 (1.75)	38 (33.33)	8 (7.02)	23 (20.18)	16 (14.04)	69 (60.53)	114 (45.24)	21.30	11	0.03 (S)
Christian	0 (0.00)	2 (66.67)	0 (0.00)	1 (33.33)	0 (0.00)	0 (0.00)	1 (33.33)	2 (66.67)	0 (0.00)	0 (0.00)	0 (0.00)	2 (66.67)	3 (37.50)			
Total	**39 (33.33)**	**45 (38.46)**	**10 (8.55)**	**7 (5.98)**	**12 (10.26**	**9 (7.69)**	**3 (2.56)**	**40 (34.19)**	**8 (6.84)**	**23 (19.66)**	**16 (13.66)**	**71 (60.68)**	**117 (45.00)**			
Caste																
SC/ST	11 (30.56)	11 (30.56)	1 (2.78)	4 (11.11)	1 (2.78)	9 (25.00)	1 (2.78)	15 (41.67)	4 (11.11)	8 (22.22)	4 (11.11)	25 (69.44)	36 (67.92)	29.67	11	0.001 (S)
Others	28 (34.57)	34 (41.98)	9 (11.11)	3 (3.70)	11 (13.58)	0 (0.00)	2 (2.47)	25 (30.86)	4 (4.94)	15 (18.52)	12 (14.81)	46 (56.79)	81 (39.13)			
Total	**39 (33.33)**	**45 (38.46)**	**10 (8.55)**	**7 (5.98)**	**12 (10.26**	**9 (7.69)**	**3 (2.56)**	**40 (34.19)**	**8 (6.84)**	**23 (19.66)**	**16 (13.66)**	**71 (60.68)**	**117 (45.00)**			
Family type																
Nuclear Family	28 (34.15)	29 (35.37)	7 (8.54)	5 (6.10)	5 (6.10)	4 (4.88)	1 (1.22)	27 (32.93)	6 (7.32)	16 (19.51)	12 (14.63)	53 (64.63)	82 (57.75)	10.39	11	0.49
Joint Family	11 (31.43)	16 (45.71)	3 (8.57)	2 (5.71)	7 (20.00)	5 (14.29)	2 (5.71)	13 (37.14)	2 (5.71)	7 (20.00)	4 (11.43)	18 (51.43)	35 (29.66)			
Total	**39 (33.33)**	**45 (38.46)**	**10 (8.55)**	**7 (5.98)**	**12 (10.26**	**9 (7.69)**	**3 (2.56)**	**40 (34.19)**	**8 (6.84)**	**23 (19.66)**	**16 (13.66)**	**71 (60.68)**	**117(45.00)**			

(Contd...)

Education																
Illiterate	4 (30.77)	7 (53.84)	1 (7.69)	0 (0.00)	0 (0.00)	1 (7.69)	0 (0.00)	5 (38.46)	0 (0.00)	4 (30.77)	3 (23.08)	12 (92.31)	13 (46.43)	42.77	66	0.98
Primary	8 (27.59)	7 (24.14)	4 (13.79)	2 (6.90)	3 (10.34)	2 (6.90)	0 (0.00)	10 (34.48)	2 (6.90)	6 (20.69)	4 (13.79)	21 (72.41)	29 (42.03)			
Middle	10 (40.00)	12 (48.00)	1 (4.00)	1 (4.00)	3 (12.00)	0 (0.00)	2 (8.00)	9 (36.00)	1 (4.00)	4 (16.00)	4 (16.00)	14 (56.00)	25 (48.08)			
High school	11 (45.83)	13 (54.17)	2 (8.34)	2 (8.34)	3 (12.55)	3 (12.50)	0 (0.00)	6 (25.00)	2 ()8.33	2 (8.34)	3 (12.50)	12 (50.00)	24 (39.34)			
Hr. Secondary	2 (22.22)	1 (11.11)	0 (0.00)	0 (0.00)	0 (0.00)	0 (0.00)	0 (0.00)	3 (33.33)	1 (11.11)	1 (11.11)	0 (0.00)	4 (44.44)	9 (50.00)			
Graduate	3 (20.00)	5 (33.34)	2 (13.33)	2 (13.33)	3 (20.00)	3 (20.00)	1 (6.67)	6 (40.00)	2 (13.33)	5 (33.34)	2 (13.33)	7 (46.67)	15 (50.00)			
Professional	1 (50.00)	0 (0.00)	0 (0.00)	0 (0.00)	0 (0.00)	0 (0.00)	0 (0.00)	1 (50.00)	0 (0.00)	1 (50.00)	0 (0.00)	1 (50.00)	2 (100.00)			
Total	**39 (33.33)**	**45 (38.46)**	**10 (8.55)**	**7 (5.98)**	**12 (10.26**	**9 (7.69)**	**3 (2.56)**	**40 (34.19)**	**8 (6.84)**	**23 (19.66)**	**16 (13.66)**	**71 (60.68)**	**117(45.00)**			
Present Age																
≤ 19	7 (66.67)	0 (0.00)	0 (0.00)	0 (0.00)	0 (0.00)	0 (0.00)	0 (0.00)	0 (0.00)	0 (0.00)	0 (0.00)	0 (0.00)	0 (0.00)	3 (16.67)	229.9	44	0.001 (S)
20-24	0 (0.00)	5 (26.32)	1 (5.26)	0 (0.00)	0 (0.00)	2 (10.53)	0 (0.00)	4 (21.05)	1 (5.26)	2 (10.53)	1 (5.26)	5 (26.32)	19 (23,46)			
25-29	4 (56.00)	10 (38.46)	3 (11.54)	3 (11.54)	5 (19.23)	4 (15.38)	1 (3.85)	9 (34.62)	1 (3.85)	5 (19.23)	3 (11.54)	18 (69.23)	26 (40.00)			
30-34	13 (51.00)	8 (29.63)	3 (3.70)	1 (11.11)	3 (11.11)	2 (7.41)	0 (0.00)	9 (33.33)	4 (14.81)	7 (25.93)	5 (18.52)	19 (70.37)	27 (60.00)			
Above 35	15 (38.10)	22 (52.38)	3 (7.14)	3 (7.14)	4 (9.52)	1 (2.38)	2 (4.76)	18 (42.86)	2 (4.76)	9 (21.43)	7 (16.67)	29 (69.05)	42 (82.35)			
Total	**39 (33.33)**	**45 (38.46)**	**10 (8.55)**	**7 (5.98)**	**12 (10.26**	**9 (7.69)**	**3 (2.56)**	**40 (34.19)**	**8 (6.84)**	**23 (19.66)**	**16 (13.66)**	**71 (60.68)**	**117(45.00)**			

(Contd...)

Age at Menarche																
≤12	1 (20.00)	1 (20.00)	2 (40.00)	1 (20.00)	3 (60.00)	1 (20.00)	3 (60.00)	1 (20.00)	1 (20.00)	3 (60.00)	3 (60.00)	1 (20.00)	5 (35.71)	22.99	44	0.001 (S)
13	1 (12.50)	1 (12.50)	3 (37.50)	1 (12.50)	8 (100.00)	1 (12.50)	0 (0.00)	3 (37.50)	3 (37.50)	3 (37.50)	8 (100.00)	4 (50.00)	8 (34.78)			
14	7 (53.84)	5 (38.46)	5 (38.46)	2 (1538)	0 (0.00)	7 (53.84)	0 (0.00)	4 (30.77)	4 (30.77)	5 (38.46)	4 (30.77)	8 (61.54)	13 (48.15)			
15	17 (39.53)	15 (34.88)	0 (0.00)	3 (6.98)	1 (2.33)	0 (0.00)	0 (0.00)	18 (41.86)	0 (0.00)	12 (41.86)	0 (0.00)	26 (60.47)	43 (47.78)			
Above 16	13 (27.08)	23 (47.92)	0 (0.00)	0 (0.00)	0 (0.00)	0 (0.00)	0 (0.00)	14 (29.17)	0 (0.00)	0 (0.00)	1 (2.08)	32 (66.67)	48 (45.28)			
Total	**39 (33.33)**	**45 (38.46)**	**10 (8.55)**	**7 (5.98)**	**12 (10.26**	**9 (7.69)**	**3 (2.56)**	**40 (34.19)**	**8 (6.84)**	**23 (19.66)**	**16 (13.66)**	**71 (60.68)**	**117(45.00)**			
Occupation																
Agriculture	11 (37.93)	7 (24.14)	4 (13.79)	0 (0.00)	2 (6.90)	4 (13.79)	0 (0.00)	11 (37.93)	1 (3.45)	5 (17.24)	5 (17.24)	14 (48.27)	29 (29.90)	33.89	33	0.42
Coolies/wages	17 (32.69)	21 (40.38)	2 (3.85)	6 (11.54)	4 (7.69)	4 (7.69)	0 (0.00)	13 (25.00)	3 (5.77)	11 (21.15)	7 (13.26)	35 (67.31)	52 (58.43)			
Business/ Trade	5 (45.45)	7 (63.64)	2 (18.18)	1 (9.09)	3 (37.27)	1 (9.09)	1 (9.09)	4 (96.36)	2 (18.18)	1 (9.09)	3 (27.27)	6 (54.54)	11 (40.74)			
Employed	6 (24.00)	10 (40.00)	2 (8.00)	0 (0.00)	3 (12.00)	0 (0.00)	2 (8.00)	12 (48.00)	2 (8.00)	6 (24.00)	1 (4.00)	16 (64.00)	25 (53.19)			
Total	**39 (33.33)**	**45 (38.46)**	**10 (8.55)**	**7 (5.98)**	**12 (10.26**	**9 (7.69)**	**3 (2.56)**	**40 (34.19)**	**8 (6.84)**	**23 (19.66)**	**16 (13.66)**	**71 (60.68)**	**117(45.00)**			

(Contd...)

Annual Household Income																
≤ 10,000	13 (34.21)	11 (28.95)	4 (10.53)	2 (5.26)	3 (7.89)	3 (7.89)	0 (0.00)	9 (32.68)	3 (7.89)	5 (13.15)	8 (21.05)	27 (71.05)	38 (38.00)	44.96	66	0.97
10,001-20,000	14 (33.33)	20 (47.62)	3 (7.14)	4 (9.52)	6 (14.29)	5 (11.90)	2 (4.76)	18 (42.86)	1 (2.28)	9 (21.43)	6 (14.29)	24 (57.14)	42 (45.16)			
20,001-30,000	5 (41.67)	3 (25.00)	1 (8.33)	0 (0.00)	1 (8.33)	0 (0.00)	0 (0.00)	3 (25.00)	1 (8.33)	2 (16.67)	0 (0.00)	8 (66.67)	12 (57.14)			
30,001-40,000	1 (25.00)	3 (75.00)	1 (25.00)	0 (0.00)	0 (0.00)	0 (0.00)	0 (0.00)	2 (50.00)	1 (25.00)	2 (50.00)	0 (0.00)	4 (100.00)	4 (40.00)			
40,001-50,000	2 (33.33)	1 (16.67)	0 (0.00)	0 (0.00)	0 (0.00)	0 (0.00)	0 (0.00)	2 (33.33)	1 (16.67)	1 (16.67)	1 (16.67)	1 (16.67)	6 (75.00)			
50,001-60,000	1 (33.33)	0 (0.00)	0 (0.00)	0 (0.00)	0 (0.00)	1 (33.33)	0 (0.00)	2 (66.67)	0 (0.00)	2 (66.67)	0 (0.00)	1 (33.33)	3 (37.50)			
Above 60,001	3 (25.00)	7 (58.33)	1 (8.33)	1 (8.33)	2 (16.67)	0 (0.00)	1 (8.33)	4 (33.33)	1 (8.33)	2 (16.67)	1 (8.33)	6 (50.00)	12 (60.00)			
Total	**39 (33.33)**	**45 (38.46)**	**10 (8.55)**	**7 (5.98)**	**12 (10.26**	**9 (7.69)**	**3 (2.56)**	**40 (34.19)**	**8 (6.84)**	**23 (19.66)**	**16 (13.66)**	**71 (60.68)**	**117(45.00)**			
Medical Expenditure																
≤ 500	17 (38.64)	14 (31.82)	4 (9.09)	4 (9.09)	6 (13.64)	4 (9.09)	0 (0.00)	12 (27.27)	2 (4.55)	5 (11.36)	11 (25.00)	23 (52.27)	44 (38.94)	41.39	55	0.91
501-1000	15 (39.47)	13 (34.21)	3 (7.89)	2 (5.26)	3 (7.89)	4 (10.53)	0 (0.00)	10 (26.31)	3 (7.89)	9 (23.68)	1 (2.63)	26 (68.42)	38 (54.29)			
1001-1500	2 (20.00)	4 (40.00)	1 (10.00)	0 (0.00)	1 (10.00)	1 (10.00)	1 (10.00)	4 (40.00)	1 (10.00)	3 (30.00)	1 (10.00)	7 (70.00)	10 (40.00)			
1501-2000	3 (30.00)	5 (50.00)	1 (10.00)	0 (0.00)	1 (10.00)	0 (0.00)	1 (10.00)	7 (70.00)	1 (10.00)	3 (30.00)	1 (10.00)	6 (60.00)	10 (58.82)			
2001-2500	1 (20.00)	5 (100.00)	0 (0.00)	0 (0.00)	1 (10.00)	0 (0.00)	0 (0.00)	2 (40.00)	0 (0.00)	1 (20.00)	1 (10.00)	4 (80.00)	5 (45.45)			
Above 2501	1 (10.00)	4 (40.00)	1 (10.00)	1 (10.00)	0 (0.00)	0 (0.00)	1 (10.00)	5 (50.00)	1 (10.00)	2 (20.00)	1 (10.00)	5 (50.00)	10 (41.67)			
Total	**39 (33.33)**	**45 (38.46)**	**10 (8.55)**	**7 (5.98)**	**12 (10.26**	**9 (7.69)**	**3 (2.56)**	**40 (34.19)**	**8 (6.84)**	**23 (19.66)**	**16 (13.66)**	**71 (60.68)**	**117(45.00)**			

Out of 260 women assessed, 117 women reported that they have experienced one or more gynecological problems in their reproductive period. White discharge, excess bleeding, irregular period, abdomen pain/backache, urinary tract infection were the major problems reported by the women in the study area. Anemia, itching during menstruation, painful menstruation, foul smelling discharge.

While analysing the women with gynecological morbidities with their socio-economic and demographic background, it can be inferred that out of 260 women probed, 117(45 per cent) women were reported that they have experienced one or more of the problems. White discharge (60.7 per cent), was the major problem reported by a majority of respondents followed by excessive bleeding (38.5 per cent), abdominal pain/backache (34.2 per cent), and irregular menstrual periods (33.3 per cent). Other problems like urinary tract infection (19.7 per cent), Anaemic (13.7 per cent), painful menstruation (8.6 per cent), itching during menstruation (10.3 per cent) and scanty bleeding (7.7 per cent) were also reported by a considerable proportion of women in the study area. The cross-classification of these women the socio-economic and demographic characteristics inferred that a higher proportion of SC/ST women, women belong to nuclear families, and women engaged as coolies/daily wagers reported the problem of white discharge. The Chi-square test analysis shows that respondents' Caste, present age and age at menarche are the variables having significant association with the prevalence of gynecological problems as the $p<0.05$.The other socio-economic and demographic variable are not significantly associated with these gynecological problems.

5.12 Contraceptive Prevalence Among Women and their Socio-economic and Demographic Background

Contraceptive prevalence rate is the percentage of women who are practicing, or whose sexual partners are practicing, any form of contraception. It is usually measured for married women ages 15-49 only. The contraceptive prevalence (percentage of women ages 15-49) in India was reported at 54 in 2008, according to the World Bank. Contraceptive prevalence rate is the percentage of women who are practicing, or whose sexual partners are practicing, any form of contraception. It is usually measured for married women ages 15-49 only. In the study area, information regarding the use of contraceptive methods was collected and correlated with their socio-economic and demographic background. The following table shows the distribution of respondents by their use of contraceptive methods and socio-economic and demographic variables. From the table it is evident that, nearly, 35 per cent of the women in the study area reported that they have practiced any form of contraception.

The cross-classification revealed that, contraceptive prevalence was found to be higher (52.8 per cent) among the women belong to SC/ST than the non-SC/ST (29.9 per cent) women and the difference was statistically significant. The above table shows the number and percentage of current contraceptive usage by the women according to the Type of Family. Current contraceptive prevalence among women of nuclear families was higher (48.6 per cent) than women in joint families (17.8 per cent) and the difference was statistically significant ($p < 0.001$). Contraceptive prevalence was found to increase significantly with increase in present age of the women as the prevalence increased from 5.6 per cent with women of age <19 to 74.5 per cent with women aged 35 years and above ($p < 0.001$). A similar trend in adoption of family planning methods was observed which increased progressively from 21.4 per cent in women with the age at menarche of <12 to 52.2 per cent in women with the age at menarche of 16 years and above.

Table-5.21: Distribution of Respondents by Use of Contraceptive Method and Socio-economic and Demographic Variables

SED/Sub-variables	*No*	*Yes*	*Total*	*Chi-Square*	*df*	*P value*
Religion						
Hindu	165(65.5)	87(32.1)	252(100)	0.030	1	0.862
Christian	5(62.5)	3(37.5)	8(100)			
Total	**170(65.4)**	**90(34.6)**	**260(100)**			
Caste						
SC/ST	25(47.2)	28(52.8)	53(100)	9.75	1	0.002 (S)
Others	145(70.1)	62(29.9)	207(100)			
Total	**170(65.4)**	**90(34.6)**	**260(100)**			

(Contd...)

Family Type						
Nuclear family	73(51.4)	96(48.6)	142(100)	27.003	1	0.0001 (S)
Joint family	97(82.2)	21(17.8)	118(100)			
Total	**170(65.4)**	**90(34.6)**	**260(100)**			
Education						
Illiterate	17(60.7)	11(39.3)	28(100)	12.118	6	0.05 (S)
Primary	45(65.2)	24(34.8)	69(100)			
Middle	31(59.6)	21(40.4)	52(100)			
High school	47(77.0)	14(22.9)	61(100)			
Hr. Secondary	15(83.3)	3(16.7)	18(100)			
Graduate	14(46.7)	16(53.3)	30(100)			
Professional	1(50.0)	1(50.0)	2(100)			
Total	**170(65.3)**	**90(34.6)**	**260(100)**			
Present Age						
≤19	17(94.4)	1(05.6)	18 (100)	85.511	4	0.000 (S)
20-24	78 (96.3)	3(03.7)	81(100)			
25-29	42(64.6)	23(35.4)	65 (100)			
30-34	20(44.4)	25(55.6)	45 (100)			
Above 35	13 (25.5)	38(74.5)	51(100)			
Total	**170(65.4)**	**90(34.6)**	**260(100)**			
Age at Menarche						
≤12	11(78.6)	3(21.4)	14(100)	7.471	4	0.113
13	18(78.3)	5(21.7)	23(100)			
14	21(77.8)	6(22.2)	27(100)			
15	59(65.6)	31(34.4)	90(100)			
Above 16	61(57.6)	45(42.5)	106(100)			
Total	**170(65.4)**	**90(34.6)**	**260(100)**			
Age at Marriage						
≤18	21(53.9)	18(46.2)	39(100)	7.54	3	0.05 (S)
18-20	79(71.8)	31(28.2)	110(100)			
21-23	59(67.5)	29(32.9)	88(100)			
Above 24	11(47.8)	12(52.2)	23(100)			
Total	**170(65.4)**	**90(34.6)**	**260(100)**			
Age at First Birth						
≤20	26(81.3)	6(18.8)	32(100)	7.19	4	0.08
21-22	23(76.7)	7(23.3)	30(100)			
23-24	58(64.4)	32(35.6)	90(100)			

(Contd...)

25-26	28(65.2)	15(34.9)	43(100)			
Above 27	35(53.9)	30(46.2)	65(100)			
Total	**170(65.4)**	**90(34.6)**	**260(100)**			
Children Ever born						
1	46(71.9)	18(28.1)	64(100)	76.77	4	0.001 (S)
2	44(56.4)	34(43.6)	78(100)			
3	42(62.7)	25(37.3)	67(100)			
4	27(81.8)	6(18.2)	33(100)			
Above 5	11(61.1)	7(38.9)	18(100)			
Total	**170(65.4)**	**90(34.6)**	**260(100)**			
Family Size						
1	93 (87.7)	13(12.3)	106(100)	44.55	2	0.001 (S)
2	65 (61.3)	41(38.7)	106(100)			
Above 3	12(25.0)	36(75.0)	48(100)			
Total	**170(65.4)**	**90(34.6)**	**260(100)**			
Occupation						
Agriculture	83(85.6)	14(14.4)	97(100)	32.299	3	0.000 (S)
Coolies/wages	46(51.7)	43(48.3)	89(100)			
Business/Trade	19(70.4)	8 (29.6)	27(100)			
Employed	22(46.8)	25(53.2)	47(100)			
Total	**170(65.4)**	**90(34.6)**	**260(100)**			
Annual Household Income						
≤10,000	78 (78.0)	22(22.0)	100(100)	24.258	6	0.000 (S)
10,001-20,000	58(62.4)	35(37.6)	93(100)			
20,001-30,000	12(57.1)	9(42.9)	21(100)			
30,001-40,000	8(80.0)	2(20.0)	10(100)			
40,001-50,000	4(50.0)	4(50.0)	8(100)			
50,001-60,000	5 (62.5)	3(37.5)	8(100)			
Above 60,001	5(25.0)	15(75.0)	20(100)			
Total	**170(65.4)**	**90(34.6)**	**260(100)**			
Medical Expenditure						
≤500	83(73.5)	30(26.6)	113(100)	17.78	5	0.003 (S)
501-1000	42(60.0)	28(40.0)	70(100)			
1001-1500	12(48.0)	13(52.0)	25(100)			
1501-2000	12(70.6)	5(29.4)	17(100)			
2001-2500	6(54.6)	5(45.5)	11(100)			
Above 2501	15(62.5)	9(37.5)	24(100)			
Total	**170(65.4)**	**90(34.6)**	**260(100)**			

The same trend was also observed in the adoption of contraceptive methods which increased from 18.8 per cent in couples of aged 20 at first birth to 46.2 per cent in women of age 27 years and above.

It is inferred from the above table that regarding Distribution of Respondent's by Use of any contraceptive method across SED variables, the caste, family type, respondent's education, respondent's present age, respondent's age at marriage, child ever born, family size, respondent's annual household income, respondent medical expenditure is significantly associated $p<0.05$. The Religion, age at menarche is not significantly associated with Distribution of Respondent's by Use of any contraceptive method across SED variables $P>0.05$.

Chapter – 6

Summary and Conclusions

The recent years have witnessed major paradigm shifts in the way population and health issues have been conceptualised and articulated. A significant transformation is the inclusion of the concept of reproductive health under the rubric of population policies and programmes which received global endorsement at the International Conference on Population and Development at Cairo. Reproductive health means that people have the ability to reproduce and regulate their fertility; women are able to go through pregnancy and childbirth safely; the outcome of pregnancy is successful in terms of maternal and infant survival and well being; and couples are able to have sexual relations free of the fear of pregnancy (Fathallah, 1988). A reproductive health approach thus demands more than the delivery of maternal and child health and family planning services since it is inextricably bound with individuals', particularly women's, reproductive rights and freedom. According to the World Health Organisation, "Reproductive and sexual ill-health accounts for 20 per cent of the global burden of ill-health for women, and 14 per cent for men and the percentage will increase substantially very high in near future. In order to address women's reproductive health as envisaged under the national programme, it becomes necessary to assess the magnitude of reproductive morbidity among the women across the country. While the studies reviewed earlier have provided valuable insights into women's health and treatment seeking patterns, most of them are in-depth studies and the magnitude of morbidity among various groups of women cannot be ascertained. Thus, data are needed on the varied health problems of women in all regions of the country as well as the magnitude of these problems. It is in these context, the present study has explored the status of reproductive health problems of women through this sample survey in rural areas of a backward district of Tamil Nadu so that data on the prevalence and magnitude of these problems are available to the programme managers for various regions of the country on a periodic basis. It is also felt that such information would help in the development of a suitable package of health services as well as design appropriate training of the grassroots level health workers so as to address women's varied health needs as envisaged under the re-oriented Reproductive and Child Health Programme.

In this regard the present study aims at understanding the varied reproductive health problems of women and their treatment seeking patterns for the management of these problems, in various villages of Cuddalore district of Tamil Nadu.

6.1 Socio-economic and Demographic Profile

The findings of the present study of 300 women to understand their reproductive health status in rural areas of Cuddalore district, across five villages of the district, have important implications for the newly re-oriented Reproductive and Child Health Programme of the country. While interpreting the findings of the study, it is important to bear in mind that the sample of women is drawn from the villages that are socio-economically relatively better developed villages in the district. The magnitude of reproductive health problems, which is large here, may still be on the lower side for rural Tamil Nadu as a whole, since such problems are likely to be much higher in the backward villages of the state.

The background characteristics of the sample women in rural areas confirm that they come from relatively better developed villages of the state. Ninety-six per cent of the respondents were Hindus and a meager of four per cent was belonging to Christians and Muslims. The caste of the respondents has been classified broadly SC/ST and Others as it is study of analysing the Reproductive Health Status of Women in General, the need has not been arise to categorise the women further. Nearly one-fourth of the respondents were belonging to Scheduled Castes and Tribes. In the study area more than two-third of the women belong to nuclear families. Distribution of women on the basis of their household size reveals that 28.0 per cent of the women belongs to households with size four followed by 27.7 per cent of households with size six. Considerable proportions of women (23.7 and 20.8 per cent) were belonging to the households with size 5 and ≤ 3 respectively. The mean household size of the sample area has been calculated as 2.53. It was found that, majority (71.0 per cent) of the respondents was found to be engaged in agriculture and as agricultural labourers followed by (18.7 per cent) women employed in other than agricultural activities. About annual income of the family, 37.3 per cent of the families had annual income below ₹ 10,000. Another 36.0 per cent of the families had income between ₹ 10,000-20,000. 8.3 per cent of the families fall in the category of ₹ 20,000-30,000. The remaining 18.4 per cent of the families had income more than ₹ 30,000. The average Annual Household Income of the families in the study area has been calculated as ₹ 19,133.33.

It can be revealed that the annual household expenditure of 38 per cent of the respondents were ₹ < 10,000. 41 per cent of the family's expenditure was between ₹ 10,000-20,000. Remaining 21 per cent were lie between ₹ 30,001-60,000. The distribution of respondents by their present age shows that nearly 54.0 per cent of the respondents belong to the age group of 20-29 years. The average age of the respondents has been calculated as 26.7 years. Place of birth is an important factor which will determine the reproductive health status of women. The women in the sample area have been distributed according to their place of birth and the distribution shows that 97.0 per cent were rural born respondents. Age at marriage is an important variable because early age at consummation of marriage leads to early child bearing, which is considered as a risk factor for reproductive health of women. The table revealed regarding age at marriage that 13.0 per cent of the married women have got married before the legal age at marriage of 18 years. The mean age at marriage has been calculated as 20.9 years. The distribution of respondents by their educational status revealed that 9.3 per cent of the women in the sample area were illiterate. Nearly 24.0 per cent of the respondents were educated up to primary level of education. Only 22.6 per cent of the respondents have got higher education such as Higher Secondary, Graduation and Professional courses. Distribution of spouses with their age at marriage shows that, a majority (51.2 per cent) of the spouses married at the ages between 25-29 years. The average age at marriage of the spouses has been calculated as 27.1 years. In rural areas of India, most of the parents think that their daughters are ready to start reproductive life as soon as the daughters attain menarche which hinders all the opportunities like education and employment in their life. Hence they will be deprived from these opportunities and face many problems in their future life as they were sent to their husband's house by the parents as soon as they reach menarche. Thus, age at reaching menarche decides her future reproductive life. An examination of the table revealed regarding age at menarche that, higher percentage (55.0 per cent) of respondents reached menarche when they were in the age group of 13-15 years and the mean age at menarche was found to be 14.8 years. Sooner the adolescent become pregnant, higher the complication she has to face during pregnancy and delivery. Most of the studies revealed that most of the married adolescent mothers experienced their first pregnancy and child birth before they reached the age of 18 years. In the sample area, regarding age at first birth, it was found that majority of the respondents (58.46 per cent) had their first birth before 23 years of age. The mean age at first birth was found to be 24.1 years in the sample area. The results of the distribution of respondents by their age at last birth were that a higher percentage (36.5 per cent) of women had their last birth between 25-29 years. But a considerable (30 per cent) proportion of women had their last birth only after the age of 30 years. The number of living children is an important demographic variable influencing the reproductive health and acceptance of contraceptive methods of women. The average number of living children of women in the sample area was found to be 1.5. Majority (53.46 per cent) of the respondents in the sample area had only one living children. The analysis of children ever born also shows that more than 56.0 per cent of the respondents had only one ever born child. A small percentage (3.84 per cent) of women had more than 4 ever born children. The average number of children ever born in the sample area has been found to be 1.6.

6.2 Reproductive Health Problems of Women before Marriage

Out of 300 women assessed, 195(65 per cent) reported reproductive health problems during their premarital stage. Among the 195 respondents who have experienced problems, more than two-third of women had reported abdominal pain and leg pain and back pain. Profuse bleeding was also a common problem experienced by 60 per cent of the women. White discharge, irregular periods and vomiting sensation were also the problems of 50 per cent of the women. only 62(32 per cent) women sought care for their problems with a majority (64.5 per cent) using private providers followed by (19.35 per cent) government providers. 16.13 per cent of women in the sample area still sought locally available traditional medicines for their illness. The average duration of treatment taken for their problems has been calculated as 2.03 days. Hence, women's reproductive health seeking behaviour appears far from optimum. Future intention for home delivery and unskilled child birth was highly indicated. Inadequate awareness and decision-making were obvious. Effective measures need to be considered at the community and health sector level.

6.3 Problems during Pregnancy and Health Care Seeking Behaviour

It was noted that majority 253 (97.3 per cent) of the women were reported to have at least one health problem related directly or indirectly to their pregnancy in the preceding three months of their antenatal period. The important morbidities reported were swelling of feet and face 200 (79 per cent), White discharge 132 (50.6 per cent), Paleness/ Anaemia120 (47.4 per cent), Nausea/Vomiting 101 (39.9 per cent) and pregnancy-induced hypertension 60 (23.7 per cent). Other morbidities included morning sickness 68 (26.1 per cent), fever 36 (13.9 per cent), diarrhoea 7 (2.5 per cent), vaginal bleeding 4 (1.5 per cent) and urinary tract infections 29 (11.1 per cent). The average duration of illness has been calculated as 3.6 days. The above discussion shows high prevalence of problems among women in the study area during prenatal period. These results are in line with the studies conducted by various researchers in India as well as in many countries. About 48.9 per cent of the mothers visited private health facilities during illness, while

34.1 per cent visited government general hospital. But a considerable proportion of women (16.8 per cent) sought still traditional practices of healthcare.

6.4 Antenatal Health Care Check Up

The percentages of mothers seeking antenatal healthcare consultation for the first time in less than two, three, four and five months were 16.15, 38.08, 7.30 and 38.47 respectively. The most mentioned places of latest consultation were the private hospital (75.8 per cent) followed by government clinics. In the present study, only 54 per cent of the mothers sought antenatal healthcare checkup in first trimester which is lower than the NFHS-3 data of 75 per cent for the state of Tamil Nadu. The tetanus toxoid immunisation coverage of 94.23 per cent and regular intake of iron-foliate tablets of 90.38 per cent, were more or less similar to NFHS-3 data for Tamil Nadu. With regard to healthcare advices received by the mothers in the sample area, 61.0 per cent of the women reported that they have received advices relating to nutrition and nearly 70.0 per cent of them reported that they have received some sort of advices relating to Family Planning. More than 70.0 per cent of the mothers in the sample area reported that they have taken green leafy vegetables, milk and fruits as special food items during pregnancy.

6.5 Reproductive Health Problems during Delivery and Within Seven Days of Delivery

It was found in the present study that, more than half (51.2 per cent) of the respondents faced problems in this period. Among them majority (53.4 per cent) faced problems of Malpresentation. Rupture of Membrane was also a problem faced by 46.6 per cent of the respondents. Excessive bleeding and prolonged labour after delivery were the other problems reported by a considerable proportion of respondents. Episiotomy/Perineal tear and Retained Placenta were also the problems reported by some of the respondents. Regarding place of delivery in the present study majority (54.2 per cent) of respondents were found to have delivered at private hospitals. Nearly 40.0 per cent of the respondents delivered children at government hospitals. Interestingly, 5.4 per cent of the women in the sample area were still found to have delivered at home. Among these respondents, majority were assisted by their family members during their deliveries. As such, it was natural for some of the respondents in the sample area, to have suffered complications during child birth. In this context, women in the sample area were likely to be exposed to unhygienic delivery, which lead to the risk of morbidity and mortality of mother and child during and after the childbirth. The mothers were classified according to their type of last delivery. This classification shows that nearly 79 per cent of the mothers delivered normally their children. Around 12 per cent of them had Caesarean section type of births. Among 260 women assessed, more than one-fourth (25.4 per cent) of them reported that they had some complications during the time of delivery. Out of 66 women with delivery complications, prolonged labour was the major complication experienced by 55 women (83.3 per cent). Excessive bleeding and delayed delivery of placenta were also the problems reported by a considerable proportion of women in the sample area. The classification of women with the weight of their last child at the time of delivery shows that, the weight of the children at the time of delivery was below 2.5 kilograms for more than one-fourth of the mothers in the study area. But the average weight of the children during delivery in the study area has been calculated as 2.85 kilograms.

More than one-fourth of the respondents faced problems of excessive bleeding during this period, nearly one-fourth of the respondents reported that they have experienced lower abdomen pain and foul smelling discharge was also a problem during this period and the other problems reported by a considerable proportion of respondents. All these problems were due to the improper or lack of treatment and care during pre and perinatal periods. The duration of illness ranges 1 day to more than 10 days. The average duration of these problems has been calculated as 6.4 days. Regarding treatment taken for these problems, among 185 women had problems during this period only 143(77.3 per cent) women sought treatment. The remaining 42(22.7 per cent) women did not seek any treatment for their problems. While probing about the general medical check up after delivery, 81 per cent of the women had general medical check up after delivery. The remaining 35 women (19.0 per cent) did not go for any postnatal checks up. Poor quality of medicines, non-cordial behaviour of the health personnel and unsuitable timings were the reasons reported by the respondents for their non-utilisation of healthcare services. Poor quality of medicines resulted in poor recovery and dissatisfaction among the respondents, which lead to subsequent non-utilisation of the facility. Regarding place of postnatal care services, in the present study majority of respondents (68.5 per cent) were found to have sought healthcare at private hospitals. Only 28.5 per cent of the respondents sought postnatal healthcare services from government facilities. With regard to breast feeding, 191 women (73.5 per cent) were breast feed their children within three hours of delivery. The other 26.5 per cent of the women in the sample area breast feed their children only after 3 hours and some respondents breast feed their children even after 12 hours of delivery. During this period, the children were given plain water or water mixed with sugar/ honey. The analysis of distribution of mothers with their duration of breast feeding shows that, nearly 24.6 per cent of the mothers in the sample area breast feed their children only up to 12 months. Nearly half of the women (48.9 per cent) in the study area breast feed their children up to 18 months. Only 26.5 per cent of women breast feed more than 19 months. The average duration of breast feeding of the mothers in the sample area has been calculated as 15.3 months. Women in the sample area reported reasons for the stoppage of breast feeding as became pregnant (26.9 per cent), outdoor work (21.5 per cent), wearing age (20.8 per cent), Child refused (16.2 per cent) and insufficient milk (14.6 per cent). Breast problem, Mother's sickness, Use of contraception were also the reasons reported by a considerable size of women in the sample area.

6.6 General Gynecological Problems

Out of 260 respondents, 45 per cent (117) of the women reported that they had one or the other gynecological problems. Menstrual problems constitute one class of gynecological problems. Nearly one third of the total women reported that they had irregular periods of menstruation. Painful menstruation was also a problem reported by 8.6 per cent of the women. White discharge (60.7 per cent), Lower abdominal pain/Backache (34.2 per cent), Anaemia (13.7 per cent),

Excessive bleeding (38.5 per cent), Itching during menstruation (10.3 per cent), Foul smelling discharge (6.0 per cent), Burning and frequent urination (19.7 per cent), were the other problems reported by the respondents. Prolepses problems, Passes clots and scanty bleeding were also some of the problems reported by a considerable proportion of the respondents. Regarding duration of the gynecological problems of the women in the study area, nearly 30.0 per cent of the women reported that the duration of their problems last long for more than 13 days. 43.1 per cent of the women reported that their illness duration last long for 7-12 days. The average duration of illness has been calculated as 9.4 days. Among 117 women with gynecological problems, 63.0 per cent of women did not seek any healthcare for their problems. Negligence, Laziness, Not serious problem, not get time were the reasons reported by the respondents for not taking any healthcare for the gynecological problems.

6.7 Reproductive Health Problems of Women before Marriage and Socio-economic and Demographic Background

Women suffered by these problems were cross-classified with their socio-economic and demographic characteristics and the inferences are as follows. As far as the religion is concerned, nearly 65 per cent of the respondents belong to Hindu Religion were suffered by many of the reproductive health problems before their marriage. The percentage of women suffered by these problems among scheduled castes women (79.7 per cent) is higher than that of the women belong to other castes (60.2 per cent). It is also inferred that there is no significant variation among the percentages of women belong to Nuclear and Joint family suffered by reproductive health problems before their marriage. Surprisingly, the prevalence of problems was higher among the women with higher education than the women with relatively lower education and illiterates. While examining the women reported reproductive health problems with their present age, it was found that, more than 45 per cent of the women who suffered reproductive health problems were in the age group of less than 24 years. The age group wise analysis of the women who suffered one or more reproductive health problems revealed that higher percentage

(70 per cent) of the women in the age group of 25-29 years reported reproductive health problems than the women in the other age groups. The analysis shows that there is no significant association between the occupational status of the respondents and the prevalence of reproductive health problems. As most of the respondents belong to the income category of less than ₹20,000 per annum, the women suffered reproductive health problems were also high among the women belong to low income category of less than ₹20,000.The medical expenses per annum of the family has been cross-classified with the prevalence of reproductive health problems among women. It was also found to be that more than 63.3 per cent of the women spending lesser amount of money as their medical expenses reported reproductive health problems. The percentages of women in the higher income and higher medical expenses categories were less in number it is not meaningful to corroborate these variables with the women reported reproductive health problems before their marriage.

While the reproductive health problems of the women before marriage were cross-classified with the socio-economic and demographic variables, it can be inferred that there was no significant association between religion, caste, and their socio-economic and demographic variables. But the family type is significantly associated with the health problems before marriage ($p<0.05$). The annual house hold income, is significantly associated ($p>0.05$) whereas, the other variables like education, age, age at menarche, occupation, medical expenses have no significant association ($p>0.05$).

It is inferred from the above table that, regarding place of treatment before marriage, the Chi-square result proves that there is no association between the religion, caste, family type, respondent's present age, respondent's education and age at menarche are not significant ($P>0.05$). But the occupation alone is significantly associated with the place of treatment before marriage ($P<0.05$), whereas the other variables the child ever born, family size, respondents age at marriage, age at first birth, respondent's annual household income and respondent's expenditure on medical are not significantly associated ($P>0.05$).

6.8 Reproductive Health Problems of Women during Pregnancy and Socio-economic and Demographic Variables

The percentage of women reported reproductive health problems during pregnancy and their socio-economic and demographic background. Religion, Caste, Family type, educational status, present age, age at marriage, age at menarche, age at first birth, children ever born, family size, occupation, household annual income and annual medical expenditure are the variables correlated with the women reported reproductive health problems during their pregnancy. The above discussion reveals that, out of 260 married women, 97.3 per cent of them reported one or more reproductive health problems during their pregnancy. While cross-classifying the women reported reproductive health problems with their background characteristics, it was found that there is no significant relation between the variables and women with reproductive health problems.

While considering the religion, the Chi-square result proves that there is no association between religion of the respondent and their health problems. Similarly the caste, family type, respondent's education, present age, age at menarche, age at marriage and age at first birth are not significant. Further children ever born, family size, occupation, annual income and expenditure on medical are not significant. Since all the calculated Chi-square values are not significant ($P>0.05$).

Out of 253 women reported reproductive health problems in the study area, 185(73.1 per cent) and 128(50.5 per cent) women reported that they have suffered by the problem of Swelling of Feet/Face and White discharge respectively. The analysis of women reported problem of swelling of feet/face and their socio-economic and demographic characteristics revealed that majority of women reported swelling of feet/face were belong to non-SC/ST, nuclear family, women belong to higher age, women with higher age at menarche, women with higher age at first birth, women with lower number of children ever born, women with lower family size, women occupied in agriculture and as coolies/daily wagers, women in the families of lower income groups and spent less money for their medical expenditures. The second reproductive health problem reported by more number of women was white discharge during their pregnancy. More than 50.5 per cent of the women reported that they have experienced this problem during their pregnancy period. While these women were cross-classified with their socio-economic and demographic characteristics, the analysis shows that the same trend has been inferred as in the case of swelling of feet/face. As far as the educational status is concerned, it has no significant relation with the percentage of women reported reproductive health problems. The overall discussion of the above table reveals that the percentage of women reported reproductive health problems were higher among the women belong to the categories of non-SC/ST, nuclear family, higher age group, higher menarcheal age, higher age at first birth, agriculture and coolies/daily wagers, families of low income groups and spending less money for their medical expenses irrespective of the problems. Hence special efforts should be made to safeguard the women in these categories in order to prevent them from contracting these reproductive health problems.

It is inferred from the above table that regarding any health problems during pregnancy on the basis of all yes variables, the caste, Age at first birth is associated $P<0.05$. The annual house hold income, is not significantly associated ($P>0.05$). Also the other variables religion, education, age, age at menarche, family size, Children born ever, occupation, medical expenses are no significant association $P>0.05$.

6.9 Place of Healthcare Treatment after Marriage

Out of 53 SC/ST women, more than 52 per cent of them sought healthcare from the government health facilities such as government hospitals and primary health centres in the study area. Whereas the family type is concerned, there is no significant relation between the family type and the place of healthcare treatment. Surprisingly, the women sought healthcare treatment for their health problems from private health facilities were higher than the women sought healthcare treatment irrespective of their educational status. Present age of the women is also an important variable to be taken into consideration while assessing the reproductive health status and treatment seeking behaviour. In the study area, higher percentage of women in the higher age groups sought healthcare from government health facilities. Women with younger ages prefer private health facility for their health problems. Hence, there is an urgent need to create an awareness among young women about health services rendered by the government health facilities at free and low cost and the quality of healthcare services of the government healthcare facilities have to be improved so as to enable the young rural women to make use of the healthcare services. The age at menarche of the respondents in the study area has also been cross-classified with the place of treatment sought by them. The analysis shows that, there is no significant association between the age at menarche of the respondents and the place of healthcare treatment. The same trend can also be inferred while analysing the age at marriage with the place of healthcare treatment of the women in the sample area. The percentage of women sought healthcare treatment from private healthcare facility has increased with their age at first birth. Hence, it can be inferred that a positive association is exist between the ages at first birth and the percentage of women sought healthcare treatment in private health facility.

Among the women sought healthcare treatment in private health facility, the women with lesser number of children ever born were higher in proportion than women with higher number of ever born children. The percentage of women seeking healthcare treatment from private health facility is decreasing with the increase in the family size. Hence, an indirect association is being exists between the family size and the number of women sought healthcare treatment from private healthcare facility. The higher cost for medical treatment in private health facilities is the major reason for the decrease in the treatment seekers from the private health facilities. Hence, stringent efforts should be taken to streamline the fees collected by the private health facilities and reformative measures should also be accelerated to enrich the quality as well as quantity of the healthcare services rendered by the government health facilities. Surprisingly, higher percentage of women engaged in agricultural occupation and engaged as coolies/daily wagers sought private health facility than government health facilities for their reproductive health problems. Higher percentage of women from the families of higher income groups sought healthcare treatment from the private health facility than the women in the lower income group families. Similarly the higher percentage of women in the families spending more money for their medical expenditure sought healthcare from private healthcare facilities. Higher the money spent on medical expenses higher the percentage of women sought medical care from private health facility.

It is inferred from the above table that regarding any health problems during pregnancy on the basis of all yes variables, the caste, age at first birth is associated P<0.05. The annual house hold income, is not significantly associated (P>0.05). Also the other variables religion, education, age, age at menarche, Family size, children born ever, occupation, medical expenses are no significant association P>0.05.

6.10 Antenatal Care and Background Characteristics

The average number of antenatal checks up was lower for the women belong to the category of SC/ST, joint families, illiterate and lower educational status, with lower age groups and low age at menarche, women with low age at first birth, women with higher family size, and the families of low income groups than their counterparts. It is inferred from the analysis, regarding Times of ANC, the Chi-square result proves that there is no association between the religion, caste, family type, respondent's present age and respondent's education are not significant (P>0.05). But the age at menarche, age at first birth is significantly associated with the Times of ANC (P<0.05). Also the child ever born, family size, occupation are significantly associated (P<0.05), whereas the other variables respondents age at marriage, respondent's annual household income and respondent's expenditure on medical are also not significantly associated (P>0.05).

6.11 TT Injection and IFA Supplements Received and Background Characteristics

In the study area, more than 90 per cent of the women received TT injection and IFA supplements. More than 94 per cent of the women received TT injection irrespective of their caste category. While analysing percentage of women received TT injection and IFA supplementary with their family type, it can be found that there was no significant association between these two variables. Interestingly, even educational status of the women in the study area does not have any bearing on the number of women received TT injection and IFA tablets.

The percentage of illiterate women received TT injection and IFA tablets was higher than the women with higher educational status. It can also be inferred that the percentage of women received TT injection and IFA supplements is increases with the present age of the women in the study area. Hence, there is a direct association between the present age and the percentage of women received these vaccines and supplements. The same trend is prevailing while analysing the age at menarche of the women and the percentage of women received TT injections and IFA supplements. The analysis of women received TT injection and IFA supplements with their age at marriage shows that, the percentages of women with lower age at marriage (below 18 years) and higher age at marriage (24+ years) received TT injection were lower than the women with age at marriage of 18-23 years. Whereas in receiving the IFA supplements, the percentage women increase with the increase in the age at marriage. The same trend can also be found that the percentage of women received TT injection and IFA supplements increase with their age at first birth. The family size of the respondents has an inverse relation with the percentage of women received IFA supplements. Lower the family size higher the percentage of women received IFA supplements. The percentage of women received TT injection and IFA supplements were lower among the women engaged in agricultural occupation and as daily wagers than the women engaged in other occupations. The percentages of women received TT injection and IFA supplementary were high among all the women in the study area irrespective of their annual household income and the amount spent for medical expenses. Though the overall percentage of women received TT injection and IFA supplementary were high, there were some special groups like higher educational status, lower age group women, women with lower age at menarche, women with lower and higher age at marriages, women with lower age at first birth and women with higher family size need to be taken special care in order to achieve an equity in receiving TT injection and IFA supplementary.

6.12 Health Advices Received During Antenatal Visits

Only 51 per cent-72 per cent of the pregnant women were advised on at least one of the components. Moreover, socioeconomic inequalities in providing advice were significant and the provision of advice concentrated disproportionately among the rich. Inequalities were highest in the case of advice on family planning methods. Advice on breastfeeding was least unequal. Public health workers working in lower level health facilities were significantly less likely than their counterparts in the higher level health facilities to provide specific advice. A significant proportion of women were not advised on recommended components of maternal and child health in rural India. Moreover, there were enormous socioeconomic inequalities. The findings of this study raise questions about the capacity of the public healthcare system in providing equitable services in India. The Government of India must focus on training and capacity building of the public health workers in communication skills so that they can deliver appropriate and recommended advice to all clients, irrespective of their socioeconomic status.

Women belong to SC/ST were less provided (66.04 per cent) about nutrition advices than other category women (81.16 per cent). But the advices provided regarding family planning to SC/ST and other category women were equal. The percentage of women belong to joint families received advice regarding nutrition and healthcare measures to be taken during pregnancy was higher than the women belong to nuclear families. In contrary, the family planning advice was provided to higher percentage of women belong to nuclear families than the joint families. The health personal in the health facilities have some fear over the elders in the joint families to provide family planning advices. While educational status of the respondents correlated with the health advices received, it can be inferred that, higher proportion of women with higher education received health advices than the women with less educated and illiterates. Similarly, the women with higher education were not provided advice regarding family planning by the health workers. This may be because of the fear over the educated women. Only 50-56 per cent of the educated women were provided advices relating to family planning. At the same time higher proportion of younger age women were provided advices regarding to nutrition and family planning. Equal proportion of women in the study area received advice relating to healthcare to be taken during pregnancy irrespective of their age group. It can also be inferred that there was no significant relationship between the age at menarche of the women and the health advices received. The age at marriage of the respondents is an important variable to be correlated with the percentage of women received healthcare advices. In the study area, lesser proportion of women with low age at marriage received nutrition and family planning advices than the women with higher age at marriage. Higher the age at marriage higher the percentage of women received health advices during antenatal period. The proportion of women received healthcare advices decreases with the increase in the family size. At the same time, the proportion of women received family planning advice increases with the family size. Higher percentage of employed women and women engaged in business were received advices regarding nutrition and antenatal healthcare measures than the women occupied in agriculture and as daily wagers. At the same time, the family planning advice provided to lesser proportion of employed women (59.57 per cent) than the women engaged in agriculture and as daily wagers (73.20 per cent). Similarly, lesser proportion of women in the higher income group and the women belong to the families spent more on medical expenses were provided advices relating to family planning. Hence, the above discussion reveals that, a significant proportion of women were not advised on recommended components of maternal and child health in the study area. Moreover, there were enormous socioeconomic inequalities. The findings of this study raise questions about the capacity of the public healthcare system in providing equitable services. The government must focus on training and capacity building of the public health workers in communication skills so that they can deliver appropriate and recommended advice to all clients, irrespective of their socioeconomic status.

It is also inferred that milk, green leafy vegetables and fruits were the special foods taken by the mothers in the study area. Though 74 per cent of the respondents reported that they took milk as special food during pregnancy, only 52.8 per cent of the women belong to SC/ST reported that they have taken milk during pregnancy. Further, only a lesser proportion of women with low age at menarche (50 per cent), low age at marriage (66.7 per cent) were taken milk during pregnancy compared with the women belong to higher age at menarche and higher age at marriage. Only 64.04 percentage of the respondents engaged as coolies/wagers have taken milk during pregnancy. Green leafy vegetables were consumed by majority of the respondents irrespective of the socio-economic and demographic background as it was easily available at low cost in the study area. As far as the fruits are concerned, though, more than 73 per cent of the respondents in general took more fruits during pregnancy, the percentages of women took fruits belong to lower (<24 years) and higher age groups (35+ years), women with higher number of ever born children, women with higher family size and women belong to the occupation of agriculture were lesser compared with their counterparts. Hence, the above discussion shows that there was a significant association between the socio-economic and demographic background and the special food taken during pregnancy.

6.13 Prevalence of Reproductive Health Problems During Delivery

While the caste is correlated with the prevalence of reproductive health problems, interestingly lower proportion of women reported reproductive health problems than the women belong to other category. Similarly, higher percentage of women reported reproductive health problems were belong to nuclear families, higher educated women, women of higher age groups, women with higher age at menarche, women with higher number of children ever born, women with higher family size, women engaged in agricultural occupation and as coolies/ daily wages, women with lower household income, and the women belong to the families spent lesser amount for their medical expenses. A lower proportion of women among illiterates reported reproductive health problems than other higher educated women. The overall discussion of the above table shows that there were some socio-economic inequalities exist in the prevalence of reproductive health problems among the women in the study area.

It is inferred from the analysis that, regarding problems at the time of delivery, the Chi-square result proves that there was no association between religion, caste, family type, respondent's present age, respondent's education and age at menarche were not significant ($P>0.05$) with socio-economic and demographic background. But the age at first birth, children ever born was significantly associated with the problems at the time of delivery ($P<0.05$), whereas the other variables like, respondent's age at marriage, family size, occupation, respondent's annual household income and respondent's expenditure on medical were also not significantly associated ($P>0.05$).

It shows that, higher percentage of women belong to joint family, higher age group women, women with higher age at menarche, women with higher age at first birth, higher number of children ever born, and higher family size, were reported the problem of foetal malpresentation. The analysis also shows that there was no significant association between the variables such as caste, educational status, age at marriage, occupation, household income and money spent for medical expenses.

While analysing the prevalence of the problem of excessive bleeding during delivery with the socio-economic and demographic characteristics of the women in the study area, higher proportion of women belong to other than SC/ST, nuclear family, married below the age of 18 years, women with higher number of children ever born, and higher family size reported the problem of excessive bleeding during delivery. The analysis also shows that there was no significant association between the variables such as, educational status, age at menarche, age at first birth, occupation, household income and money spent for medical expenses. As far as the other diseases such as prolonged labour, Episiotomy/Perineal tears and retained placenta were concerned the same trend has been witnessed.

It is inferred from the statistical analysis, regarding at the time of delivery, the variables like, religion, caste, family type, respondent's education, respondent's present age, age at menarche, age at first birth, age at marriage, family size, occupation, expenditure on medical, are not significantly associated with the problems during delivery as the calculated value $p>0.05$. The Respondent's annual household income and the number of children ever born and family type are significantly associated with the problems during delivery (P<0.05).

6.14 Place of Delivery

Irrespective of the socio-economic and demographic background of the mothers in the study area, nearly 5.4 per cent of the respondents delivered their babies in their home itself. More than 54 per cent of the respondents accessing private hospitals, nearly 40 per cent of the respondents accessing government health facilities for delivery, and a meager of 0.8 per cent of the respondents delivered in maternity homes. Though the number of respondents delivered children in their homes (14), the higher percentages were among nuclear families, belong to SC/ST, Illiterate women, higher age group women (35+ years), women with higher number of children ever born, women with higher family size and women of the families spending less amount for their medical expenses.

It is inferred from the analysis that, regarding place of delivery the Chi-square result proves that there is no association between the religion, respondent's education, respondent's present age and age at menarche are not significant (P>0.05). But the caste, family type, respondent's annual household income is significantly associated with the place of delivery (P<0.05). Also the child ever born, family size, occupation are significantly associated (P<0.05), whereas the other variables respondents age at marriage, age at first birth, and respondent's expenditure on medical are also not significantly associated (P>0.05).

6.15 Reproductive Health Problems During Post Partum Period

The percentage of women experienced problems in this period was higher among the women belong to other than SC/ST, nuclear families, higher age group, higher menarcheal age group, higher age at first birth, women with lower number of children ever born, lower family size and women with higher income groups. The analysis further shows that there was no significant association between religion, educational status, and age at marriage.

It is also proved statistically that the Chi-square analysis shows the variables like religion, caste, family type, respondent's education, respondent's present age, respondent's age at marriage, children ever born, is are not significantly associated with the problems during post-partum period as $p>0.05$. The age at menarche, age at first birth, family size, respondent's annual household income, respondent medical expenditure, occupation are significantly associated with the prevalence of problems immediately after delivery as $p<0.05$.

The analysis of socio-economic and demographic variables with the problems during postpartum period shows that, majority of the respondents (60.1 per cent) respondents reported that they have experienced the problem of lower abdominal pain during their post-natal period. Excessive bleeding was also a problem reported by 47.6 per cent of the respondents. Fever, fainted for more than 15 minutes, foul smelling discharge and pus formation were the other problems faced by a considerable proportion of the respondents in the study area. The percentage of women experienced lower abdominal pain during their postpartum period was higher among the women belong to the category of non-SC/ST, joint families, illiterates, mothers of lower ages, mothers of low age at menarche, mothers of higher number of children ever born, mothers of lower family size, and mothers engaged in agriculture occupation. While analysing the second highest reported problem of heavy bleeding after birth with the socio-economic and demographic back ground, it is inferred that, women belong to SC/ST, nuclear families, higher educated women, higher age group, women with higher ages at first birth, and women spending higher amount for medical expenses. The other variables like, religion, age at marriage, children ever born, family size, and income were not significantly associated with the prevalence of the problems.

The association between the background characteristics of the women and the problems faced during postpartum period has also been proved that religion, caste, family type, respondent's education, respondent's present age, respondent's age at marriage, children ever born are not significantly associated $p>0.05$. The age at menarche, age at first birth, occupation family size, respondent's annual household income, respondent's medical expenditure, are significantly associated with the problems during postpartum period as the calculated value $P<0.05$.

The percentage of women taken treatment were high among the women belong to non-SC/ST, joint families, higher educated, higher age groups, higher age at marriage, higher age at first birth, and women employed with other than agricultural activities. The other variables such as religion, age at menarche, children ever born, family size, annual income and amount spent for medical expenses were not associated with the percentage of women taken treatment for their problems during post-partum period.

The Chi-square test values of the analysis of background characteristics and the treatment taken for the problems during post-partum period shows that except family of the respondents other variables such as, the religion, caste, respondent's education, respondent's present age, respondent's age at marriage, age at menarche, age at first birth, children ever born, family size, occupation, respondent's annual household income, and respondent's medical expenditure, are not significantly associated ($p>0.05$). The family type is significantly associated with treatment taking behaviour of the respondents as $P<0.05$.

Health programmes should invest to ensure that all women receive early postpartum visits after delivery at home and after discharge from institution to detect and manage maternal morbidity. Further, health programmes should also ensure that women are properly screened for complications before their discharge from hospitals after delivery.

6.16 Post Natal Care Treatment

While analysing the mothers who took postnatal care with their socio-economic and demographic background, it can be inferred that the percentage of mothers took postnatal care was higher among the mothers belong to joint families, with low age at menarche, low age at first birth, lesser number of children ever born, higher family size, of agriculture occupation and coolies/daily wagers, and spending more money for their medical expenses. The variables like religion, caste, educational status, present age, age at marriage were not significantly associated with the women took postnatal care.

The above table shows the details about medical check up after delivery. Considering the religion, the Chi-square result proves that there is no association between religion of the respondent and their complication. Similarly the caste, respondent's education, age at first birth, age at menarche, age at marriage, family size, expenditure on medical, occupation and annual income are not significant. Since the calculated Chi-square values are not significant ($P>0.05$). Further, the Chi-square result proves that there is association between family type, children ever born, and respondent's present age are significant. Since the calculated Chi-square values are significant ($P<0.05$).

6.17 Place of Post Natal Care

The above table shows that 68.5 per cent of the 260 women assessed, received post natalcare services from private hospitals. Only 28.5 per cent of the respondents received postnatal care services from government health facilities. Only 3.0 per cent of the respondents received postnatal care services from the health workers during their home visits. The percentage of women received postnatal care services from government health facility were higher among the women belong to SC/ST, higher age group, higher age at menarche, lower age at marriage, higher age at first birth, higher number of children ever born, and women engaged as coolies/daily wagers. While the women received postnatal care services from private hospitals were cross-classified with their socio-economic and demographic characteristics, the analysis showed that women belong to non-SC/ST, joint families, lower age group women, lower age at menarche, higher age at marriage, women with lower age at first birth, and women with fewer number of children ever born were higher in percentage than their counterparts.

It is inferred from the analysis that, the Chi-square results prove that there is no association between the religion, respondent's education and age at menarche with the percentage of women received postnatal care services as the calculated value of ($P>0.05$). But the caste, family type, respondent's present age are significantly associated with the percentage of women received postpartum care services ($P<0.05$). The variables like the number of children ever born, family size, occupation are also significantly associated

(P<0.05), whereas the other variables respondents age at marriage, age at first birth, respondent's annual household income and respondent's expenditure on medical care are not significantly associated (P>0.05). The findings suggest the need for strengthening PNC services to keep pace with advances in coverage for care at birth and prenatal services in India through targeted policy interventions.

6.18 Gynecological Problems

The prevalence of gynecological problems were high among the mothers belong to SC/ST, nuclear families, higher age group, higher age at menarche, low age at marriage, and higher family size. The characteristics like religion, education of the respondents, age at first birth of the mother, children ever born, household income and household expenditure on medical care were not significantly associated with the prevalence of gynecological morbidity. The percentage of women reported gynecological morbidity was higher among the mothers engaged as coolies/daily wagers.

While analysing the women with gynecological morbidities with their socio-economic and demographic background, it can be inferred that out of 260 women probed, 117(45 per cent) women were reported that they have experienced one or more of the problems. White discharge (60.7 per cent), was the major problem reported by a majority of respondents followed by excessive bleeding (38.5 per cent), Abdominal pain/backache (34.2 per cent), and irregular menstrual periods (33.3 per cent). Other problems like urinary tract infection (19.7 per cent), Anaemic (13.7 per cent), painful menstruation (8.6 per cent), itching during menstruation (10.3 per cent) and scanty bleeding (7.7 per cent) were also reported by a considerable proportion of women in the study area. The cross classification of these women the socio-economic and demographic characteristics inferred that a higher proportion of SC/ST women, women belong to nuclear families, and women engaged as coolies/daily wagers reported the problem of white discharge. The Chi-square test analysis shows that respondents' caste, present age and age at menarche are the variables having significant association with the prevalence of gynecological problems as the p<0.05. The other socio-economic and demographic variable are not significantly associated with these gynecological problems.

6.19 Contraceptive Prevalence

Contraceptive prevalence was found to be higher (52.8 per cent) among the women belong to SC/ST than the non-SC/ST (29.9 per cent) women and the difference was statistically significant. The above table shows the number and percentage of current contraceptive usage by the women according to the type of family. Current contraceptive prevalence among women of nuclear families was higher (48.6 per cent) than women in joint families (17.8 per cent) and the difference was statistically significant ($p<0.001$). Contraceptive prevalence was found to increase significantly with increase in present age of the women as the prevalence increased from 5.6 per cent with women of age <19 to 74.5 per cent with women aged 35 years and above ($p < 0.001$). A similar trend in adoption of family planning methods was observed which increased progressively from 21.4 per cent in women with the age at menarche of $\leq$12 to 52.2 per cent in women with the age at menarche of 16 years and above.

Regarding reproductive health problems unrelated to maternity, it was found that most of the respondents complained about menstrual problems. These imply the prevalence of menstrual problems and negligence regarding hygiene and sanitation. Hence, ill effects of this problem have to be explained to the respondents to seek medical treatment in the initial stage itself.

Regarding utilisation of government health services, it was found that, majority of the respondents failed to utilise the government health services effectively. The results indicate the need to make respondents aware about the advantages of utilising government health services.

6.20 Policy Suggestions

Women's reproductive healthcare seeking behaviour during premarital stage appears far from optimum. Future intention for home delivery and unskilled child birth was highly indicated. Inadequate awareness and decision-making were obvious. Effective measures need to be considered at the community and health sector level to enhance the awareness and increase the utilisation of healthcare services.

Awareness campaigns for menstrual hygiene along with an active participation from these women themselves, in voicing their problems and solving them mutually with women community action, is the immediate need of the hour.

In the study area, higher percentage of women in the higher age groups sought healthcare from Government health facilities. Women with younger ages prefer private health facility for their health problems. Hence, there is an urgent need to create an awareness among young women about health services rendered by the government health facilities at free and low cost and the quality of healthcare services of the government healthcare facilities have to be improved so as to enable the young rural women to make use of the healthcare services.

The higher cost for medical treatment in private health facilities is the major reason for the decrease in the treatment seekers from the private health facilities. Hence, stringent efforts should be taken to streamline the fees collected by the private health facilities and reformative measures should also be accelerated to enrich the quality as well as quantity of the healthcare services rendered by the government health facilities.

Though the overall percentage of women received TT injection and IFA supplementary were high, there were some special groups like higher educational status, lower age group women, women with lower age at menarche, women with lower and higher age at marriages, women with lower age at first birth and women with higher family size need to be taken special care in order to achieve an equity in receiving TT injection and IFA supplementary.

In the study area, the family planning advices were provided to higher percentage of women belongs to nuclear families than the joint families. The health personal in the health facilities have some fear over the elders in the joint families to provide family planning advices. Similarly, the women with higher education were not provided advice regarding family planning by the health workers. This may be because of the fear over the educated women. Only 50-56 per cent of the educated women were provided advices relating to family planning. Hence the health personnel were advised to provide information relating to family planning and other aspects of reproductive health without any biasness irrespective of the socio-economic and demographic background of the women.

As a significant proportion of women were not advised on recommended components of maternal and child health in the study area. Moreover, there were enormous socioeconomic inequalities. The findings of this study raise questions about the capacity of the public healthcare system in providing equitable services. The government must focus on training and capacity building of the public health workers in communication skills so that they can deliver appropriate and recommended advice to all clients, irrespective of their socioeconomic status.

Nearly one-fourth of the women in the sample area did not seek any healthcare treatment for their reproductive health morbidities during postpartum period. Hence, health programmes should invest to ensure that all women receive early postpartum visits after delivery at home and after discharge from institution to detect and manage maternal morbidity. Further, health programmes should also ensure that women are properly screened for complications before their discharge from hospitals after delivery.

The findings also suggest the need for strengthening PNC services to keep pace with advances in coverage for care at birth and prenatal services in India through targeted policy interventions.

Among the various problems reported by women were the possible symptoms of reproductive tract infections (white discharge, backache, abdominal pain), urinary tract infection (pain/burning sensation during urination, abnormal frequency of urination), anemia (excessive tiredness/weakness during the performance of normal household activities, fatigue, backache), menstrual disorders (excessive bleeding, painful menstruation, aches and pains during menstruation and irregular menstruation) and finally fever of any type.

The assessment of women's health status, particularly as reflected by their obstetric and gynecological morbidity, reveals the heavy burden of ill health among the sample of rural women.

Reproductive health concerns cut across many socio-economic aspects. Indeed, the health sector alone cannot resolve them. Yet, many problems and their costly consequences can be averted if reproductive health is routinely addressed within the context of primary healthcare as a first line of prevention and care. To achieve this, it is vital to strengthen health systems, build trust among the communities they serve and expand access to reproductive health programmes that take in to account to social, cultural, economic and gender dimensions.

Bibliography

Abdul Salam, S.A Siddiqui. **Socio Economic Inequalities in use of Delivery care Services in India.** The Journal of Obstetrics and Gynecology of India vol. 56, No.2 : March / April, 2006, p. 123-127.

Abrahams N, Jewkes R and Laubser R. **I do not Believe in Democracy in the Home. Men's Relationships with and Abuse of Women** (Technical Report). South Africa: Medical Research Council, 1999.

Abusaleh Sharriff and Geetha Singh, **"Determinants of Maternal Health Care Utilization of India; Evidence from a Recent Household,** "www.ncaer.org/wp.pdd. Recent publication, 1994.

Acharya, L.B. and Cleland. J. **Maternal and Child Health Services in Rural Nepal: Does Access or Quality Matter More?** Health Policy and Planning, 2000, 15(2):223-229.

Adamchak S. et al., **A guide to Monitoring and Evaluating Adolescent Reproductive Health Programs,** Washington, DC FOCUS on Young Adults, 2000

Ahmad, et al., **Induced abortions in Mat lab, Bangladesh: Trends and determinates** International Family Planning Perspectives vol. 24, No. 3 (Sep. 1998) pp. 128-138, Published by: Guttamacher Institute.

Ajayi et al., (1991) **Adolescent sexuality and fertility in Kenya : A survey of knowledge perceptions and practices** Studies in Family Planning 22(4) : 205-16.

Akhter, H.H. **Menstrual Regulate Among Adolescents in Bangladesh; Risks and Experiences,** in S. Bott and other (eds),

Adolescent Sexual and Reproductive Health, Evidence and Programme Implications for South Asia, (Geneva, WHO), 2002.

Alan Guttmacher Institute (AGI). Into a New World: Yoting Woolens Sexual and Reproductive Lives. New York, NY: AGI, 1998.

Amita Pitra and Bhogyashrec Khaire (2004). Gender Sensitive Health Care System. Need for a Gender Sensitive Health Care System, Health Action, vol. 17, No. 9, Sept. 2004. Pg. 17-19.

Anuratha Mathu. **Women's Health a major area of concern.** Social welfare, 52(1), April 2005, pg. 5-9.

Aoyama A.S. **Reproductive Health in the Middle East and North Africa: Well – being for all Washington,** DC: The World Bank (2001).

Ashford, Lori S. **Women's New Population Policies: Advancing Health and Rights,** Population Bulletin, 2001, 56(1): 1-44.

AYARH. Population Reference Bureau, the World's Youth 2000. Washington, P.C Population Reference Bureau, 2001.

Bacci. A, Manhica GM, Machungo F, et al., **Outcome of Teenage Pregnancy in Maputo, Mozambique.** International Journal of Gynaecol Obstetrics, 1993, 40(1):19-23.

Banerjee, B. **A Qualitative Analysis of Maternal and Child Health Services of an Urban Health Center,** Indian Journal of Community Medicine. 2003; 28: 153-156

Bang, R. and Bang, A. **A Community Study of Gynecological Diseases in Indian Villages in Zeidenstein and Moore (eds.) Learning about Sexuality: A Practical Beginning,** New York: Population Council, 1989.

Baridalyne, N., and V.P. Reddaian **Menstruation: Knowledge, Beliefs and Practices of Women in the Reproductive Age Group Residing in an Urban Resettlement** Colony of Perspectives and Issues, 2004, 27(1): 9-16

Barua, A and Kurtz, Cathleen. **Reproductive Health Seeking by Married Adolescent Girls in Maharastra, India,** Reproductive Health Matters, 2001, vol. 9(17).

Beard, J. **Effectiveness and Strategies of iron Supplementation During pregnancy.** American Journal of Clinical Nutrition, 2000, 71 (Suppl): 12885 – 12945

Bhatia, J.C and Cleland, J. **Self Reported Symptoms of Gynecological Morbidity and their Treatment in South India,** Studies in Family Planning, 1995, Vol. 26(4), pp. 203-216

Biswas. R. **Maternal Care in India Reveals Gaps between Urban and Rural Rich and Poor, West Bengal** World Health Organization (WHO) United Nations Children's Fund (UNICEF) and United Nations Population Fund (UNFPA), Maternal Mortality Database (1995) Accessed Online at www.child info.org/eddb/mat_mortal/database.htm, 2003, on May 7, 2003

Blanc, Annk. And Anna. **Way Sexual Behavior and Contraceptive Knowledge and use Developing countries** Studies in Family Planning, 1998, 29(2), p. 99-105

Bongaarts, John and Barney Cohen. **Introduction and overviews** Studies in Family planning, 1998, 29(2), p. 99-105

Carroli G, Rooney C, Villar J. **How Effective is antenatal care in preventing maternal mortality and serious morbidity? An overview of the evidence.** Pediatrics Perinatal Epidemiology, 2001, 15(1 Suppl): 1-42.

CDC – **Trends in Fertility and Infant and Maternal Health-**United States, 1980 – 1988, MMWR, 1991; 40: 381-3, 389-90.

CEDPA, **Advocating for Increased Awareness of Adolescents Reproductive Health and Family Planning Needs** in Mali Submitted to the World Bank by the Centre for Development and Population Activities (CEDPA), 2000.

Centre for Development and Population Activates (CEDPA) **Adolescent Girls in India Choose a Better Future**: An Impact Assessment Washington DC : CEDPA, 2001

Chen, Lincoth C., Melitia C., Gesche, Shamsa Ahmed, A.I. Chowdhury and W.H. Mosley. **Maternal Mortality in Rural Bangladesh,** Studies in Family Planning, 1974, 5(11), p. 334-341.

Chowdhury S. **Pregnancy and Postpartum Experience Among First-Time Young Parents in Bangladesh: Preliminary Observations.** In Boa So Jejeebhoy S, Shah I, et al., eds. Towards Adidthood: **Exploring the Sexual and Reproductive Health of Adolescents in South Asia** (Geneva: World Health Organization, 2003) 59-61.

Dabi DR. Parak Manish et al., **"A Study of Maternal Vitamin 'A' Status and its Relationship with Intrauterine Growth Restriction.** The Journal of Obstetrics and Gynecology of India, vol. 56, No.6, November/December 2006, p. 489-497.

Demographic Development in Europe Belgium 1998-1999.

Department of family welfare, ministry of Health and family Welfare, GOI, New Delhi, 2000.

Dilip. T.R. **Utilisation of RCH Care Servicers: Some Observations from Kerala.** Journal of Health Management April – 2002, 4:19-30

Easterly R.A and Crimmins EM:. **The Fertility Revaluation the University of Chicago Press.** Pilanesberg National Park. South Africa, 1985

Ford, Clellans. S. **A comparative study of human reproduction.** Yale university publications in anthropology. No. 32 New haven Yale University Press, 1945

Freedman. R. **Fertility Determinants. In the World Fertility Survey: An Assessment** (Ed. J. Cleland and C. Scott), pp. 773-795. Oxford University Press, Oxford, 1987

Gittelsohn, J., Bentley, M.E., Pelto P. J., Nag, M., Paachauri S., Harrision, A.D. and Landman, L.T. (eds.) **Listening to Women Talk about their Health: Issues and Evidence from India,** New Delhi : Har Anand Publication, 1994.

Govindasamy P. Stewart MK, Rutstein SO, et al., **High – Risk Births and Maternity Care.** Columbia, MD: Macro International, Inc., 1993.

Govt. of India. National Population Policy Department of Family Welfare, Ministry of Health and Family Welfare, GOI, New Delhi, 2000.

Govt. of India. National Population Policy Department of Family Welfare, Ministry of Health and Family Welfare GOI, New Delhi, 2001

Govt. of India. National Population Policy. Department of Family Welfare. Ministry of Health and Family Welfare, GOI, New Delhi, 1998.

Gregson, S.C.A. Nyamukapa, G.P Gaehtt. et al., **Sexual Mixing Patterns and Sex Differentials in Teenage Exposure to HIV Infection Rural Zimbabwe,** The Lencet, 2002, 359 (9321) : 1896-1903.

Griffiths, P. and Stephenson, R. **Understanding users Perspectives of Barriers to Maternal Health Care use in Maharashtra,** India. Journal of Biosocial science, 2001, 33; 339-359.

Hensaw, StanleyK, **Induced Abortion: A World Review,** Family Planing Perspectives".1990, 22:76-89.

Hoj, L. et al., **Factors Associated with Maternal Mortality in Rural Guinea – Bissau. A Longitudinal Population – Based Study.** British Journal of Obstetrics and Gynecology, 2002, 109: 792-299.

Indra Pathamanathan, Jerker Kiljestrand. **Investing in Maternal Health: Learning from Malaysia and Srilanka.** World Bank Publications 01, March, 2003, p. 182

Jejeebhoy, S.J., **Maternal Mortality and Morbidity in India,** Priorities for Social Science Research. The Journal of Family Welfare, 1996, 43(2): 31-51

Jejeebhoy, Sthireen. **Adolescent Sexual and Reproductive Behaviour: A Review of the Evidence from India in Ramasubban and Jejeebhoy, (eds.)** Women's Reproductive Health in India, New Delhi: Rawat Publication, 2000.

Jensen, R and a Thornton. **Early Female Marriage in the Developing World,** Gender and Development, 2003, 11(2) : 9-19.

Jothy, K. **Reproductive and Child Health Status Differentials in Tamilnadu,** in the **Research Journal of Humanities and Social Sciences,** (Print ISSN-0975-6795), Vol.4, Issue-2, Pp.223-230, April-June, 2013.

Kapadia, S.V. Shah ad Sikni, 1997, **Women's RH Understanding Explanatory models of illness within a socio – Psychological Context Report of Study Funded by the Population Council.** Department of human Development and Family Studies. Faculty of Home Science. M.S university of Baroda. Baroda.

Khan, M.E., Ghosh Dastitar S.K., and Ratanjeet Singh, **Nutrition and Health practices Among Rural Women: A case study of Uttar Padesh, India.** The journal of family welfare, 1998, 33(1): p. 3-18.

Khanna, Anoop and Goyal R.S. **A study of Adolescent Girls in Rajasthan,** Journal of Health Management, 2005, Vol. 7 (1), pp: 91-107.

Koblinsky M, Conroy C, Kureshy N, et al. **Issues in Programming for Safe Motherhood.** Arlington, VA: MotherCare/john Snow, Inc., 2000.

Luke, Nancy and Watkins, Susan Cotts, **Reactions of Developing Country Elites to International Policy,** Population and Development Review, 28 (4); 2002.

M. Fathalla, **Research Needs in Human Reproduction** in E. Diczfalusy, P.D. Griffin and J. Kharina (eds), **Research in Human Reproduction.** Geneva: World Health Organization, 1988.

M. Fathalla, **Research Needs in Human Reproduction,** in E. Direfully, PD. Griffin, and J. Kharlne (eds), Research in Human Reproduction. Biennial Report (1986-87), World Health Geneva, 1988 IIPS (2000), National Family Health Survey India 1998-99 MOHFW Population polity Government of India, 2000.

M. Jodie Dodd, S. Jeffery Robinson and A. Carolis Gowther, **"'Guiding Antenatal Care** "www.i-nja.comau/ public/issues /I 76-06-180302/ dod 10052.html.

Magadi, M. et al., **Analysis of Factors Associated with Maternal Mortality in Kenyan Hospital.** Journal of Biosocial Science, 2001, vol. 33(3): July 2001. Pg. 375-389

Mc Cauley A P and Salter C, **Meeting the Needs of Young Adults,** Population Reports, 1995, Series J, No. 41

Mc. Caw – Binns. A. **Access to care and Maternal Mortality in Jamaican hospitals:** 1993 – 1995. International Journal of Epidemiology 2001. Aug. 30(4) : 796-801

McDonagh. M., et al., **Reproductive health and health sector reform: opportunities and challenges.** John snow international UK forthcoming, 2000.

Mmari KN, Magnani RJ. **Does Making Clinic-Based Reproductive Health Services More Youth-Friendly Increase Service use by Adolescents? Evidence from Lusaka, Zambia.** Journal of Adolescent Health, 2003, 33 (4):259-70.

Munjanja. S.P. et al., **Randomized Controlled Trial of a Reduced Visits Programme of Antenatal care in Harare Zimbabwe.** Lancet, 1996, 348:364-9.

Naveneetham K and A Dharmalingam. **Utilisation of Maternal Health Care Services in Southern India.** Social Science and Medicine, 2002, 43: 459-471

NFHS –2, India. National Family Health Survey (NFHS-2) 1998-99, India, International Institute for Population Sciences, Mumbai and ORC Macro, USA, 2000

Pallikadavath. S. Foss. M., and Stones. R.W. **Antenatal Care: "Provision and Inequality in Rural North India.** Social Science and Medicine (1982), 2004, 59(6): 1147-1158.

PRB. Adolescent Women in Sub – Saharan Africa. Washington, D.C. Yinger and other PRB, Demographic and Health surveys project of Macro International and the Division of RH of the Centers for Disease Control. 1992. **Adolescent Sexual Activity and Childbearing in Latin America and the Caribbean: Risks and Consequences.** Washington D.C. International Programs, 1992.

PRB. The World's Youth, Washington DC, Population Reference Bureau, Measure Communications, 2000

Prema Ramachandran. Nutrition in Pregnancy. In Gopalan. C, Kaur. S., editors. **Women and Nutrition in India.** Special Publication No. 5, New Delhi. Nutrition Foundation of India, 989, p. 153-93.

Prual, A. et al., **The Quality of Risk Factor Screening during Antenatal Consultations in Niger.** Health Policy and Planning, 2000, 15(1): 11 -16.

Ramarao. S. et al., **"Safer maternal Health in Rural Uttar Pradesh: Do primary Health Services Contribute?** International Programs Division, Population Council, New York. 10017, USA. Health Policy and Planning (Impact Factor: 2.65), 2001, 10/2001: 16(3) : 256-63."

Rameshwar Sarma K.V. and Prahlad Rao. N. **Strengthening Nutrition programme for Women** IASSI quarterly Oct – Dec 1992.

Ravindran. T.K.S. **Women's Health in Rural Population of TN.** In : M. Dasgupta L. Chen and T.K. Krishna (eds.). Women's Health in India. Risk and vulnerability Bombay : Oxford University Press.1995

Reynolds et al., World Health Organization **Unsafe Abortion. Global and Regional Estimates of the Incidence of Unsafe Abortion and Associated mortality in 2003,** 5th ed. Generva: World Health organisation: 2007

Rutstein et al., **"Unsafe Abortion Higher no of Pregnancies".** National Institute of Population Studies 1992, Pakistan Demographic and Health Survey 1990-91. Islamabad, 1990.

S. Pachauri and J. Gittlesohn, Summary of Research Studies and Implications for Health policy and Prosralications New Delhi, 1994.

S. Pachauri, **Relationship between AIDS and Family Paling Programmes: a Ratio Native for Developing Integrated Reproductive Health Services,** Health Transition Review, Supplement to No.4 331-347,1995.

Sen, G. (2004), **Whether Women Health,** www. India – seminar. Com/ 2004, 25 August

Sender wiz J: A **Review of Program Approaches to Adolescent Reproductive Health** Poptech Assignment Number 200 – 176, June 1, 2000, review on 13 may 2005.

Senderowit Z J, **Adoleseent Health Reassessing the Passage to Adulethood,** Washington, D C world Bank, 1995

Shatrugha Govt. of India, National Nutrition Policy, Department of Women Child Development ministry of Human Resource development, GOI, New Delhi, 1993

Sivakami. M., and Kulkarni. P.M., **Are Socially and Economics Weaker Sections Deprived of Maternal Health Care in Tamil Nadu, India,** Journal of Health and Population in Developing Countries, 2003, Aug. 7:15

Srinivasan. K. et al., Population profile of the state of Uttaranchal Paper Presented at the State Level conference on **"Health Development and Population Stabilization Issues in Uttaranchal,** Dehradun, 22-23 May, 2001.

Steketee RW,Wirima JJ, Slutsker. L, et. al. **The problem of Malaria and Malaria Control in Pregnancy in Sub-Saharan Africa.** Ain J Trop Med Hyg 1996, 55(l Suppl): 2-7.

Stoltzfus Rj. **Iron-Deficiency Anemia: Reexamining the Nature and Magnitude of the Public Health Problem. Summary: Implications for Research and Programs.** NWr, 2001;131 (2S-2): 697S-701S.

Sumedha M. Joshi, (Mrs.) N.P. Pai. **Effect of the Maternal Biosocial Determinates on the Birth Weight in a Slum Area of Greeter Mumbai,** Indian Journal of Community Medicine, 2000, Vol. XXV, No. 3, July – Sept.

T.K. Sundari Ravindran 1993. **Women and the Polities Population and Development in India.** Reproductive Health Matters. vol. 1, No. 1. Population and Family Planning Polices : Women – Centercd Perspectives may (1993), pp. 26-38. Published by: Reproductive Health Matters (RHM).

T.V. Antony. **Population Policy and Reproductive Health Proceedings of the Seminar on Policy Direction and Strategy of Action in Population and Reproductive. Health in India,** New Delhi, December 1995, Edited by K. Srinivasan, Hindustan, Pub. Cor. (India) New Delhi (marry Martin Book sellers), 2001, XVI, 361, p. 123.

Thaddeus Dudes, S. Marine D. **Too Far to Walk : Maternal Mortality in Context** Social Science and Medicine. 1994: 38(8): 109-110.

Thengaleela, T. and P. Vijayalakshmi **Prevalence of Anemia Pregnancy.** The India Journal of Nutrition and Dietetics, 1994, 31(2), p. 26-29.

Thersa O. Scholl et al., **"Prenatal Care and Maternal Health During Adolescent Pregnancy: A Review and Meta – Analysis.** Journal of Adolescent Health vol. 15, Issue 6, pg : 444-456, Sept. 1994

Tsui, A.O., Wasserheit, J.N. and Hagga, J.G (eds.), **Reproductive Health in Developing Countries,** Expanding Dimensions Building Solutions National Academy Press, Washington OC, 1997.

Uddlin, Nassir. Case study, **Bangladesh, Communication and Advocacy Strategies, Adolescent Reproductive and Sexual Health Bangkok,** UNESCO PROAP, 1999.

UNFPA, The South Asia Conference

UNFPA. **Reproductive Tract Infection in India: The HIV / AIDS Connection,** New Delhi.(1999).

UNICEF (2001). The Progress of Nations 2001, New York, United Nations Children's Fund

UNICEF, The Progress of Nation, 1991, New York, p. 21.

United Nations (1994) Population and Development Review, New York.

United Nations (UN). Report of the International Conference on Population and Development, Cairo: UN, 1994.

United Nations 1999. Demographic Year Book, 1997, New York.

United Nations, **Adolescent Reproductive Behaviour.** Vol.II Eviolence from Developing Countries, New York: UN,1989

UPS, International Institute for Population Sciences (UPS) and ORS macro. NFHS – 2, 1998 – 99 Mumbai UPS 2000.

Van Der Straten, A.R., King O. Grinsteal et al., **Sexual Coerction, Physical in Steady Relationship** in Kingali, Rwanda, AIDS and Bahavious, 1998, 2(1) : 61-73.

Vanneste, A.M. et al., **Prenatal Screening in Rural Bangladesh; from Predication to Care.** Health Policy and Planning, 2000, 15(1): 1-10.

W. Parker Maudlin and Sheldon J. Segal. **Prevalence of Contraceptive use: Trends and Issues.** Studies in Family Planning Vol. 19, No. 6 (Nov – Dec, 1988), pp. 335-353, Published by Population Council.

Wang et al., **Access to Adolescent Reproductive Health Services Financial and Structural Barriers to Care Prospect** Sex Report Health, 2003, May: 35(3): 144-7.

Westoff and Luis Hernando Ochoa. **Unmet Need and the Demand for Family Planning.** DHS, Comparative Studies No.5 Columbia, Md. Macro Systems/Institute for Resource Development 1999.

Westoff C.F., **Trends in Marriage and Early Childbearing in Developing Countries, Calverton, M D., U S A., ORC Marco, 2003.**

WHO, **Antenatal Care Randomized Trial Manual for the Implementation of the New Model.** World Health Organization. Department of Reproductive Health and Research, 2001.

WHO, **Approaches to Adolescent Health and Development: A Compendium of Projects and Programming,** 1992a. Geneva

WHO, Division of Reproductive Health, 1998. WHO, Geneva.

WHO, Women's Health, across age and Frontier 1992c: Geneva.

WHO, World Population Report, 2003.

World Bank, 1993.

World Bank, World Development Report: **Investing in Health** Oxford University Press New York, 1993, pg. 117, 216.

World Bank. **Safe Motherhood and the World Bank: Lessons from Ten Years of Experience.** Draft Washington, D.C, 1999.

World Development Report, 2006.

World population Monitoring. Population and development review 1998 24(4) : 697-737, December.

Zabin LS. Expiration. K., **The health consequences of Adolescent sexual and fertility behavior in sub – Saharan Africa** Studies Family Journal Planning 1998, 29(2) : 2010-232.

Zurayk **"Concepts and Measures of Reproductive Morbidity".** Health Transition Review, 1993, 3(1): 17-39.

Index